DAD'S ARMY
a companion

compiled by Tony Pritchard & Paul Carpenter

A Dad's Army Appreciation Society Publication

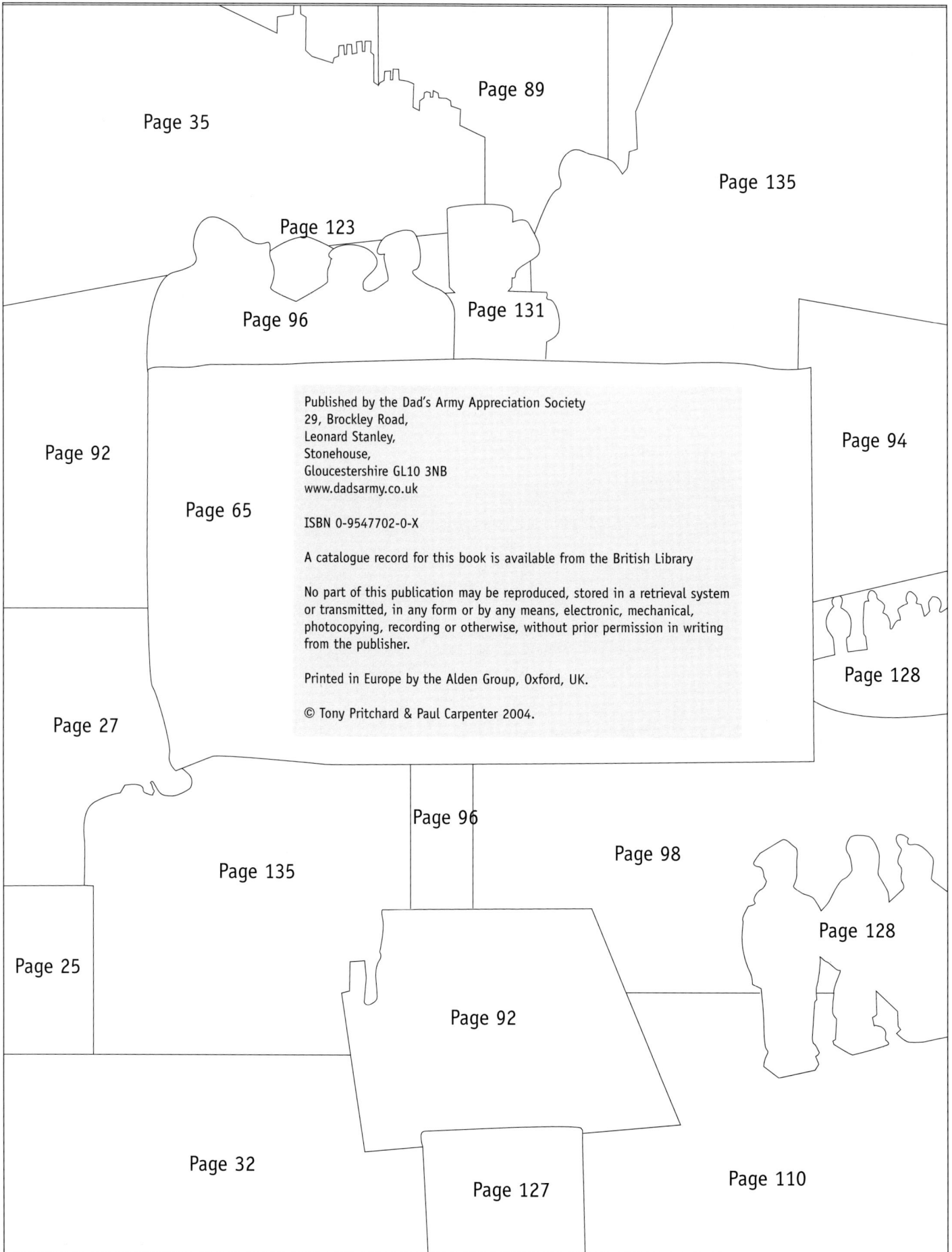

Page 89

Page 35

Page 135

Page 123

Page 96

Page 131

Page 92

Published by the Dad's Army Appreciation Society
29, Brockley Road,
Leonard Stanley,
Stonehouse,
Gloucestershire GL10 3NB
www.dadsarmy.co.uk

ISBN 0-9547702-0-X

A catalogue record for this book is available from the British Library

Printed in Europe by the Alden Group, Oxford, UK.

© Tony Pritchard & Paul Carpenter 2004.

Page 94

Page 65

Page 128

Page 27

Page 96

Page 98

Page 135

Page 128

Page 25

Page 92

Page 32

Page 127

Page 110

A book of this kind would not be possible were it not for the assistance of the many enthusiastic followers of Dad's Army:

Jimmy Perry OBE and David Croft OBE for supporting the Society in everything they do.
David Hamilton, Alan and Alys Hayes for the original manuscript (Dad's Army, A Guide to TV, Radio & Stage 1996).
Iain Wilson, who has supplied current vehicle whereabouts and information
Andy Howells for details of the cartoon versions.
Dyllan Tappenden who supplied and wrote the section on model vehicles
David Homewood of the New Zealand DAAS
David Noades for discography details and sleeve images.
Anne Webster at Stanta for imparting her great knowledge on filming at the MOD training area and her kind friendship.
Harold Snoad - for providing valuable information on the production of Dad's Army and one or two difficult locations and for being there at the time!

The following have kindly supplied photographs for inclusion:
Tim Ball, Ross Barrett, The late Hugh Cecil, Joan Chamberlain, Brian Fisher, Len Hutton, S Oatley, Richard Palmer, Bill Pertwee, John Riffles, Don Smith, John Smith, Fred Thrulow, Iain Wilson. and the residents of the many properties we have visited in our quest for locations.

The following also helped with the eight-years task of tracking down the filming locations:
Tim Ball, Ron Barrell, Ross Barrett, Vernon Brand, Eric and Diana Burroughes, David Croft OBE, Joyce Dooley, Keith Eldred, Dave Homewood, Sid Hoskins, R Leonard, Mary Olly, David Osborne, Richard Palmer, Richard Parrott, Tim Rudderham, Dr. Giles Smith, Harold Snoad, Philip Standley, John Steel, Fred Thrulow, Lt. Col. Tullett (Ret'd), Richard Webber, Anne Webster, Jonathan Wheeler, Iain Wilson

And finally, those who have helped in one way or another during the production of this book:
Linda Andrews, Claire Green, Andrew Hopwood (Alden Press), Chrissie Jones, MOD Stanta, Bill Pertwee, Julie Pritchard, Mark Stephens, Thetford Town Council, Jack Wheeler and anyone else we have forgotten to mention.

Every attempt has been made to trace the origin of the photographs used in this book and no copyright infringement is intended.

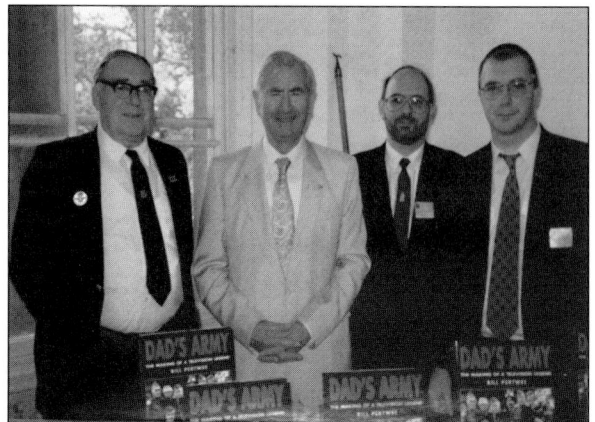
Left to right: The Appreciation Society team, Jack Wheeler, Bill Pertwee (President), Tony Pritchard and Paul Carpenter.

This latest edition of the 'Dad's Army Companion' is really a work of art. It is a great experience, for example, to be able to, at last take in, in one volume, locations for the filming of the many television episodes and feature film that have been discovered by Tony and Paul with thoroughness of research that is quite amazing.

I wonder if the BBC archives department realise the importance of a document like this concerning one of their finest situation comedies which has brought so much pleasure to so many people and generations of all ages over the past 35 years. This document is to some, their only knowledge of that part of our history in the 1940's. It was a dark, but finest hour, and there really was a band of warriors, not some fictitious group, called 'The Home Guard' who would have given their lives to defend this island from the potential invaders. Senior citizens and very young men from all walks of life who lived in communities, large or small, just like the areas depicted in the surrounds of those which were used in the TV series 'Dad's Army'.

To me personally it is a joy to be able to go back in time when reading this and remembering those sunny days in Norfolk and Suffolk.

This compilation is really a Dad's Army experience which I am sure will give those followers of the series, and those who are not too familiar with it, a new dimension to the programme.

Well done the Appreciation Society.

Bill Pertwee, Surrey 2004

Welcome to this Companion dedicated to the BBC comedy programme, 'Dad's Army'.

It is the intention of The Dad's Army Appreciation Society (DAAS) to make this Companion the complete and definitive reference for those who enjoy 'Dad's Army'.

Originally the hard work of David Hamilton, Alan Hayes and Alys Hayes, and published as their 'Homefront' publication 'Dad's Army, A Guide to Television, Radio, Film and Stage' in 1996, the DAAS later revised, added and updated the information in the form of the 'Dad's Army Handbook'.

At that time, the only book available on Dad's Army, apart from the 1976 scripts book, was Bill Pertwee's 'The Making of a Television Legend'. Since then, the popularity of the series has grown, no doubt fuelled by TV nostalgia. There are now many books on the series and most of the main cast have their own dedicated autobiographies, from Arthur Lowe to Colin Bean.

This book assumes that the reader is familiar with the concept and premise of the programme, and has a basic knowledge of the cast and character names.

As with the original guide, the plot outlines, in most cases, are those that appeared in the BBC listings magazine Radio Times and the broadcast details are those from the UK terrestrial television. We have added new information to this text, as it has become available. Information on the outside filming locations used in each episode has been enhanced. All those identified have been photographed and compared with scenes from the original programme and in some cases we have obtained photographs taken by local people during the actual filming.

Ordnance Survey map and grid references have also been included to assist you. It must be noted that many of these locations are on a restricted (Ministry of Defence) area or private property and therefore visiting is not always possible. To find these locations has proved to be a major undertaking and as with any such project there were many people involved, including the cast, technicians and society members. Some actively searched whilst others provided hints and clues.

Many hours of work from people named and many unnamed have made this publication possible, to the very best of our knowledge the details in this companion are correct. The Dad's Army Appreciation Society hope that you will find its contents interesting and useful. Should you wish to make any comments, suggestions or if there is something we've missed, please write to or email the Dad's Army Appreciation Society, at 29 Brockley Road, Leonard Stanley, Stonehouse, Gloucestershire, Engalnd GL10 3NB (info@dadsarmy.co.uk). Please mark your envelope or head your email 'Companion'.

There has been no attempt to copy or reproduce any other published material and every effort has been made to identify the originators of the photographs used in this book.

Jimmy Perry was walking past Buckingham Palace one day, and started to nostalgically recall the days when the Home Guard manned the sentry posts there during World War II. An actor, with experience in Joan Littlewood's Theatre Workshop, Perry had been in the Home Guard himself, in the Hertfordshire 1st Battalion, while he was too young to be conscripted. His instructor at the time had kept telling his men that the enemy 'didn't like it up 'em!' By the end of his walk, Jimmy had an idea for a comedy series.
He showed the idea to his friend, David Croft, then a BBC producer. Croft showed it to his boss, Michael Mills, the Head of Comedy. Mills said, 'This could run forever.'

'Dad's Army' is based, at heart, on a single class joke that Huw Weldon, when he first met the cast, failed to get. He assumed that John Le Mesurier was Captain Mainwaring and Arthur Lowe was Sergeant Wilson. In truth, that was how it was going to be, but Perry and Croft changed their minds. The central conflict in the show is that of a lower middle-class bank manager who finds himself commanding a man from the upper classes. Wilson is the voice of sanity, he always has the easier answer. If it wasn't for Wilson's unwillingness to get involved in anything, he'd make a much better officer.

The other central issue in the show is summed up by a line from the first episode: 'The machine guns could have a clear field of fire from here to Timothy White's if it wasn't for that woman in the telephone box.' We laugh with the men of the Home Guard because of the contradictions between warfare and 'Little England'. However, in 1940, those contradictions were utterly real. As Alan Coren said in The Times, 'Clive Dunn might well have been the only thing standing between us and Dachau. Mills had defended the fledgling series against internal claims of bad taste, and he was again correct. We can't laugh at the Walmington-on-Sea platoon because not only is their situation truly desperate, but, in the best tradition of Fred Karno, Evelyn Waugh, and the lowly soldiers in Henry V, they're doing the best they can. Tom Hutchinson summed it up when he called the show 'a sweetly comic celebration of the British amateur'.

Mainwaring's platoon contained not only the laconic Wilson, but the hyper-loyal butcher, Lance Corporal Jack Jones. Jonesie had first seen service in 1885 in the Rifle Brigade, 'trying to relieve General Gordon', and the 12 medals he occasionally wore were lovingly selected by the writers and the costume designer, Barbara Kronig. They were exactly correct for the military career Perry and Croft had constructed for Jonesie, from Khartoum, through the Sudan, on to the North West Frontier, back under Kitchener for the battle of Omdurman, the Frontier again, then the Boer War and the Great War in France. Dunn himself had been made a POW on the night before he was due to be promoted to

Lance Corporal, spending the rest of the war in a prison camp in Austria.

Tremendous accuracy was insisted upon, surely a factor in the series' popularity. The boots, watches, and Arthur Lowe's glasses were all originals, and similar attention was paid to newly-created items. Mainwaring's uniform, because of his wealth, was of a slightly better material than those of his men. The line 'I couldn't care less' was cut from one episode as being too modern, although it was used by Pike in the episode 'Brain Versus Brawn'. E.V.H. Emmett's voice was heard giving actual newsreel announcements, and period songs were played across scene breaks, Perry writing the lyrics to the authentic-sounding title music 'Who Do You Think You Are Kidding Mister Hitler?'. It was the last thing Bud Flanagan was to record before he died.

If the little butcher with the habit of asking for 'Permission to speak, sir' was a bit of a hero on the quiet, so was Godfrey, the medic who, more often than not, wanted to relieve his bladder when he spoke up. In 'Branded', Godfrey is revealed to have been a Conscientious Objector in the Great War. The other men consequently shun him, until he rescues Mainwaring from death in a smoke-filled room. He reveals that he won the Military Medal for his courage as an ambulance man.

The rest of the platoon was made up of Walker, the spiv who avoided military service in the Army by developing an allergy to corned beef, Pike, too young for war but eager to join in because of all the gangster movies he watches, and Frazer, the Scottish undertaker whose 'We're doomed!' was the obvious answer to Jones' 'Don't panic!' Apart from a thorough knowledge of the characters' backgrounds (they were sure that Pike's 'uncle Arthur' was secretly his Dad), Perry and Croft both had theatrical experience, and let the actors' personalities influence them. Croft commented to the Radio Times that John Laurie was like Frazer in some ways. 'He starts a show saying "I don't know if it will work" and ends it saying "Well, I thought it would be all right".' Rounding out the cast were Hodges, the ARP man ('Wellington' to Mainwaring's 'Napoleon'), the somewhat critical vicar and his more forceful verger, all devoted to putting common sense (and thus, somehow, defeatism) in the way of the platoon's schemes. It wasn't all spite, though. Croft had been an air-raid warden himself.

'Dad's Army' caught on very quickly, achieving its greatest fame (books, a movie version, board games, a radio adaptation, even a stage musical) and highest ratings (18.5 million) in the early 70s. It was reported to be the Queen Mother's favourite programme, won a Writers' Guild award in 1970, and the BAFTA award for Best Comedy in 1971. Len Brown and David Quantick, writing in the NME, have made some interesting assertions as to what made the series tick - notably that, like much great TV comedy, 'Dad's Army' works because it centres on people trapped (in this case, a bunch of free spirits trapped in the bodies of old men, along with a 'stupid boy' and a lazy spiv).

In August 1973, James Beck died, and the show was thrown into crisis. No new character was to be created to replace the well-loved actor's performance as Walker, but occasional characters including the eccentric Welsh War Correspondent Cheeseman and the podgy Private Sponge were introduced or given a little more to do. A sort of regular Perry and Croft repertory company, containing such people as Michael Knowles, Don Estelle, Felix Bowness and Jeffrey Holland, was already building up to continually provide walk-ons, but the show was never short of guest stars. Fred Trueman and Barbara Windsor graced the early seasons, with Perry himself making an appearance as comedian Charlie Cheeseman in the final show of the first season. Trueman appears in 'The Test', which involves a game of cricket between the Wardens and the Home Guard. The match is won by a six from, of all people, Godfrey. As the players leave the pitch, air-raid warnings sound. 'Here they come again,' says a resigned Mainwaring as the episode ends without laughter.

Typical moments included Mainwaring and Wilson finding themselves holding onto an unexploded bomb in their bank, Frazer and Godfrey disguising themselves as a panto cow (and, of course, meeting a bull) and Mainwaring holding the mooring line of a runaway barrage balloon and thus having to be pursued by Jones' converted butcher's van. These sequences gained a standing ovation from the studio audience who watched the recordings. Mainwaring got to play through his own version of Brief Encounter, presumably to the worry of his never-seen wife, Elizabeth, and the whole cast dressed up as Nazi sympathisers (including Pike in memorable gangster outfit). In 'A Soldier's Farewell', Mainwaring dreams the entire cast to Waterloo, after he takes the platoon to see Napoleon (and has a cheese supper with Wilson and Jones). Another dream sequence / flashback occurs in 'The Two and a Half Feathers', in which Jones is accused of gaining his medals through cowardice. In 'Absent Friends' the men do not turn up for patrol in order to finish a darts game. Mainwaring orders them back and, after some hesitation, they comply, simply because they are unable to let the Captain down, walking into an ambush of Irish fifth columnists. 'Don't Fence Me In' concerns the suspicion that Walker is aiding Italian POWs to escape. There was also pathos, in the form of Wilson's eventual promotion to bank manager: his branch is destroyed by a bomb a few minutes after he has taken up the position.

Most of the stars of 'Dad's Army' are dead now, the only survivors of the main seven at the time of writing being the youngest, Ian Lavender (then aged 27, playing 17), and the 'oldest', Clive Dunn (then 48, playing late 70s). In their time, and in their incredible ratings revival on television and radio in the 80s and 90s, they could, as Tom Stoppard said in The Guardian, 'bring a smile and a tear to every lover of England and Ealing.'

Perry and Croft went on to develop 'It Ain't Half Hot Mum' and 'Hi-De-Hi!'. Both were very successful, but they hadn't quite the heart of their predecessor, featuring stereotyped foreigners and homosexuals in a way that never would have befitted the little Kent town of Walmington-on-Sea. The terrors of war may have threatened Bombardier Beaumont, but they actually arrived for Captain Mainwaring, most notably in the form of Philip Madoc's snarling U-boat captain. And, despite having the mickey taken out of them, they were as frightening as England had imagined them. 'Vot is your name?' the Captain asks after Pikey has sung an anti-Nazi version of 'Whistle While You Work'. 'Don't tell him, Pike,' replies Mainwaring with superb timing.

The last time the end theme, played by the Band of the Coldstream Guards, was heard was on Remembrance Sunday 1977. In the episode 'Never Too Old', Jonesie married the buxom widow, Mrs. Fox, as he had threatened to do all season. The series ended with a toast to the Home Guard, champagne in tin mugs.

The whole humour of the show was summed up by the platoon's attempt at a sea patrol. Having practised rowing in the church hall, they go to sea and get lost in the fog. Hearing French voices, they think that they've drifted across the Channel, and, hitting land, sneak aboard a train. When they open the van doors again, a man in a bowler hat is standing there. 'Qu'est-ce que c'est la gare?' asks Mainwaring. The man replies that, actually, it's Eastbourne!

series ONE 31 JUL 68 - 11 SEPT 68

1   The Man and the Hour
2   Museum Piece
3   Command Decision
4   The Enemy Within the Gates
5   The Showing Up of Corporal Jones
6   Shooting Pains
Audience viewing figures for series one 8.2 million

series TWO 1 MAR 69 - 5 APR 69

7   Operation Kilt
8   The Battle of Godfrey's Cottage
9   The Loneliness of the Long-Distance Walker
10 Sgt. Wilson's Little Secret
11 A Stripe For Frazer
12 Under Fire
Audience viewing figures for series two 12.2 million

series THREE 11 SEP 69 - 11 DEC 69

13 The Armoured Might of Lance Corporal Jones
14 Battle School
15 The Lion Has 'Phones
16 The Bullet is Not for Firing
17 Something Nasty in the Vault
18 Room at the Bottom
19 Big Guns
20 The Day the Balloon Went Up
21 War Dance
22 Menace from the Deep
23 Branded
24 Man Hunt
25 No Spring for Frazer
26 Sons of the Sea
Audience viewing figures for series three 12.1 million

series FOUR 25 SEPT 70 - 18 DEC 70

27 The Big Parade
28 Don't Forget the Diver
29 Boots, Boots, Boots
30 Sergeant - Save My Boy!
31 Don't Fence Me In
32 Absent Friends
33 Put That Light Out!
34 The Two and a Half Feathers
35 Mum's Army
36 The Test
37 A. Wilson (Manager)?
38 Uninvited Guests
39 Fallen Idol (34 minutes)
Audience viewing figures for series four 14.4 million

SPECIAL CHRISTMAS 1971

40 Battle of the Giants! (60 minutes)

series FIVE 6 OCT 72 - 29 DEC 72

41 Asleep in the Deep
42 Keep Young and Beautiful
43 A Soldier's Farewell
44 Getting the Bird
45 The Desperate Drive of Corporal Jones
46 If the Cap Fits ...

47 The King was in his Counting House
48 All is Safely Gathered In
49 When Did You Last See Your Money?
50 Brain Versus Brawn
51 A Brush with the Law
52 Round and Round Went the Great Big Wheel
53 Time On My Hands
Audience viewing figures for series five 16.3 nillion

series SIX 31 OCT 73 - 12 DEC 73

54 The Deadly Attachment
55 My British Buddy
56 The Royal Train
57 We Know Our Onions
58 The Honourable Man
59 Things that Go Bump in the Night
60 The Recruit
Audience viewing figures for series six 12.3 million

series SEVEN 15 NOV 74 - 23 DEC 74

61 Everybody's Trucking
62 A Man of Action
63 Gorilla Warfare
64 The Godiva Affair
65 The Captain's Car
66 Turkey Dinner
Audience viewing figures for series seven 14.8 million

series EIGHT 5 SEPT 75 - 10 OCT 75

67 Ring Dem Bells
68 When You've Got to Go
69 Is There Honey Still for Tea?
70 Come In, Your Time is Up
71 High Finance
72 The Face on the Poster
Audience viewing figures for series eight 13.5 million

SPECIAL CHRISTMAS 1975

73 My Brother and I (40 minutes)

SPECIAL CHRISTMAS 1976

74 The Love of Three Oranges (35 minutes)

series NINE 2 OCT 77 - 13 NOV 77

75 Wake-Up Walmington
76 The Making of Private Pike
77 Knights of Madness
78 The Miser's Hoard
79 Number Engaged
80. Never Too Old
Audience viewing figures for series nine 10.5 million

ARTHUR LOWE as Captain Mainwaring
JOHN LE MESURIER as Sergeant Wilson
CLIVE DUNN as Lance Corporal Jones
JOHN LAURIE as Private Frazer
JAMES BECK as Private Walker
ARNOLD RIDLEY as Private Godfrey
IAN LAVENDER as Private Pike

All programmes produced by the BBC are in colour unless otherwise indicated.
Newsreel Narration: E.V.H. Emmett (all Series One episodes)
All Series One titles were preceded with an episode number.

series ONE

The Man and the Hour (B/W)   Episode 1
Recorded: First Broadcast:
Monday 15/04/68   Wednesday 31/07/68, 8.20-8.50pm
Rpts. 17/1/69, 8/10/82,14/7/98†, 22/3/99†
Original viewing figures 7.2 million
In which our heroes band together to form a platoon of Local Defence Volunteers to defend our island home. With: Janet Davies (Mrs Pike), Caroline Dowdeswell (Janet King), John Ringham (Bracewell), Bill Pertwee (the A.R.P. Warden), Neville Hughes (the Soldier) and Jack Wright (Despatch Rider).
Locations: Opening scene inside 'The Nordic Room' of The Anchor Hotel, Thetford, 3/04/68.
Originally due for transmission on Monday 5 June.

Museum Piece (B/W)   Episode 2
Recorded: First Broadcast:
Monday 22/04/68   Wednesday 7/08/68, 7.00-7.30pm
Rpts. 24/1/69, 31/12/88 (C4), 21/7/98†, 10/5/99†
Original viewing figures 6.8 million
In which our heroes go to great lengths in their endeavours to equip themselves as a fighting force powerful enough to repel a ruthless enemy. With: Janet Davies (Mrs Pike), Caroline Dowdeswell (Janet King), Eric Woodburn (Museum Caretaker), Leon Cortez (the Milkman) and Michael Osborne (the Boy Scout).
Locations: Armoured car training; the platoon try to stop a steam roller using a garden roller (*Weeting*). The Platoon and the milk float march towards the Museum (*Newtown, Thetford*). The platoon try to gain entry to the Peabody Museum (*Oxburgh Hall, Oxborough*).

Command Decision (B/W)   Episode 3
Recorded: First Broadcast:
Monday 29/04/68   Wednesday 14/08/68, 8.20-8.50pm
Rpt. 31/1/69, 28/7/98†, 17/5/99†
Original viewing figures 8.6 million
In which our poorly-armed heroes receive an offer of rifles. All Captain Mainwaring has to do to secure their delivery is hand over command of the Walmington-on-Sea Platoon to Colonel Square. With: Caroline Dowdeswell (Janet King), Geoffrey Lumsden (Colonel Square), Charles Hill (the Butler) and Gordon Peters (the Soldier). Animals by Winships Circus.
Locations: Newsreel: Jones and statue, Butler opening door (*Oxburgh Hall, Oxborough*), Block of flats (*Richmond Green, Surrey*). Swift silent mounted training at Marsham Hall (*Buckenham Tofts, Stanford MOD*).

The Enemy Within the Gates (B/W)   Episode 4
Recorded: First Broadcast:
Monday 6/05/68   Wednesday 28/08/68, 8.20-8.50pm
Rpts 7/2/69, 4/8/98†, 24/5/99†
Original viewing figures 8.1 million
In which our heroes capture two German airmen. However, Private Godfrey complicates matters when he releases them from his charge to go for a tinkle. With: Caroline Dowdeswell (Janet King), Carl Jaffe (Captain Winogrodzki), Denys Peek / Nigel Rideout (German Pilots), Bill Pertwee (A.R.P Warden) and David Davenport (Military Police Sgt.).

The Showing Up of Corporal Jones (B/W)   Episode 5
Recorded: First Broadcast:
Monday 13/05/68   Wednesday 4/09/68, 8.20-8.50pm
Rpts 14/2/69, 11/8/98†, 31/5/99†
Original viewing figures 8.8 million
In which Corporal Jones's fitness is tested and our heroes ensure that he is not found wanting. With: Janet Davies (Mrs Pike), Martin Wyldeck (Major Regan), Patrick Waddington (the Brigadier), Edward Sinclair (the Caretaker) and Therese McMurray (the Girl at the Window).
Locations: Platoon members digging for Victory by the church, window box scene, climbing over garden wall (*No 59 Newtown, Thetford*). Assault course training ground (*Stanford Training Area*).

Shooting Pains (B/W)   Episode 6
Recorded: First Broadcast:
Monday 20/05/68   Wednesday 11/09/68, 8.20-8.50pm
Rpts. 21/2/69, 18/8/98†, 7/6/99†
Original viewing figures 9.7 million
In which our heroes use their rifles and their wits to compete for the honour of guarding a V.I.P. With: Guest Star: Barbara Windsor (Laura La Plaz), Janet Davies (Mrs Pike), Caroline Dowdeswell (Janet King), Martin Wyldeck (Major Regan), Jimmy Perry (Charlie Cheeseman) and Therese McMurray (the Girl at the Window). Marksmanship by Geoff Winship.
Location: Charlie Cheesman sequence (*Richmond Theatre, Surrey*)

Broadcast dates marked '†' were episodes newly digitally enhanced by the BBC.

series TWO

Episodes marked * do not exist in the BBC Archives

Operation Kilt (B/W)   Episode 7
Recorded: First Broadcast:
Sunday 13/10/68   Saturday 1/03/69, 7.00-7.30pm
Rpt. 28/12/01, 05/05/03.
Original viewing figures 13.9 million
In which our heroes defend their HQ from the regular Army by laying a trap in Pinner Woods. With: Janet Davies (Mrs Pike),James Copeland (Captain Ogilvy) and Colin Bean (Private Sponge).
Location: Farm and field (*Hatches Farm, Great Kingshill, Bucks*)

The Battle of Godfrey's Cottage (B/W)   Episode 8
Recorded: First broadcast
Sunday 20/10/68   Saturday 8/03/69, 7.00-7.30pm
Rpt 22/8/69, 28/12/01, 05/05/03.
Original viewing figures 11.3 million
The bells ring a false alarm. The platoon arrive at Godfrey's cottage at different times and each think that the other is the enemy. With: Janet Davies (Mrs Pike), Amy Dalby (Dolly), Nan Braunton (Cissy), Bill Pertwee (the A.R.P. Warden) and Colin Bean (Private Sponge).

The Loneliness of the Long Distance Walker (B/W)*   Episode 9
Recorded: First broadcast
Sunday 27/10/68   Saturday 15/03/69, 7.00-7.30pm
Not Repeated.
Original viewing figures 11.3 million
Private Walker is called up for National Service. Every attempt by the platoon to fix the medical fails, then corned beef comes to the rescue. With: Anthony Sharp (Brigadier-War Office), Diana King (the Chairwoman), Patrick Waddington (the Brigadier), Edward Evans (Mr Reed), Michael Knowles (Captain Cutts), Gilda Perry (Blondie), Larry Martyn (Soldier), Colin Bean (Private Sponge) and Robert Lankesheer (Medical Officer).
Location: Walker at Barracks (*Regents Park Barracks, London*).

Sgt. Wilson's Little Secret (B/W)   Episode 10
Recorded: First Broadcast:
Friday 15/11/68   Saturday 22/03/69, 7.00-7.30pm
Rpts 2/9/98 BBC2 9pm, 29/8/99 BBC2 7.10pm.
Original viewing figures 13.6 million
In which Sergeant Wilson finds it difficult to concentrate on Home Guard activities as he has a little problem of his own. With: Janet Davies (Mrs Pike) and Graham Harboard (Little Arthur) and Colin Bean (Private Sponge).

A Stripe for Frazer (B/W)*   Episode 11
Recorded: First Broadcast:
Friday 15/11/68   Saturday 29/03/69, 7.00-7.30pm
Rpt. 5/9/69.
Original viewing figures 11.3 million

Captain Mainwaring has a vacancy for a Corporal, Jones and Frazer compete for promotion. With: Geoffrey Lumsden (Corporal-Colonel Square), John Ringham (Captain Bailey), Gordon Peters (Policeman) and Edward Sinclair (the Caretaker).

Under Fire (B/W)*   Episode 12
Recorded: First Broadcast:
Wed. 27/11/68   Saturday 5/04/69, 7.00-7.30pm
Rpt. 29/8/69.
Original viewing figures 11.6 million
A local resident is suspected of signalling to the enemy, the platoon go and investigate. With: Janet Davies (Mrs Pike), Geoffrey Lumsden (Corporal-Colonel Square), John Ringham (Captain Bailey), Ernst Ulman (Sigmund Murphy), Bill Pertwee (the A.R.P. Warden), Queenie Watts (Mrs Keene), June Petersen (Woman) and Gladys Dawson (Mrs Witt).

series THREE

The Armoured Might of Lance Corporal Jones   Episode 13
Recorded: First Broadcast:
Sunday 25/05/69   Thursday 11/09/69, 7.30-8.00pm
Rpts. 4/4/70, 18/8/71, 4/1/77 (not Wales / Scotland), 21/6/92, 25/5/96, 7/6/99 BBC2, 22/6/02.
Original viewing figures 10.5 million
In which our heroes convert Jones' van into an armoured car, ambulance and troop transport. With: Janet Davies (Mrs Pike), Bill Pertwee (the A.R.P. Warden), Frank Williams (the Vicar), Pamela Cundell (Mrs Fox), Jean St. Clair (Miss Meadows), Nigel Hawthorne (the Angry Man), Queenie Watts (Mrs Peters), Olive Mercer (Mrs Casson), Harold Bennett (the Old Man) and Dick Haydon (Raymond).
Locations: Stretcher and Ambulance practice in Percy Street, Walmington. (*Nether Row, Thetford*).

Battle School   Episode 14
Recorded: First Broadcast:
Sunday 1/06/69   Thursday 18/09/69, 7.30-8.00pm
Rpts. 11/7/70 (originally scheduled for 11/4/70), 22/10/82, 21/7/92, 7/9/96, 4/9/99.
Original viewing figures 11.4 million
In which our heroes practice the art of war with live ammunition. With: Alan Tilvern (Captain Rodrigues), Alan Haines (Major Smith) and Colin Bean (Private Sponge).
Locations: The Railway Station & marching to the Battle School Camp (*Wendling Railway Station*).

The Lion Has 'Phones   Episode 15
Recorded: First Broadcast:
Sunday 8/06/69   Thursday 25/09/69, 7.30-8.00pm
Rpts. 2/5/70, 29/10/82, 15/8/92, 6/1/96, 31/5/97
Original viewing figures 11.3 million
In which an enemy aircraft crash lands in the town reservoir and our heroes make the crew surrender. With: Janet Davies (Mrs Pike), Bill Pertwee (the A.R.P. Warden), Avril Angers (the Telephone

Operator), Timothy Carlton (Lieut. Hope Bruce), Stanley McGeagh (Sgt. Waller), Richard Jacques (Mr Cheesewright), Pamela Cundell, Bernadette Milnes and Olive Mercer (the Ladies in the Queue), Linda James (Betty), Gilda Perry (Doreen), Colin Daniels and Carson Green (the Boys).

Locations: A street full of dustbins, excellent camouflage. (*Newtown, Thetford*), More camouflage training Churchyard (*West Tofts Church, MOD*). Walmington reservoir where the young boys have been swimming (*Bury St Edmunds, Sugar Works*). The working title of this episode was 'Sorry, Wrong Number', which was used for the radio version.

The Bullet is Not for Firing　　　Episode 16
Recorded:　　　　　　　　　　　　First Broadcast:
Sunday 22/06/69　　　　Thursday 2/10/69, 7.30-8.00pm
Rpts. 25/4/70, 22/8/92, 15/6/96, 14/06/99.
Original viewing figures 11.8 million
In which our heroes use up their ammunition on a passing aircraft and Captain Mainwaring calls a Court of Enquiry. With: Janet Davies (Mrs Pike), Frank Williams (the Vicar), Tim Barrett (Captain Pringle), Michael Knowles (Captain Cutts), Edward Sinclair (the Verger), Harold Bennett (Mr Blewitt), May Warden (Mrs Dowding) and Fred Tomlinson, Kate Forge, Eilidh McNab, Andrew Daye and Arthur Lewis (the Choir).
Locations: Collecting their empty bullet cases. (*Stanta MOD*).

Something Nasty in the Vault　　　Episode 17
Recorded:　　　　　　　　　　　　First Broadcast:
Sunday 15/06/69　　　　Thursday 9/10/69, 7.30-8.00pm
Rpts. 18/4/70, 16/3/71 (see below), 15/10/82 (b/w), 17/10/89, 19/12/92, 13/1/96, 11/9/99.
Original viewing figures 11.1 million
In which our heroes discover an unexploded bomb in the vault of Captain Mainwaring's bank. With: Bill Pertwee (the A.R.P. Warden), Robert Dorning (the Bank Inspector), Norman Mitchell (Captain Rogers) and Janet Davies (Mrs Pike).
The 16/3/71 repeat was to mark this episode's winning of the SFTA Award for Best Light Entertainment Production and Direction.

Room at the Bottom (B/W)　　　Episode 18
Recorded:　　　　　　　　　　　　First Broadcast:
Sunday 29/06/69　　　Thursday 16/10/69, 7.30-8.00pm
Rpts. 9/5/70, 9/9/98 BBC2 9pm
Original viewing figures 12.4 million
In which Captain Mainwaring discovers that he is not a commissioned Officer. With: Anthony Sagar (Drill Sergeant Gregory), John Ringham (Captain Bailey), Edward Sinclair (the Verger) and Colin Bean (Private Sponge).
Locations: Jones goes out scouting and finds an ants nest. (*Frog Hill, MOD*).

Big Guns　　　Episode 19
Recorded:　　　　　　　　　　　　First Broadcast:
Sunday 6/07/69　　　Thursday 23/10/69, 7.30-8.00pm
Rpts. 16/5/70, 29/8/92, 20/7/96, 18/9/99.
Original viewing figures 13.2 million
In which the platoon receive heavy artillery. With: Edward Evans

(Mr Rees), Edward Sinclair (the Verger), Don Estelle (the Man from Pickfords) and Roy Denton (Mr Bennett).

The Day the Balloon Went Up　　　Episode 20
Recorded:　　　　　　　　　　　　First broadcast
Thursday 23/10/69　　　Thursday 30/10/69, 7.30-8.00pm
Rpts. 23/5/70, 5/9/71, 5/11/82, 19/9/92, 30/12/95, 30/10/99.
Original viewing figures 12.5 million
In which our heroes capture a runaway barrage balloon. With: Bill Pertwee (the A.R.P. Warden), Frank Williams (the Vicar), Edward Sinclair (the Verger), Nan Braunton (Miss Godfrey), Jennifer Browne (the W.A.A.F. Sergeant), Andrew Carr (the Operations Room Officer), Therese McMurray (the Girl in the Haystack), Kenneth Watson (the R.A.F. Officer), Vicki Lane (the Girl on the Tandem), Harold Bennett (Mr Blewitt), and a fleeting appearance of Jack Haig (as the Gardener).
Locations: The Platoon, Vicar, Verger and Warden take the barrage balloon to Pinner Fields (*Croxton Heath, Stanford MOD*). The pruning gardener & the haystack Mainwaring crashes into (built in the garden) (*The Red House, West Tofts*). Mainwaring dangling from the railway bridge (*Wendling Railway Station*).

War Dance　　　Episode 21
Recorded:　　　　　　　　　　　　First Broadcast:
Thursday 30/10/69　　　Thursday 6/11/69, 7.30-8.00pm
Rpts. 30/5/70, 26/9/92, 1/6/96, 27/6/2000
Original viewing figures 12.6 million
In which Captain Mainwaring decides to lift the morale of the troops by giving a Platoon Dance. With: Frank Williams (the Vicar), Edward Sinclair (the Verger), Janet Davies (Mrs Pike), Nan Braunton (Miss Godfrey), Olive Mercer (Mrs Yeatman), Sally Douglas (Blodwen), The Graham Twins (Doris and Dora), Hugh Hastings (the Pianist) and Eleanor Smale (Mrs Prosser).

Menace from the Deep　　　Episode 22
Recorded:　　　　　　　　　　　　First Broadcast:
Friday 7/11/69　　　Thursday 13/11/69, 7.30-8.00pm
Rpts. 6/6/70, 12/11/82, 4/9/89, 29/1/91, 9/1/93, 12/7/96.
Original viewing figures 13.3 million
In which our heroes are very nearly blown to kingdom come by a mine under the pier. With: Bill Pertwee (the A.R.P. Warden), Stuart Sherwin (the 2nd A.R.P. Warden), Bill Treacher (the 1st Sailor) and Larry Martyn (the 2nd Sailor).
The 12/7/96 repeat was as part of Dawn and Jennifer's Comedy Zone (the comedy choices of Dawn French and Jennifer Saunders).
Locations: Getting into the boat from the Pier (*Britannia Pier, Great Yarmouth*). Warden in paddle boat (*Lowestoft*).

Branded　　　Episode 23
Recorded:　　　　　　　　　　　　First Broadcast:
Friday 14/11/69　　　Thursday 20/11/69, 7.30-8.00pm
Rpts. 13/6/70, 19/11/82, 3/10/92, 22/6/96, 11/7/2000.
Original viewing figures 11.1 million

In which the bravery of Private Godfrey is called into question. With: Bill Pertwee (the Chief Warden), Nan Braunton (Miss Godfrey), Roger Avon (the Doctor), Stuart Sherwin (the 2nd A.R.P. Warden).

Man Hunt   Episode 24
Recorded: First Broadcast:
Friday 21/11/69   Thursday 27/11/69, 7.30-8.00pm
Rpts. 20/6/70, 26/11/82, 10/10/92, 8/6/96.
Original viewing figures 11.8 million
Walker makes up 10 dozen pairs but cannot remember the colour and platoon enlist a recruit with four feet. With: Bill Pertwee (the Chief Warden), Janet Davies (Mrs Pike), Patrick Tull (the Suspect), Robert Aldous (the German Pilot), Robert Moore (the Large Man), Leon Cortez (the Small Man), Olive Mercer (the Fierce Lady), Miranda Hampton (the Sexy Lady) and Bran the dog (as himself).
Locations: Mainwaring, Wilson and Walker in the street looking for knickers (*Nether Row, Thetford*). Hodges pulls the parachute from a tree (*Black Rabbit Warren, Stanford MOD*), Walker is hot on the trail with his tracker dog (*Froghill, Stanford MOD*), Farm buildings where they capture the spy (*Stanford MOD*).

No Spring for Frazer   Episode 25
Recorded: First Broadcast:
Friday 28/11/69   Thursday 4/12/69, 7.30-8.00pm
Rpts. 25/7/70, 3/12/82, 19/9/89, 24/2/96, 01/07/2000.
Original viewing figures 13.6 million
In which Frazer loses the Lewis gun butterfly spring. With: Frank Williams (the Vicar), Edward Sinclair (the Verger), Harold Bennett (Mr Blewitt), Joan Cooper (Miss Baker) and Ronnie Brandon (Mr Drury).
Locations: Looking over the wall with the bomb notice and the churchyard (*Langford Church, Stanford MOD*).

26. Sons of the Sea   Episode 26
Recorded: First Broadcast:
Friday 5/12/69   Thursday 11/12/69, 7.30-8.00pm
Rpts. 1/8/70, 10/12/82, 17/10/92, 6/6/94, 27/1/96.
Original viewing figures 13.3 million
In which our heroes acquire a Platoon boat. With: Michael Bilton (Mr Maxwell), John Leeson (the 1st Soldier), Jonathan Holt (the 2nd Soldier) and Ralph Ball (the Man on Station).
Locations: Trying out the new boat (*River Waveney, Beccles*). Picking up the rifle bolts along the railway track (*Great Yarmouth railway station - sidings north of*). Landing on coast and Lifeboat house (*Lowestoft*).

series FOUR

The Big Parade   Episode 27
Recorded: First Broadcast:
Friday 17/07/70   Friday 25/09/70, 8.00-8.30pm
Rpts. 30/5/71, 12/9/89, 16/7/93, 17/2/96, 4/8/2000.
Original viewing figures 14 million
Captain Mainwaring decides that Walmington-on-Sea Home

Guard should have a mascot to lead them on parade. But he soon discovers that trusting Private Walker to supply one was a serious error of judgment. With: Bill Pertwee (the A.R.P. Warden), Janet Davies (Mrs Pike), Edward Sinclair (the Verger), Colin Bean (Private Sponge) and Pamela Cundell (Mrs Fox).
Locations: Pike in bog (*Stanton Lake, MOD*), The dirty platoon march past a speechless Warden and Verger (*Nether Row, Thetford*). Home Guard and the Wardens race to the finish (*Brandon, railway station yard*).

Don't Forget the Diver   Episode 28
Recorded: First Broadcast:
Friday 24/07/70   Friday 2/10/70, 8.00-8.30pm
Rpts. 6/6/71, 3/3/85, 24/10/92, 10/2/96, 19/11/2000.
Original viewing figures 12.3 million
The Walmington-on-Sea Home Guard come up with an ingenious plan to capture Captain Square's HQ, in the windmill, which does not quite go according to plan. With: Bill Pertwee (the A.R.P. Warden), Frank Williams (the Vicar), Edward Sinclair (the Verger), Geoffrey Lumsden (Captain Square), Robert Raglan (the H.G. Sergeant), Colin Bean (Private Sponge), Don Estelle (the 2nd A.R.P. Warden) and Verne Morgan (the Landlord).
Locations: The windmill which Jones has to climb (*Drinkstone Mill*). Walker is helping with the diversions (*Bardwell*). The Vicar answers the field telephone (*West Tofts Church, Stanford MOD*). Boat house, Jones in river (*Manor House, Coltishall*).

Boots, Boots, Boots   Episode 29
Recorded: First Broadcast:
Friday 31/07/70   Friday 9/10/70, 8.00-8.30pm
Rpts. 13/6/71, 10/3/85, 31/10/92, 29/6/96, 16/7/2000.
Original viewing figures 13.2 million
The Walmington-on-Sea Home Guard are instructed in the three Fs - all of which, it seems, involve feet. So begins a gruelling programme of exercises and route marches to toughen up their metatarsals. With: Bill Pertwee (the A.R.P. Warden), Janet Davies (Mrs Pike) and Erik Chitty (Mr Sedgewick).
Locations: Foot hardening on the beach (*Winterton Beach*). Football match - bare feet style (*Buckenham Tofts, Stanford MOD*).

Sergeant, - Save My Boy!   Episode 30
Recorded: First Broadcast:
Saturday 27/06/70   Friday 16/10/70, 8.00-8.30pm
Rpts. 20/6/71, 31/12/90, 21/10/95, 17/5/97, 31/3/01.
Original viewing figures 14.5 million
When Private Pike is trapped in a minefield, Private Godfrey risks his life to save him. With: Bill Pertwee (the A.R.P. Warden), Janet Davies (Mrs Pike) and Michael Knowles (the Engineer Officer).

Don't Fence Me In   Episode 31
Recorded: First Broadcast:
Friday 10/07/70   Friday 23/10/70, 8.00-8.30pm
Rpts. 27/6/71, 7/11/92, 24/5/94, 10/5/97, 25/05/03.
Original viewing figures 7.2 million

The men of the Walmington-on-Sea Home Guard are sent to watch over the local Italian Prisoner of War Camp. With: Edward Evans (General Monteverdi), John Ringham (Captain Bailey) and Larry Martyn (the Italian P.O.W.).
Locations: Italian POW camp (*Thorpe Camp MOD*).

Absent Friends   Episode 32
Recorded: First broadcast
Friday 7/08/70   Friday 30/10/70, 8.00-8.30pm
Rpt. 4/7/71
Original viewing figures 13.9 million
Our heroes take advantage of Captain Mainwaring's absence and undermine his authority. But Mainwaring receives help from an unexpected quarter. With: Bill Pertwee (the A.R.P. Warden), Janet Davies (Mrs Pike), Edward Sinclair (the Verger), J.G. Devlin (Regan), Arthur English (the Policeman), Patrick Connor (Shamus), Verne Morgan (the Landlord), and Michael Lomax (the 2nd A.R.P. Warden).
This must be the least repeated epiosde by the BBC. The mention of the IRA in the script is probably the reason for this.

Put That Light Out   Episode 33
Recorded: First Broadcast:
Friday 30/10/70   Friday 6/11/70, 8.00-8.30pm
Rpts. 11/7/71, 21/11/92, 6/5/01.
Original viewing figures 13 million
Episode based on an idea by Harold Snoad
Walmington-on-Sea Home Guard are sent to guard the local lighthouse but end up accidentally turning the light on the town - making an inviting target for enemy planes overhead. With: Bill Pertwee (the A.R.P. Warden), Avril Angers (the Telephone Operator), Stuart Sherwin (the 2nd A.R.P. Warden) and Gordon Peters (the Lighthouse Keeper).

The Two and a Half Feathers   Episode 34
Recorded: First Broadcast:
Friday 6/11/70   Friday 13/11/70, 8.00-8.30pm
Rpts. 18/7/71, 24/2/85, 28/11/92, 20/1/96, 14/6/01.
Original viewing figures 15.6 million
The glorious history of Lance Corporal Jones comes under a cloud when an old comrade-in-arms dredges up their service in the Sudan. With: Bill Pertwee (A.R.P. Warden), John Cater (Private Clarke), Wendy Richard (Edith), Queenie Watts (Edna), Gilda Perry (Doreen), Linda James (Betty), Parnell McGarry (Elizabeth) and John Ash (Raymond).
Locations: Jones recalls his days in the desert (*Leziate Sands, Kings Lynn*).

Mum's Army   Episode 35
Recorded: First broadcast
Friday 13/11/70   Friday 20/11/70, 8.00-8.30pm
Rpts. 25/7/71, 3/10/89, 12/12/92, 23/11/97, 21/6/01.
Original viewing figures 16.4 million
Captain Mainwaring involves the ladies of the town for the local War Effort and becomes involved himself with one of their number... With: Carmen Silvera (Mrs Gray), Janet Davies (Mrs Pike), Wendy Richard (Edith Parish), Pamela Cundell (Mrs Fox), Julia Burbury (Miss Ironside), Rosemary Faith (Ivy Samways), Melita Manger (the Waitress), David

Gilchrist (the Serviceman), Eleanor Smale (Mrs Prosser), Deirdre Costello (the Buffet Attendant) and Jack Le White (the Porter).

The Test   Episode 36
Recorded: First Broadcast:
Friday 20/11/70   Friday 27/11/70, 8.00-8.30pm
Rpts. 1/8/71, 5/12/92, 6/7/96, 14/8/01
Original viewing figures 16 million
The Wardens, with a secret weapon, challenge the Home Guard to a cricket match. With: Bill Pertwee (A.R.P. Warden), Frank Williams (Vicar), Edward Sinclair (Verger), Don Estelle (Gerald), Harold Bennett (Mr Blewitt) and the special appearance of Freddie Trueman (E.C. Egan).
Locations: The cricket pitch (*Buckenham Tofts, Stanta MOD*).

A. Wilson (Manager)?   Episode 37
Recorded: First Broadcast:
Friday 27/11/70   Friday 4/12/70, 8.00-8.30pm
Rpts. 8/8/71, 23/11/83, 8/1/91, 23/7/93, 31/8/96. 5/7/01.
Original viewing figures 15.4 million
Captain Mainwaring is left smarting when he is informed that promotion is in the air for Sergeant Wilson - both at Swallow Bank and in the Home Guard. With: Frank Williams (the Vicar), Edward Sinclair (the Verger), Janet Davies (Mrs Pike), Blake Butler (Mr West), Robert Raglan (Captain Pritchard), Arthur Brough (Mr Boyle), Colin Bean (Private Sponge) and Hugh Hastings (Private Hastings).

Uninvited Guests   Episode 38
Recorded: First Broadcast:
Friday 4/12/70   Friday 11/12/70, 8.00-8.30pm
Rpts. 22/8/71, 15/1/91, 6/11/93, 21/9/96, 10/7/01.
Original viewing figures 13.1 million
After the A.R.P. Headquarters is damaged in an air raid, Hodges moves his Wardens into Mainwaring's H.Q. at the Church Hall, much to the Home Guard Platoon's irritation. A battle for territory ensues which leads to a blazing climax on the roof. With: Bill Pertwee (the A.R.P. Warden), Frank Williams (the Vicar), Edward Sinclair (the Verger), Rose Hill (Mrs Cole) and Don Estelle (Gerald).
N.B. This episode was erroneously billed in Radio Times on first broadcast as Unwanted Guests.

Fallen Idol   Episode 39
Recorded: First Broadcast:
Friday 11/12/70   Friday 18/12/70, 8.00-8.30pm
Rpts. 29/8/71, 17/3/85, 26/2/2000, 4/6/02. 01/06/03.
Original viewing figures 13.1 million
An Officers' drinking session at the weekend training school leaves Captain Mainwaring more than a little the worse for wear, only an heroic action can restore his wounded reputation. With: Geoffrey Lumsden (Captain Square), Rex Garner (Captain Ashley-Jones), Michael Knowles (Captain Reed), Anthony Sagar (the Sergeant Major), Tom Mennard (the Mess Orderly) and Robert Raglan (Captain Pritchard).
Locations: Stick bomb training (*Genade Training Area, Stanta MOD*). Electricity sub station (*possibly Honington to Euston Road, Thetford*).

SPECIAL

Battle of the Giants   Episode 40
Recorded: First Broadcast:
Sunday 19/09/71   Monday 27/12/71, 7.00-8.00pm
Rpts. 26/8/72, 10/1/83, 8/1/86, 26/12/92, 18/12/93,
27/12/96, 20/1/01.
Original viewing figures 18.7 million
Captain Mainwaring's Walmington-on-Sea Platoon take part in
an initiative test against old rivals - the Eastgate Platoon. The
contest is umpired by the Warden, the Vicar and the Verger.
With: Bill Pertwee (the A.R.P. Warden), Geoffrey Lumsden (Captain Square),
Frank Williams (the Vicar), Edward Sinclair (the Verger), Robert Raglan (the
Colonel), Charles Hill (the Sergeant), Colin Bean (Private Sponge) and
Rosemary Faith (the Barmaid).
N.B. The original one hour version of Battle of the Giants was
broadcast in 1993 for the first time in over a decade and again
on 27/11/96, the 1986 and 1992 repeats being broadcast
from a separate 2-inch master tape which had been edited to
55 minutes duration.
Locations: The crossroads where Square and Mainwaring drive
round and round (*West Tofts, Stanta MOD*). Walmington and
Eastgate meet face to face on the bridge (*Buckenham Tofts,
Stanta MOD*). The platoon enter the tower to raise the winning
flag (*Eleveden Estate, Thetford*).

series FIVE

Asleep in the Deep   Episode 41
Recorded: First Broadcast:
Friday 26/05/72   Friday 6/10/72, 8.30-9.00pm
Rpts. 30/6/73, 10/10/89, 30/7/93, 20/12/96, 17/7/01.
Original viewing figures 17 million
The Platoon are trapped in an underground room at the Water
Works. They happily await rescue - until a water main begins
to leak. With: Bill Pertwee (the A.R.P. Warden) and Colin Bean (Private
Sponge).

Keep Young and Beautiful   Episode 42
Recorded: First Broadcast:
Friday 9/06/72   Friday 13/10/72, 8.30-9.00pm
Rpts. 7/7/73, 26/9/89, 6/8/93, 10/1/97, 21/2/99, 24/7/01.
Original viewing figures 16 million
It is decided in parliament that some of the Home Guard
veterans and the younger A.R.P wardens should change
places. Mainwaring's outfit set out to thwart it with the young
look. With: Bill Pertwee (the A.R.P. Warden), Robert Raglan (the Colonel),
James Ottaway (the 1st Member of Parliament), Charles Morgan (2nd Member
of Parliament), Derek Bond (The Minister), and local Thetford man, Ron
Barrell (The General).
Locations: The age and fitness parade in the rain (*High Lodge,
Thetford*).

A Soldier's Farewell   Episode 43
Recorded: First Broadcast:
Friday 2/06/72   Friday 20/10/72, 8.30-9.00pm
Rpts. 14/7/73, 14/11/92, 27/7/96, 2/5/2000.
Original viewing figures 17.7 million
London/South East Regional Repeat: 18/1/77
Mainwaring dreams that he is Napoleon. With: Bill Pertwee (the
A.R.P. Warden), Frank Williams (the Vicar), Robert Gillespie (Charles Boyer),
Joan Savage (Greta Garbo), Colin Bean (Private Sponge) and Joy Allen (the
Clippie).
Locations: Cinema interior (*Palace Cinema, Thetford*). The
battlefield of Napoleon and Wellington, Napoleon surrenders
(*Lodge Fram, Kilverstone, Thetford*).

Getting the Bird   Episode 44
Recorded: First Broadcast:
Friday 19/05/72   Friday 27/10/72, 8.30-9.00pm
Rpts. 21/7/73, 5/4/85, 22/1/91, 13/11/93, 5/10/96,
21/2/99, 22/8/01.
Original viewing figures 17.5 million
London/South East Regional Repeat: 25/1/77
Walker arranges for Jones to get some off-ration pigeons, but
did they come from Trafalgar Square? With: Bill Pertwee (A.R.P.
Warden), Frank Williams (Vicar), Edward Sinclair (Verger), Pamela Cundell (Mrs
Fox), Olive Mercer (Mrs Yeatman), Seretta Wilson (Wren) and Alvar Lidell (the
Newsreader).

The Desperate Drive of Corporal Jones   Episode 45
Recorded: First Broadcast:
Friday 16/06/72   Friday 3/11/72, 8.30-9.00pm
Rpts. 28/7/73, 16/4/91, 28/10/95, 15/3/97, 7/8/01.
Original viewing figures 15.8 million
London/South East Regional Repeat: 1/2/77
Mainwaring's Platoon are sitting in a barn which is the target
for some 25-pounders, only Jones knows of the danger. With:
Bill Pertwee (the A.R.P. Warden), Frank Williams (the Vicar), Edward Sinclair
(the Verger), Robert Raglan (the Colonel), Larry Martyn (the Signals Private)
and James Taylor (the Artillery Officer).
Locations: Jones and Godfrey's Control Point (*High Lodge,
Thetford*). The platoon marching towards the barn (*Stanta
MOD*). Jones is towing Godfrey to rescue the platoon (*Santon
Downham, Brandon Road*).

If the Cap Fits...   Episode 46
Recorded: First Broadcast:
Friday 30/06/72   Friday 10/11/72, 8.30-9.00pm
Rpts. 4/8/73, 12/2/91, 4/11/95, 7/6/97, 20/9/01.
Original viewing figures 15.5 million
London/South East Regional Repeat: 15/2/77
One way to deal with a grumbler is to let him take over - so
Mainwaring tries it with Frazer. With: Bill Pertwee (A.R.P. Warden),
Campbell Singer (Major General Menzies), Robert Raglan (Colonel), Edward
Sinclair (Verger), Alex McAvoy (Sergeant) and Dennis Blanch (2nd
Lieutenant).

The King Was in His Counting House

Episode 47

Recorded:
Friday 23/06/72
Rpts. 11/8/73, 31/10/89, 13/8/93, 07/2/97, 6/9/01.
Original viewing figures 16 million
London/South East Regional Repeat: 22/2/77

First Broadcast:
Friday 17/11/72, 8.30-9.00pm

A bomb falls on the strong room of Mainwaring's bank. He insists that the Platoon count the money and guard it. With: Bill Pertwee (the A.R.P. Warden), Frank Williams (the Vicar), Edward Sinclair (the Verger), Wendy Richard (Shirley) and Colin Bean (Private Sponge).
Locations: Loading the money onto the horse and cart (*Honington, Suffolk*). Money falling from cart (*Euston to Rushford Road*). Horse bolts across the hill (*Sapiston, Suffolk*).

All is Safely Gathered In

Episode 48

Recorded:
Friday 3/11/72
Rpts. 18/8/73, 24/10/89, 27/8/93, 24/1/97, 31/7/01.
Original viewing figures 16.5 million
London/South East Regional Repeat: 1/3/77

First Broadcast:
Friday 24/11/72, 8.30-9.00pm

The Platoon help a widowed lady friend of Private Godfrey to gather the harvest. With: Bill Pertwee (the A.R.P. Warden), Brenda Cowling (Mrs Prentice), Frank Williams (the Vicar), Edward Sinclair (Verger), Colin Bean (Private Sponge), April Walker (Judy) and Tina Cornioli (Olive).
Locations: Mrs Prentice's farm buildings, the platoon leaving by the side door, harvest scene (*Walnut Tree Farm, Bressingham*).

When Did You Last See Your Money?

Episode 49

Recorded:
Friday 10/11/72
Rpts. 25/8/73, 14/11/89, 18/9/93, 31/1/97, 27/9/01.
Original viewing figures 16 million
London/South East Regional Repeat: 8/3/77

First Broadcast:
Friday 1/12/72, 8.30-9.00pm

Jones can't remember where he put the £500 that was collected for the canteen fund, so the Platoon try to jog his memory. With: Bill Pertwee (the A.R.P. Warden), Frank Williams (the Vicar), Edward Sinclair (the Verger), Harold Bennett (Mr Blewitt) and Tony Hughes (Mr Billings).

Brain Versus Brawn

Episode 50

Recorded:
Friday 17/11/72
Rpts. 1/9/73, 19/2/91, 11/11/95, 14/6/97, 30/3/2000.
Original viewing figures 18.6 million
London/South East Regional Repeat: 15/3/77

First Broadcast:
Friday 8/12/72, 8.30-9.00pm

The Platoon disguise themselves as Firemen during an initiative exercise, but are called on to tackle a real fire. With: Bill Pertwee (the A.R.P. Warden), Robert Raglan (the Colonel), Edward Sinclair (the Verger), Anthony Roye (Mr Fairbrother), Maggie Don (the Waitress), Geoffrey Hughes (the Bridge Corporal) and David Rose (the Dump Corporal).
Locations: HQ, where the Verger starts a fire (*High Lodge, Thetford*). Army checkpoint on the bridge and village where warden Hodges diverts the fire engine (*Santon Downham*). House on fire (*Walnut Tree Farm, Bressingham*).

A Brush with the Law

Episode 51

Recorded:
Sunday 26/11/72
Rpt. 26/2/91, 18/11/95, 4/10/01.
Original viewing figures 15.4 million
London/South East Regional Repeat: 22/3/77

First Broadcast:
Friday 15/12/72, 8.30-9.00pm

A light is left burning from the Church Hall, so the Chief Warden puts Mainwaring in Court. With: Bill Pertwee (the A.R.P. Warden), Frank Williams (the Vicar), Edward Sinclair (the Verger), Geoffrey Lumsden (Captain Square), Jeffrey Gardiner (Mr Wintergreen), Stuart Sherwin (the Junior Warden), Marjorie Wilde (the Lady Magistrate), Chris Gannon (the Clerk of the Court), and Toby Perkins (the Usher).

Round and Round Went the Great Big Wheel

Episode 52

Recorded:
Friday 1/12/72
Rpts. 11/1/74, 5/3/91, 25/11/95, 21/6/97, 11/10/01.
Original viewing figures 13.7 million

First Broadcast:
Friday 22/12/72, 8.30-9.00pm

The Platoon are chosen for Special Duties during the test of a secret weapon which runs amok. With: Bill Pertwee (the A.R.P. Warden), Geoffrey Chater (Colonel Pierce), Edward Underdown (Major General Sir Charles Holland), Michael Knowles (Captain Stewart), Jeffrey Segal (the Minister) and John Clegg (the Wireless Operator). 'Great Big Wheel' operated by Mr D. Harding.
Locations: Secret weapon trials on the airfield (*Watton Airfield, MOD*), Jones dangles from the railway bridge (*Wash Lane, Wacton*), Thatched cottage and house where they borrow the motorbike and clippers (*Wacton Common, Norfolk*).

Time On My Hands

Episode 53

Recorded:
Friday 8/12/72
Rpts. 18/4/74, 10/7/81, 7/11/89, 3/9/93, 14/2/97, 18/10/01.
Original viewing figures 16.6 million
London/South East Regional Repeat: 29/3/77

First Broadcast:
Friday 29/12/72, 8.30-9.00pm

An enemy pilot bails out and becomes tangled up with the town clock - and so does Mainwaring's Platoon. With: Bill Pertwee (the A.R.P. Warden), Frank Williams (the Vicar), Edward Sinclair (the Verger), Harold Bennett (Mr Blewitt), Colin Bean (Private Sponge), Joan Cooper (Miss Fortescue), Eric Longworth (Mr Gordon) and Christopher Sandford (the German Pilot).
Locations: The platoon enter the Town Hall (*Guildhall, Thetford*), The crowd watch the pilot dangling (*Nether Row, Thetford*).

series SIX

The Deadly Attachment

Episode 54

Recorded:
Friday 22/06/73
Rpts. 25/4/74, 24/6/78, 21/11/89, 2/10/93, 25/4/95, 28/6/97, 23/10/01, 20/03/04.

First Broadcast:
Wednesday 31/10/73, 6.50-7.20pm

Original viewing figures 12.9 million
Captain Mainwaring's Platoon are detailed to guard a captured U-Boat Captain and crew. With: Philip Madoc (as the U-Boat Captain) Bill Pertwee (Chief Warden Hodges), Edward Sinclair (the Verger), Robert Raglan (the Colonel) and Colin Bean (Private Sponge).
Locations: The platoon march with the U-Boat crew (*Mill Lane, Thetford*).

My British Buddy
Episode 55

Recorded:	First Broadcast:

Friday 8/06/73   Wednesday 7/11/73, 6.50-7.20pm
Rpts. 2/5/74, 12/3/91, 25/9/93, 21/2/97, 14/11/01, 30/04/04
Original viewing figures 12.5 million
The first contingent of American troops arrive in Walmington and the Platoon make arrangements to welcome them. With: Bill Pertwee (Chief Warden Hodges), Alan Tilvern (the U.S. Colonel), Frank Williams (the Vicar), Edward Sinclair (the Verger), Janet Davies (Mrs Pike), Wendy Richard (Shirley), Pamela Cundell (Mrs Fox), Verne Morgan (the Landlord), Talfryn Thomas (Mr Cheeseman), Suzanne Kerchiss (Ivy), Robert Raglan (the Colonel) and Blain Fairman (the U.S. Sergeant).

The Royal Train
Episode 56

Recorded: First Broadcast:
Friday 29/06/73   Wednesday 14/11/73, 6.30-7.00pm
Rpts. 9/5/74, 5/2/88, 26/3/91, 4/12/93, 8/3/97, 30/7/2000, 9/4/02*.
Original viewing figures 13.1 million
H.M. King George VI is passing through Walmington by train. The Platoon provide a Guard of Honour. With: Bill Pertwee (Chief Warden Hodges), Frank Williams (the Vicar), Edward Sinclair (the Verger), William Moore (the Station Master), Freddie Earlle (Henry), Ronnie Brody (Bob), Fred McNaughton (the Mayor), Sue Bishop (the Ticket Collector) and Bob Hornery (the City Gent).
N.B. The earlier broadcast time was to celebrate the Royal Wedding of Princess Anne and Captain Mark Philips, 14th November 1973.
* Special screening on the day of Queen Elizabeth, the Queen Mother's funeral.
Locations: On the platform waiting for the Royal Train (*Weybourne Railway Station*). Chase sequence and trackside (*North Norfolk Railway, near Sherringham*).

We Know Our Onions
Episode 57

Recorded: First Broadcast:
Friday 15/06/73   Wednesday 21/11/73, 6.50-7.20pm
Rpts. 16/5/74, 19/3/91, 27/11/93, 22/2/97, 20/6/2000.
Original viewing figures 11.6 million
Captain Mainwaring and the Platoon take part in a Home Guard Efficiency Test. With: Fulton Mackay (Captain Ramsey), Bill Pertwee (Chief Warden Hodges), Edward Sinclair (the Verger), Alex McAvoy (the Sergeant), Pamela Manson (the N.A.A.F.I. Girl) and Cy Town (the Mess Steward).
Locations: Covering the gun at St. Aldhelms Church Hall (*Honington, Suffolk*). Training Room (*St David's Hall, Whitehawk, Brighton*). Initiative testing area (*Brighton Race Course, trainer's area*).

The Honourable Man
Episode 58

Recorded: First Broadcast:
Sunday 8/07/73   Wednesday 28/11/73, 6.50-7.20pm
Rpts. 23/5/74, 2/4/91, 2/12/95.
Original viewing figures 12.1 million
A relation of Sergeant Wilson dies. This puts Wilson on the outer fringes of the aristocracy - much to Mainwarings annoyance. With: Bill Pertwee (Chief Warden Hodges), Frank Williams (the Vicar), Edward Sinclair (the Verger), Eric Longworth (the Town Clerk), Janet Davies (Mrs Pike), Gabor Vernon (the Russian), Hana-Maria Pravda (the Interpreter), Robert Raglan (the Colonel), Pamela Cundell (Mrs Fox) and Fred McNaughton (the Mayor).
The studio sequences in this episode represent James Beck's last work on the TV 'Dad's Army'. He recorded two radio episodes - Sergeant Wilson's Little Secret and A Stripe for Frazer - the following Friday night and died after a short illness on Monday 6th August 1973...
Locations: Wilson mounts the motorbike (*Honington, Suffolk*). While riding falls off the motorbike (*Sapiston, Suffolk*). The car arrives with the Russian visitor (*Bardwell Green, Suffolk*).

Things That Go Bump in the Night
Episode 59

Recorded: First Broadcast:
Sunday 15/07/73   Wednesday 5/12/73, 6.50-7.20pm
Rpts. 30/5/74, 9/4/91, 11/12/93, 24/5/97, 15/12/01
Original viewing figures 12.2 million
Jones's van, carrying the Platoon, breaks down outside an apparently deserted house where Mainwaring decides they should spend the night. With: Jonathan Cecil (Captain Cadbury) and Colin Bean (Private Sponge).
N.B. This episode features James Beck in location film work, shot prior to the studio recording of The Honourable Man, and is, in transmission order, his final appearance in the TV series.
Locations: Leaving the dog training area, bottles at the slope (*Glebe Cottage, Sapiston*). Marching across open fields and running away from the dogs, river crossing where Mainwaring keeps his feet dry (*The Black Bourn, Sapiston, Suffolk*).

The Recruit
Episode 60

Recorded: First broadcast
Sunday 22/07/73   Wednesday 12/12/73, 6.50-7.20pm
Rpts. 6/6/74, 8/1/94, 19/7/97, 20/12/01.
Original viewing figures 11.6 million
Captain Mainwaring is temporarily in hospital, during his absence Sergeant Wilson allows the Vicar and the Verger to join the Platoon. With: Bill Pertwee (Chief Warden Hodges), Frank Williams (the Vicar), Edward Sinclair (the Verger), Susan Majolier (the Nurse) and Lindsey Dunn (the Small Boy).
This episode had to be rewritten to take into account James Beck's absence due to illness.

series SEVEN

Everybody's Trucking   Episode 61
Recorded: First broadcast
Sunday 27/10/74   Friday 15/11/74, 7.45-8.15pm
Rpts. 15/5/75, 14/5/91, 19/11/94, 30/11/97, 21/12/01.
Original viewing figures 14.1 million
The platoon are to sign the route for the convoy. They discover a steam engine obstructing the road. With: Bill Pertwee (Chief Warden Hodges), Frank Williams (the Vicar), Edward Sinclair (the Verger), Pamela Cundell (Mrs Fox), Harold Bennett (Mr Bluett) (sic), Olive Mercer (Mrs Yeatman), Felix Bowness (the Driver) and Colin Bean (Private Sponge).
Locations: Steam engine blocking the road (*Blackrabbit Warren, Stanta MOD*), The crossroads with the convoy diversion sign (*Stanta MOD*).

A Man of Action   Episode 62
Recorded: First broadcast:
Tuesday 7/05/74   Friday 22/11/74, 7.45-8.15pm
Rpts. 22/5/75, 16/4/82, 28/11/89, 20/11/93, 24/8/96, 3/1/02.
Original viewing figures 16.4 million
A bomb drops on the outskirts of Walmington-on-Sea. Mainwaring declares Martial Law. With: Bill Pertwee (Chief Warden Hodges), Talfryn Thomas (Mr Cheeseman), Frank Williams (the Vicar), Edward Sinclair (the Verger), Eric Longworth (the Town Clerk), Harold Bennett (Mr Bluett) (sic), Arnold Peters (Fire Officer Dale), Jay Denyer (Inspector Baker), Robert Mill (Captain Swan) and Colin Bean (Private Sponge).
N.B.Shown as a special tribute to Arthur Lowe on Sunday 16th April 1982 at 9.25pm (after his death on 15th April 1982).

Gorilla Warfare   Episode 63
Recorded: First broadcast
Sunday 27/10/74   Friday 29/11/74, 7.45-8.15pm
Rpts. 29/5/75, 12/6/76, 5/12/89, 9/10/93, 12/4/97, 3/1/02.
Original viewing figures 14.4 million
During an exercise, Mainwaring casts himself as a Highly Important Secret Agent. The regular Army try to prevent him from completing his mission. With: Bill Pertwee (Chief Warden Hodges), Talfryn Thomas (Private Cheeseman), Edward Sinclair (the Verger), Robert Raglan (the Colonel), Robin Parkinson (Lieutenant Wood), Erik Chitty (Mr Clerk), Rachel Thomas (the Mother Superior), Michael Sharvell-Martin (the Lieutenant), Verne Morgan (the Farmer) and Joy Allen (the Lady with the Pram).
Locations: Briefing outside the hall (*Honington, Suffolk*). Nuns with broken down car, open field where the warden gets covered in yellow paint, Lady with a pram (*Stanta MOD*).

The Godiva Affair   Episode 64
Recorded: First broadcast
Sunday 3/11/74   Friday 6/12/74, 7.45-8.15pm
Rpts. 5/6/75, 30/4/91, 9/12/95, 2/8/97, 9/1/02.
Original viewing figures 13.8 million
The platoon decide to perform a Morris Dance in the Walmington-on-Sea Spitfire Fund Carnival. With: Bill Pertwee (Chief Warden Hodges), Talfryn Thomas (Private Cheeseman), Frank Williams (the Vicar), Edward Sinclair (the Verger), Janet Davies (Mrs Pike), Pamela Cundell (Mrs Fox), Eric Longworth (the Town Clerk), Peter Honri (Private Day), Rosemary Faith (the Waitress), Colin Bean (Private Sponge) and George Hancock (Private Hancock).

The Captain's Car   Episode 65
Recorded: First broadcast
Sunday 17/11/74   Friday 13/12/74, 7.45-8.15pm
Rpts. 12/6/75, 7/5/91, 26/11/94, 26/7/97, 16/1/02.
Original viewing figures 14.4 million
Captain Mainwaring is offered the use of a Rolls-Royce. On the way to be camouflaged, it gets mixed up with the Mayor's official car. With: Bill Pertwee (Chief Warden Hodges), Talfryn Thomas (Private Cheeseman), Frank Williams (the Vicar). Edward Sinclair (the Verger), Robert Raglan (the Colonel), Eric Longworth (the Town Clerk), Fred McNaughton (the Mayor), Mavis Pugh (Lady Maltby), John Hart Dyke (the French General) and Donald Morley (Glossip).
Locations: Town Hall (*Guildhall, Thetford*). Petrol taken from Motorbike /Inspecting camouflaged staff car (*Honington, Suffolk*).

Turkey Dinner   Episode 66
Recorded: First broadcast
Sunday 10/11/74   Monday 23/12/74, 8.00-8.30pm
Rpts. 19/6/75, 23/4/91, 25/12/93, 23/12/95, 23/12/98, 22/1/02.
Original viewing figures 15.8 million
The Platoon decide to give a turkey dinner to the old-age pensioners of Walmington-on-Sea. With: Bill Pertwee (Chief Warden Hodges), Talfryn Thomas (Private Cheeseman), Frank Williams (the Vicar), Edward Sinclair (the Verger), Harold Bennett (Mr Bluett) (sic), Pamela Cundell (Mrs Fox), Janet Davies (Mrs Pike), Olive Mercer (Mrs Yeatman) and Dave Butler (the Farmhand).
Locations: North Berrington Turkey farm (*Caston Hall, Norfolk*).

series EIGHT

Ring Dem Bells   Episode 67
Recorded: First broadcast
Thursday 3/07 /75   Friday 5/09/75, 8.00-8.30pm
Rpts. 24/4/76, 17/7/81, 12/12/89, 23/10/93, 14/9/96, 30/1/02.
Original viewing figures 11.3 million
Captain Mainwaring and the Platoon play the part of Nazi soldiers in a training film. With: Bill Pertwee (Chief Warden Hodges), Frank Williams (the Vicar), Edward Sinclair (the Verger), Jack Haig (the Landlord), Robert Raglan (the Colonel), Felix Bowness (the Special Constable), John Bardon (Harold Forster), Hilda Fenemore (Queenie Beal), Janet Mahoney (the Barmaid) and Adele Strong (the Lady with Umbrella).
Locations: The platoon arrive for filming (*Stanta MOD*). The thirsty troop arrive at the Six Bells (*The Six Bells, Bardwell*). Walmington Church where Hodges, Vicar and the Verger warn England (*Sapiston Church, Suffolk*). Pike giving Nazi salute from Jones' van (*Sapiston, Suffolk*).

When You've Got to Go
Episode 68
Recorded: First broadcast
Friday 6/06/75   Friday 12/09/75, 8.00-8.30pm
Rpts. 1/5/76, 28/5/91, 10/12/94, 19/4/97, 6/2/02. Original viewing figures 12.6 million
Private Pike receives his call-up papers and, to the great alarm of his mother, he is passed A1. With: Bill Pertwee (Chief Warden Hodges), Frank Williams (the Vicar), Edward Sinclair (the Verger), Janet Davies (Mrs Pike), Eric Longworth (the Town Clerk), Freddie Earlle (the Italian Sergeant), Tim Barrett (the Doctor), Colin Bean (Private Sponge) and Frankie Holmes (the Fishfryer).

Is There Honey Still for Tea?
Episode 69
Recorded: First broadcast
Thursday 26/06/75   Friday 19/09/75, 8.00-8.30pm
Rpts. 8/5/76, 4/6/91, 3/12/94, 26/4/97.
Original viewing figures 12.8 million
Private Godfrey's cottage is condemned to be bulldozed because a new airstrip is to be built. With: Bill Pertwee (Chief Warden Hodges), Gordon Peters (the Man with the Door), Robert Raglan (the Colonel), Campbell Singer (Sir Charles McAllister), Joan Cooper (Dolly) and Kathleen Saintsbury (Cissy).
Locations: Path leading to and Cherry Tree (Godfrey's) Cottage (*The Lost Nurseries, East Wretham*).

Come In, Your Time is Up
Episode 70
Recorded: First broadcast
Thursday 10/07/7   Friday 26/09/75, 8.00-8.30pm
Rpts. 15/5/76, 11/6/91, 31/12/94, 1/3/97, 1/11/02.
Original viewing figures 14.6 million
While camping they discover a German air crew, in a dinghy on a lake and endeavour to bring it ashore. With: Bill Pertwee (Chief Warden Hodges), Frank Williams (the Vicar), Edward Sinclair (the Verger), Harold Bennett (Mr Bluett) (sic) and Colin Bean (Private Sponge).
Locations: The platoon and scouts camping area by the river (*Buckenham Tofts Lake, Stanta MOD*).

High Finance
Episode 71
Recorded: First broadcast
Friday 30/05/75   Friday 3/10/75, 8.00-8.30pm
Rpts. 22/5/76, 21/5/91, 17/12/94, 22/3/97.
Original viewing figures 14.3 million
Mainwaring decides that Jones must do something about the precarious state of his bank account. With: Bill Pertwee (Chief Warden Hodges), Frank Williams (the Vicar), Edward Sinclair (the Verger), Janet Davies (Mrs Pike), Ronnie Brody (Mr Swann), Colin Bean (Private Sponge) and Natalie Kent (Miss Twelvetrees).

The Face on the Poster
Episode 72
Recorded: First broadcast
Thursday 17/07/75   Friday 10/10/75, 8.00-8.30pm
Rpts. 5/6/76, 18/6/91, 29/3/97
Original viewing figures 15.5 million
Mainwaring's plans for a recruitment campaign suffer a set back when the photographs on the poster are mixed up and Jones is mistaken as an escaped prisoner of war. With: Bill Pertwee (Chief Warden Hodges), Frank Williams (the Vicar), Edward Sinclair (the Verger), Peter Butterworth (as Mr Bugden), Harold Bennett (Mr Bluett) (sic), Gabor Vernon (the Polish Officer), Colin Bean (Private Sponge), Bill Tasker (Fred) and Michael Bevis (the Police Sergeant).
Locations: Jones in the street carrying some eggs, Free Polish Club (*Old Bury Road, Thetford*). Prisoner of War camp (*Gorse Industrial Estate, Barnham*).

SPECIAL

My Brother and I
Episode 73
Recorded: First broadcast
Friday 23/05/75   Friday 26/12/75, 6.05-6.45pm
Rpts. 29/5/76, 31/12/80, 25/12/89, 20/8/93, 11/3/2000, 18/05/03.
Original viewing figures 13.6 million
Captain Mainwaring gives a sherry party for local dignitaries. Unfortunately, an unwelcome guest arrives in the shape of Mainwaring's brother Barry. With: Bill Pertwee (Chief Warden Hodges), Frank Williams (the Vicar), Edward Sinclair (the Verger), Arnold Diamond (the Major-General), Penny Irving (the Chambermaid) and Colin Bean (Private Sponge).

SPECIAL

The Love of Three Oranges
Episode 74
Recorded: First broadcast
Friday 10/12/76   Sunday 26/12/76, 7.25-7.55pm
Rpt. 25/12/90
Original viewing figures 13.7 million
Walmington-on-Sea Home Guard Platoon decide to help the Vicar with his Bazaar to raise money for comforts for the troops. With: Bill Pertwee (Chief Warden Hodges), Frank Williams (the Vicar), Edward Sinclair (the Verger), Pamela Cundell (Mrs Fox), Janet Davies (Mrs Pike), Joan Cooper (Dolly), Eric Longworth (the Town Clerk), Olive Mercer (Mrs Yeatman) and Colin Bean (Private Sponge).

series NINE

Wake-Up Walmington
Episode 75
Recorded: First broadcast
Friday 8/06/77   Sunday 2/10/77, 8.10-8.40pm
Rpts. 11/9/78, 31/7/79, 19/12/89, 30/10/93, 5/4/97.
Original viewing figures 10.2 million
Mainwaring believes that the people of Walmington have become apathetic to the threat of invasion, so he arranges for the platoon to masquerade as Fifth Columnists to test the town's reaction. With: Bill Pertwee (Chief Warden Hodges), Edward Sinclair (the Verger), Geoffrey Lumsden (Captain Square), Sam Kydd (the Yokel), Harold Bennett (Mr Bluett) (sic), Robert Raglan (the Colonel), Charles Hill (the Butler), Jeffrey Holland (the Soldier), Barry Linehan (the Van

Driver), Colin Bean (Private Sponge), Alister Williamson (Bert) and Michael Stainton (Frenchy).
Locations: Rifle shooting practice (Lynford Hall, Mundford). Locals having a drink at the Six Bells (The Six Bells, Bardwell). The flour mill (the cut-throats and desperados' HQ) (*Ixworth Mill, Ixworth*). Walking like a rabble (*Blackrabbit Warren, Stanta MOD*).

The Making of Private Pike   Episode 76
Recorded: First broadcast
Friday 1/07/77   Sunday 9/10/77, 8.10-8.40pm
Rpts. 18/9/78, 7/8/79, 2/7/91, 28/9/96, 25/3/2000, 13/9/01.
Original viewing figures 10.3 million
Captain Mainwaring is given a staff car. It breaks down when Private Pike and a girlfriend borrow it to go to the pictures. With: Bill Pertwee (Chief Warden Hodges), Frank Williams (the Vicar), Edward Sinclair (the Verger), Jean Gilpin (Sylvia), Anthony Sharp (the Colonel), Jeffrey Segal (the Brigadier), Pamela Cundell (Mrs Fox), Janet Davies (Mrs Pike) and Melita Manger (Nora).
Locations: Pike and his girlfriend driving to the pictures and throwing smoke bombs from the car (*Lynford Hall, Mundford*).

Knights of Madness   Episode 77
Recorded: First broadcast:
Friday 22/07/77   Sunday 16/10/77, 8.10-8.40pm
Rpts. 25/9/78, 14/8/79, 20/9/91.
Original viewing figures 19 million
To help Wings for Victory Week, Mainwaring and the Platoon stage the Battle of St. George versus the Dragon. With: Bill Pertwee (Chief Warden Hodges), Frank Williams (the Vicar), Edward Sinclair (the Verger), Colin Bean (Private Sponge), Janet Davies (Mrs Pike), Olive Mercer (Mrs Yeatman), Eric Longworth (the Town Clerk) and Fred McNaughton (the Mayor).
Locations: Village church and fairground area (*Sapiston, Suffolk*). Mainwaring being lifted up by block and tackle (*Buckenham Tofts, Stanta MOD*).

The Miser's Hoard   Episode 78
Recorded: First broadcast:
Friday 24/06/77   Sunday 23/10/77, 8.10-8.40pm
Rpts. 2/10/78, 21/8/79, 25/6/91, 3/8/96.
Original viewing figures 11.1 million
Frazer keeps his savings of gold sovereigns in a tin. Mainwaring thinks the money should be in a safe place - such as a bank - his bank! Special Guest Appearance: Fulton Mackay (as Dr. McCeavedy), With: Bill Pertwee (Chief Warden Hodges), Frank Williams (the Vicar), Edward Sinclair (the Verger) and Colin Bean (Private Sponge).

Number Engaged   Episode 79
Recorded: First broadcast:
Friday 15/07/77   Sunday 6/11/77, 8.10-8.40pm
Rpts. 9/10/78, 28/8/79 13/9/91, 16/12/95, 23/8/97.
Original viewing figures 9.6 million
The Platoon are guarding a vital telephone line. They awake to find a bomb enmeshed in the wires. With: Bill Pertwee (Chief Warden Hodges), Frank Williams (the Vicar), Edward Sinclair (the Verger), Ronnie Brody (the G.P.O. Man), Robert Mill (the Army Captain), Kenneth MacDonald (the Army Sergeant), Felix Bowness (the Van Driver), Colin Bean (Private Sponge), Stuart McGugan (the Scottish Sergeant), Bernice Adams (the A.T.S. Girl).
Locations: Road works at a 'T' junction, camp area guarding the telephone wires (*Black Rabbit Warren, Stanta MOD*).

Never Too Old   Episode 80
Recorded: First broadcast:
Friday 29/07/77   Sunday 13/11/77, 8.10-8.45pm
Rpts. 16/10/78, 4/9/79, 1/12/91, 8/5/95*, 28/5/2000.
Original viewing figures 12.5 million
Love comes to Corporal Jones in this, the final episode of 'Dad's Army'. With: Bill Pertwee (Chief Warden Hodges), Frank Williams (the Vicar), Edward Sinclair (the Verger), Pamela Cundell (Mrs Fox), Janet Davies (Mrs Pike), Colin Bean (Private Sponge), Joan Cooper (Dolly) and Robert Raglan (the Colonel). The wives and partners of the cast were used as the guests in the reception scene.
* Shown as part of BBC1's programmes to celebrate the 50th Anniversary of VE Day

Series Created by Jimmy Perry
Scripts by Jimmy Perry & David Croft

Signature Tune:
Words by Jimmy Perry
Music by Jimmy Perry and Derek Taverner
Sung by Bud Flanagan (all episodes)
Closing Theme:
Band of the Coldstream Guards conducted by their Director
of Music, Lt. Col.(Retd) Trevor L. Sharpe L.V.O., O.B.E,
L.R.A.M., A.R.C.M., (all episodes)

Costumes:
George Ward (S1,4) Odette Barrow (S3) Michael Burdle (S3)
Barbara Kronig (S4) Judy Allen (BG)
Susan Wheal (S5-7) Mary Husband (S8-9, MB, L3)

Make Up:
Sandra Exelby (S1) Cecile Hay-Arthur (S3)
Cynthia Goodwin (S4-5) Penny Bell (BG)
Anna Chesterman (S5-6) Ann Ailes (S6)
Sylvia Thornton (S7-9, MB, L3)

Visual Effects:
Peter Day (S3-6,8) John Friedlander (S4) Ron Oates (S4)
Len Hutton (BG) Tony Harding (S5) Jim Ward (S7)
Martin Gutteridge (S9) Ken Bowphrey, Rhys Jones.

Studio Lighting:
George Summers (S1,2,4) Howard King (S3-9, BG, MB, L3)

Studio Sound:
James Cole (S1,2) Michael McCarthy (S3-8, L3)
John Holmes (S3-4) John Delany (S5)
Alan Machin (S8, MB) Laurie Taylor (S9)

Film Cameramen:
James Balfour (S3,5-6) Stewart A. Farnell (S4-5, BG)
Len Newson (S7) Peter Chapman (S8-9)

Film Sound:
Les Collins (S4-5, BG) Ron Blight (S5) John Gatland (S6-7)
Bill Chesneau (S8) Graham Bedwell (S9)

Film Editors:
Bob Rymer (S3,5-6, BG) Bill Harris (S4-7)
John Stothart (S8) John Dunstan (S9)

Production Assistants:
Bob Spiers (S7) Jo Austin (S8, MB, L3) Gordon Elsbury (S9)

Designers:
Alan Hunter-Craig (S1) Paul Joel (S1-6, BG)
Oliver Bayldon (S2) Ray London (S3) Richard Hunt (S3)
Bryan Ellis (S7) Robert Berk (S8, MB) Geoff Powell (S9)
Tim Gleeson (S9)

Directors:
Harold Snoad (S2-4, selected episodes) Bob Spiers (S9,
selected episodes) David Croft (all other episodes)

Producer:
David Croft (all episodes)

The many extras used were provided by the Thetford Music and
Drama Society under the direction of Mr Keith Eldred.
Coaches from Mulley's Coaches were used to transport the
actors to the various outside locations used in the series. The
owner, the late Jack Mulley, lived in Ixworth. He also provided
many other vehicles used in the programmes and his wife still
owns the lorry used as Hodges' van.
Studio Material recorded at BBC Television Centre, Wood Lane,
London W12

GUIDE TO PRODUCTION CREDIT ABBREVIATIONS:
S = Series. BG = Battle of the Giants, MB = My Brother and I
L3 = The Love of Three Oranges

Sketch 1. Untitled Sketch
(Part of 'Christmas Night with the Stars')
Recorded: Sunday 27/10/68
First Broadcast Wednesday 25/12/68, BBC1 B/W.
A 'Dad's Army' sketch formed a part of this programme, which was presented by Eric Morecambe and Ernie Wise.
Edward Sinclair guested in the item which featured the main platoon members on parade Christmas Day morning and for various reasons they are all dressed like Father Christmas.
This item does not exist in the BBC Archive.

Sketch 2. Resisting the Aggressor Down the Ages
(Part of 'Christmas Night with the Stars')
Recorded: Friday 21/11/69
First Broadcast: Thursday 25/12/69, BBC1 Colour (9 mins).
The Dad's Army team are rehearsing their Christmas town pageant written, produced by and starring George Mainwaring as John Bull. The story depicts Britain's dogged defiance of the many aggressors who had tried to overthrow her people in the past. According to Mainwaring's re-write of history, they all lost, despite Wilson pointing out that they actually

won. The platoon have gone to considerable trouble to obtain period costumes, we see Pike as King Philip of Spain, although he looks like Eddie Cantor in the Kid from Spain, Frazer as William the Conqueror, Godfrey as Julius Caesar, Jones as The Spirit of Agriculture (a country yokel) Walker as The Spirit of Commerce and Wilson as Napoleon, despite the disgusting business with Josephine. The rehearsals are interrupted by an air raid and Hodges and a warden bring in a captured German Pilot (Robert Aldous) who experiences at first hand that "They Don't Like It Up Em".
This item featured in Christmas Night with the Stars compered by Val Doonican.
The Dad's Army sketch exists in its entirety in the BBC archives, although sadly the remainder of the programme does not. An extract of 5 minutes was included in the BBC 2's Fry & Laurie Host a Christmas Night with the Stars special (27/12/94).

Sketch 3. Guarding Buckingham Palace
(Part of 'A Royal Television Gala Performance')
Recorded: 12/05/70
First Broadcast Sunday 24/5/70, BBC1 Colour.
In the presence of the Queen and the Duke of Edinburgh, the Dad's Army team perform an item at the BBCTV Theatre, Shepherd's Bush as part of the Gala Performance, proceeds from which went to aid the British Isles teams taking part in the 1970 Commonwealth Games at Edinburgh.
The Dad's Army regulars perform an 11 minute sketch, written by Jimmy Perry and David Croft, live on stage. The platoon are rehearsing for their part in the Home Guard duties of guarding Buckingham Palace. The problem is that the 'New Guard', comprising of the older members, are going to show up the 'Old Guard', comprising of the younger members. Mainwaring's solution is to put them on the back door, much to the disgust of Jones, Frazer and Godfrey. However, it did have its compensations as they were treated to mugs of cocoa by some familiar looking young ladies.
Other regulars included Colin Bean, Freddie Wiles, Desmond Cullum-Jones and Vernon Drake.
The programme was compered by Morecambe & Wise and also featured Frankie Howerd in an Up Pompeii! sketch. Directed by David Croft, Cilla Black, Basil Brush with Derek Fowlds, Dave Allen, Tony Bennett and Vera Lynn.
This item exists in the BBC Archive.

Sketch 4. The Cornish Floral Dance
(Part of 'Christmas Night with the Stars')
Recorded:
First Broadcast Friday 25/12/70, BBC1 Colour.
The Dad's Army team, featuring Bill Pertwee as the A.R.P. Warden, contributed a 15 minute item for this programme, which was introduced by Cilla Black. The item concerned a choir rehearsal for a performance of The Cornish Floral Dance by Mainwaring's men, the Wardens and some of the ladies of

Walmington-on-Sea. This item was subsequently revived for the stage show in 1975, with a few alterations. (This was also the item chosen for inclusion in the 1975 Royal Variety Performance.)

This item does not exist in the BBC Archive. However, a complete audio recording of this sketch exists in a private collection.

Sketch 5. Broadcast to the Empire

(Part of 'Christmas Night with the Stars')
Recorded: 26/11/72
First Broadcast Monday 25/12/72, BBC1 Colour 13 minutes.
Rpt. 26/12/93 (as part of "At Home with Vic & Bob")
Featuring Bill Pertwee (A.R.P. Warden), Peter Greene (Sound Engineer) and Michael Knowles (BBC Producer's voice).

The Dad's Army team, contributed a 13 minute item for this programme recorded at the same time as 'A Brush with the Law', which was presented by the Two Ronnies - Ronnie Barker and Ronnie Corbett.

The item concerned a special broadcast being made from the Church Hall, in which the Platoon are to perform a short play. The broadcast is to be followed by a speech from the King and Mainwaring is particularly pleased that his voice will be the last voice heard before he speaks. While the platoon are poised to go on air Hodges comes marching in singing and asked 'what happened to your lot then?', it's Old Mother Riley's Christmas Party on now'.

The programme also featured sketches from 'The Goodies' and 'The Liver Birds'. Other artists included Cilla Black, Lulu, and Mike Yarwood.

The programme was produced by Michael Hurll and Terry Hughes.

This sketch was recorded at the same time as the episode 'A Brush With The Law'.

This item exists in the BBC Archive.

Sketch 6. Blue Peter

Recorded 22/2/73 (live)
Captain Mainwaring and Sergeant Wilson are invited along to the Blue Peter studio to inspect a large painting produced by Moorlands County Primary School near Reading.

The picture is 4 metres in length by 1 metre high. During the inspection they discuss what to do with jelly and view a surprising picture of Mrs Mainwaring.

The sketch was written by Jimmy Perry and was followed by a clip from 'Battle of the Giants'.

Sketch 7. Blue Peter

Recorded 29/4/74 (live)
Jones' Butchers Van was to take part in the London to Brighton Historic Commercial Vehicle Run on 5 May 1974.

Captain Mainwaring drives the vehicle into the Blue Peter studio and is interviewed about the trip by John Noakes. He mentions that Clive Dunn, John Le Mesurier, Ian Lavender and Bill Pertwee will be travelling on the day.

This short sketch is followed by the scene from 'The Armoured Might of Lance Corporal Jones' in which we see how it was converted into platoon transport.

Sketch 8. Choir Practice (Part of 'The Royal Variety Performance')

Recorded: Mon 10.11.75
First Broadcast Sunday 16/11/75, ITV Colour. R/time 8.5 minutes.

This sketch taken from the Stage Show, scene 8 'Choir Practice', features the platoon and the people of Walmington rehearsing their part in the coming Saturday concert in aid of wounded soldiers. Mainwaring has decided that the choir will perform 'The Floral Dance'.

The programme was recorded at the London Palladium.

Regulars appearing are: Arthur Lowe, John Le Mesurier, Clive Dunn, Arnold Ridley, Ian Lavender, Bill Pertwee, Frank Williams, Edward Sinclair, Janet Davies, Hamish Roughead, John Bardon and Pamela Cundell.

This programme exists in the LWT TV Archive.

Sketch 9. Crossing the Road

Recorded: Thursday 23/12/76
Two short Public Information Films.

The Dad's Army regulars are employed to make a Road Safety Film demonstrating the use of Pelican Crossings for the Central Office of Information.

A special temporary crossing had to be installed for this filming which caused considerable concern amongst the shopkeepers.

In the first film we see Mainwaring and his men marching towards the crossing and then Jones getting into a panic when the green man starts flashing. The second film sees Hodges and Verger, complete with the Greengrocer van, trying to push Mainwaring off the crossing.

Both these films add up to 1 minute of footage.

These items are available on the video 'Charlie Live' volume 2 reference 7951109, Network/Sound and Media Ltd, 1998.

Location: Crockhamwell Road Centre, Woodley, near Reading.

▲ Acle New Road, Great Yarmouth.

Railway Line (just outside station) ▲

Episode 26
OS Sheet: 134 Map ref: 515 085
Additional notes:
The exact location is apx 500 yards outside the existing railway station.

▲ Training Course

Episode 5
OS Sheet: 144 Map ref: 845 905
Additional notes:
MOD Stanford is a restricted area.

▲ Assault Training Course, STANTA.

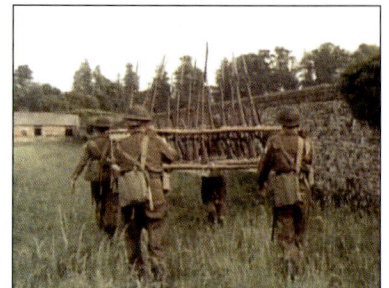

Marching with rifles behind wall ▲

Episode 28
OS Sheet: 144 Map ref: 945 738

▲ Bardwell near The Six Bells.

▲ Village Green

Episode 58
OS Sheet: 144 Map ref: 944 737

▲ Bardwell Green.

▲ Blackrabbit Warren, STANTA .

Unnamed road & camp ▲

Episodes 27, 61, 75 & 79
OS Sheet: 144 Map ref: 915 935
Additional notes:
The end credits sequence was also filmed
here. MOD Stanford is a restricted area.

▲ Walmington Station forecourt (SR)

Episode 27
OS Sheet: 144 Map ref: 784 873

▲ Brandon Station.

Initiative Training Centre ▲

Episode 57
OS Sheet: 198 Map ref: 049 329
Additional notes:
Location used due to a BBC technicians
strike. See also 'St David's Hall'.

▲ Brighton Training Stables, Brighton Race Course.

▲ Walmington Pier

Episode 22
OS Sheet: 134 Map ref: 533 078

▲ Britannia Pier, Great Yarmouth.

Walmington Pier ▲

Episode 22
OS Sheet: 134 Map ref: 533 078

▲ Britannia Pier, Great Yarmouth.

North African Desert

Episode 34
OS Sheet: 132 Map ref: 685 195

British Industrial Sands Ltd, Leziate, Kings Lynn.

Walmington Cricket & Football pitch

Episode 29 & 36
OS Sheet: 144 Map ref: 835 945

Buckenham Tofts, STANTA (Restricted MOD area).

Marsham Hall

Episode 3
OS Sheet: 144 Map ref: 838 948
Additional notes: Buckenham Tofts was
the family home of Edward Underdown
who appeared in one episode.

Buckenham Tofts, STANTA (Restricted MOD area)

Bailey Bridge ▲

Episode 40
OS Sheet: 144 Map ref: 836 953

▲ Buckenham Tofts, Bailey Bridge, STANTA (restricted MOD area).

▲ Walmington Reservoir

Episode 15
OS Sheet: 155 Map ref: 859 657

▲ Bury Sugar Beet Works, Bury St Edmunds.

▲ Caston Hall, Caston

North Berrington Turkey Farm ▲

Episode 66
OS Sheet: 144 Map ref: 974 975
Additional notes:
Private Property

Pinner Fields

Episode 20 & 63
OS Sheet: 144 Map ref: 878 917

Croxton Heath, STANTA (Restricted MOD area).

Mill

Episode 28
OS Sheet: 155 Map ref: 964 622
Additional notes:
The mill used is nowhere near a river!

Drinkstone Mill, nr Woolpit, Suffolk

Sub Station

Episode 39
OS Sheet: Map ref:
Additional notes:
Not confirmed

No Picture Available

Location still to be identified

Electric Sub Station, Honington to Euston Road, Suffolk

Elveden Hall Water Tower

Unnamed water tower

Episode 40
OS Sheet: 144 Map ref: 823 795

Unnamed road

Episode 47
OS Sheet: 144 Map ref: 805 905

Euston to Rushford Road.

Ferngate Farm, Weeting.

Unnamed road

Episode 2
OS Sheet: 144 Map ref: 775 881

Block of Flats

Episode 3
OS Sheet: 176 Map ref: 178 751
Additional notes:

Fitzwilliam Mansions, Richmond-on-Thames

Frog Hill, STANTA (Restricted MOD area).

Unnamed

Episodes 16, 24, 47 & 63
OS Sheet: 144 Map ref: 873 911

Unnamed Road

Episode 45
OS Sheet: 144 Map ref: 873 808

Santon Downham, Norfolk.

▲ Glebe Cottage, Sapiston.

Tracker Dog Training School ▲

Episode 59
OS Sheet: 144 Map ref: 918 943

▲ Prisoner of War Camp

Episode 72
OS Sheet: 144 Map ref: 875 793
Additional notes:
Nothing remains at this site.

▲ Gorse Industrial Estate, Barnham.

▲ Grenade Training Area, STANTA (Restricted MOD area).

Sticky Bomb Training ▲

Episode 39
OS Sheet: 144 Map ref: 845 905

▲ Manor Farm

Episode 7
OS Sheet: 165 Map ref: 874 981

▲ Hatches Farm, Great Kingshill, Buckinghamshire.

▲ High Lodge, Brandon

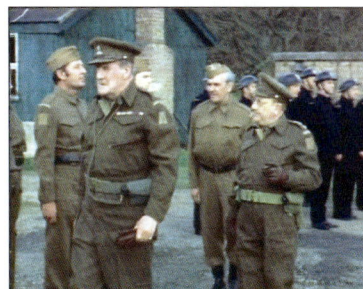

Army Depot ▲

Episodes 42, 45 & 50
OS Sheet: 144 Map ref: 813 855

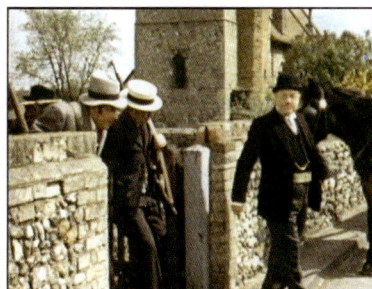

▲ St Aldhelms Church, Walmington

Episodes 47, 57, 58, 63, 65 & 67
OS Sheet: 144 Map ref: 913 746

▲ Honington, All Saints Church, Malting Row.

▲ Honington Primary School, Malting Row.

St Aldhelms Church Hall, Walmington ▲

Episodes 47, 57, 58, 65 & 67
OS Sheet: 144 Map ref: 913 746

▲ Old Flour Mill

Episode 75
OS Sheet: 144 Map ref: 928 711

▲ Ixworth Mill, Ixworth.

▲ Langford Church, St Andrews, STANTA (Restricted MOD area).

St Matthews Church, Walmington ▲

Episode 25
OS Sheet: 144 Map ref: 837 965

▲ St Matthews Church, Walmington

Episode 25
OS Sheet: 144 Map ref: 837 965

▲ Langford Church, St Andrews, STANTA (Restricted MOD area).

Farm Building ▲

Episode 43
OS Sheet: 144 Map ref: 889 842

▲ Lodge Farm, Kilverstone, Thetford.

▲ Waterloo Battle Field

Episode 43
OS Sheet: 144 Map ref: 889 842

▲ Lodge Farm, Kilverstone, Thetford.

△ Lowerstoft Lifeboat Shed.

Paddle & Rowing Boats △

Episode 22
OS Sheet: 134 Map ref: 547 925

△ Landing with boat

Episode 22
OS Sheet: 134 Map ref: 547 925

△ Lowerstoft Lifeboat Shed.

△ Lynford Hall (Hotel), nr Mundford.

The Big Hall △

Episodes 75 & 76
OS Sheet: 144 Map ref: 821 943
Additional notes:
Lynford Hall Hotel is still open for
business.

▲ Boathouse & riverbank

Episode 28
OS Sheet: 134 Map ref: 275 196
Additional notes:
It is only possible to view boathouse from
the river.

▲ Boat House, Manor House, Coltishall.

▲ Mill Lane, Thetford.

A Walmington road ▲

Episode 54
OS Sheet: 144 Map ref: 871 825

▲ Percy Street, Walmington

Episodes 13, 24, 27 & 53
OS Sheet: 144 Map ref: 872 828
Additional notes:
Although as filmed it appears there are
houses both sides, there are not!

▲ Nether Row, Thetford.

Unnamed street/estate ▲

Episode 2 & 15
OS Sheet: 144 Map ref: 866 828

▲ Newtown, Thetford

▲ Free Polish Club, Walmington

Episode72
OS Sheet: 144 Map ref: 868 829

▲ Old Bury Road, Thetford

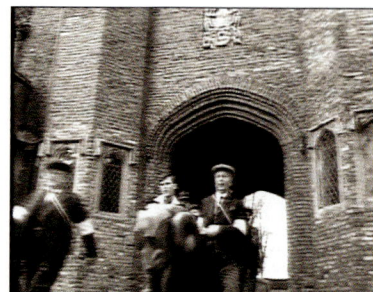

Peabody Museum ▲

Episode 2
OS Sheet: 143 Map ref: 743 014

▲ Oxburgh Hall, Oxborough

▲ Inside Cinema, Eastgate

Episode 27 & 43
OS Sheet: 144 Map ref: 873 830
Additional notes:
Cinema now a Bingo Hall

▲ Palace Cinema, Thetford

Theatre interior (Charlie Cheeseman) ▲

Episode 6
OS Sheet: 176 Map ref: 179 751
Jimmy Perry played the part of Charlie
Cheeseman.

▲ Richmond Theatre (exterior view).

▲ River

Episode 26
OS Sheet: 134 Map ref: 418 906

▲ River Waveney, Beccles.

▲ Santon Downham, nr Brandon.

Unnamed village & bridge ▲

Episode 50
OS Sheet: 144 Map ref: 817 878

▲ Wilson falls off motorcycle in lane

Episode 58 & 67
OS Sheet: 144 Map ref: 918 748

▲ Sapiston, lane to church.

▲ Sapiston Church, Sapiston

Walmington Green/St Aldhelms Church ▲

Episode67 & 77
OS Sheet: 144 Map ref: 921 743

St Aldhelms Church

Episode 67
OS Sheet: 144 Map ref: 921 743
Additional notes:
Although there is a church next to the hall
at Honington, it was never used.

Sapiston Church, Sapiston.

St Davids Hall (interior used), Brighton.

Training Room ▲

Episode 57
OS Sheet: 198 Map ref: 045 355
Additional notes:
Location used due to a BBC technicians'
dispute.

Church

Episode 5 & 6
OS Sheet: 144 Map ref: 865 828
Viewed from No53 , Newtown.

St Mary The Less (1567), Old Bury Road, Thetford.

Farm buildings ▲

Episode 14
OS Sheet: 134 Map ref: 852 956

▲ Stanford Farm, STANTA (Restricted MOD area).

▲ Unnamed lake

Episode 70
OS Sheet: 144 Map ref: 842 950

▲ Stanford Lake, Buckenham Tofts, STANTA (Restricted MOD area).

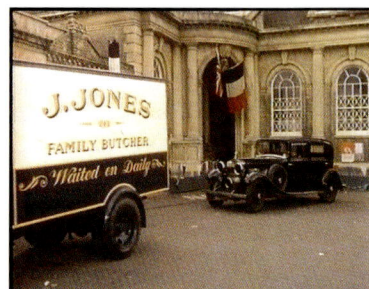

Walmington Town Hall ▲

Episode 53 & 65
OS Sheet: 144 Map ref: 870 832

▲ The Guildhall, Thetford.

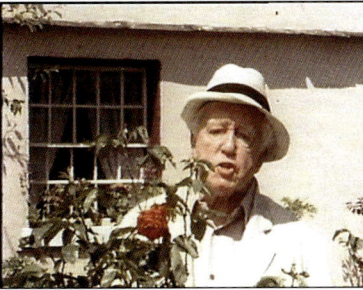

▲ Cherry Tree Cottage

Episode 69
OS Sheet: 144 Map ref: 918 924

▲ The Lost Nurseries, East Wretham.

▲ The Red House, West Tofts.

Removing bush from pot. ▲

Episode 20
OS Sheet: 144 Map ref: 833 925

▲ River crossing

Episode 59
OS Sheet: 144 Map ref: 927 744

▲ Black Bourn River, Sapiston.

The Six Bells, Bardwell.

The Six Bells ▲

Episode 67 & 75
OS Sheet: 144 Map ref: 946 737

▲ Italian POW camp

Episode 31
OS Sheet: 144 Map ref: 901 901

▲ Thorpe Camp, STANTA

Wacton Village, Wacton.

Unnamed village ▲

Episode 52
OS Sheet: 134 Map ref: 181 914

▲ Unnamed village

Episode 52
OS Sheet: 134 Map ref: 181 914

▲ Wacton Village, Wacton.

▲ Walnut Tree Farm, Wilney Green, Fersfield.

House on fire ▲

Episode 50
OS Sheet: 144 Map ref: 067 817
Additional notes:
Buildings no longer exist.

▲ Mrs Pentice's Farm

Episode 48
OS Sheet: 144 Map ref: 067 817
Additional notes:
Buildings no longer exist.

▲ Walnut Tree Farm (back door), Wilney Green, Fersfield.

Mrs Prentice's Farm ▲

Episode 48
OS Sheet: 144 Map ref: 067 817

▲ Walnut Tree Farm orchard, Wilney Green, Fersfield.

▲ Railway Bridge

Episode 52
OS Sheet: 144 Map ref: 168 917

▲ Wash Lane, Wacton.

Disused Airfield (MOD) ▲

Episode 52
OS Sheet: 144 Map ref: 943 995

▲ Watton Airfield, MOD Watton.

▲ Unnamed station

Episode 14 & 20
OS Sheet: 132 Map ref: 932 130
Additional notes:
Station demolished 1974.

▲ Wendling Railway Station, Wendling.

▲ West Tofts Church, STANTA (Restricted MOD area).

St Aldhelms Church, Walmington ▲

Episode 15
OS Sheet: 144 Map ref: 836 929

▲ St Aldhelms Church, Walmington

Episode 28
OS Sheet: 144 Map ref: 836 929

▲ West Tofts Church, STANTA (Restricted MOD area).

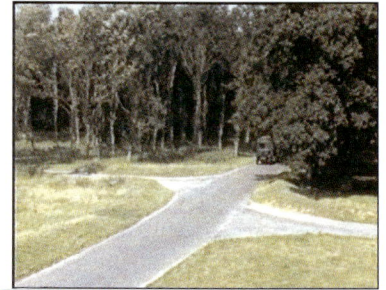

Unnamed crossroads ▲

Episode 40
OS Sheet: 144 Map ref: 837 944

▲ West Tofts Crossroads, STANTA (Restricted MOD area).

▲ Mainwaring hoisted onto a horse

Episode 77
OS Sheet: 144 Map ref: 837 930

▲ West Tofts Field, STANTA (Restricted MOD area).

Walmington Station ▲

Episode 56
OS Sheet: 133 Map ref: 118 419

▲ Weybourne Station, Weybourne.

△ Walmington Beach

Episode 29
OS Sheet: 134 Map ref: 505 185

△ Winterton Beach, Winterton.

ARTIST	CHARACTER	EPISODE
Bernice Adams	ATS Girl	Number Engaged
Robert Aldous	German Pilot	Man Hunt, Gala Sketch 1970
Joy Allen	Clippie	Soldier's Farewell
	Lady with Pram	Gorilla Warfare
Avril Angers	Tel. Operator	Lion Has Phones, Put That Light Out
Bernard Archard	Major/General Fullard	Film
John Ash	Raymond	Two and a Half Feathers
Roger Avon	The Doctor	Branded
Ralph Ball	Man at Station	Sons of the Sea
John Bardon	Harold Forster	Ring Dem Bells
Tim Barrett	Captain Pringle	Bullet is Not for Firing
	Doctor	When You've Got To Go
John Baskcomb	Mayor	Film
Colin Bean	**Pte. Sponge**	**(28 Shows)**
James Beck	**Pte. Joe Walker**	**Appeared in the first 59 episodes & the Columbia Film**
Michael Bevis	Police Sergeant.	Face On the Poster
Harold Bennett	Old Man	Armoured Might of Lance Corporal. Jones
	Mr Blewitt	**(13 Shows)**
Michael Bilton	Mr Maxwell	Sons of the Sea
Sue Bishop	Ticket Collector	The Royal Train
Dennis Blanch	2nd Lieutenant	If the Cap Fits
Derek Bond	Minister	Keep Young & Beautiful
Roger Bourne	Regular Extra	In many episodes
Felix Bowness	Driver	Everybody's Trucking, Number Engaged
	Special Constable	Ring Dem Bells
Ronnie Brandon	Mr Drury	No Spring for Frazer
Nan Braunton	Miss Cissy Godfrey	Battle of Godfrey's Cottage, Day the Balloon went Up, War Dance, Branded
Ronnie Brody	Bob	Royal Train
	Mr Swan	High Finance
	GPO Man	Number Engaged
Arthur Brough	Mr Boyle	A. Wilson Manager
Jennifer Browne	WAAF Sergeant.	Day the Balloon Went Up
Julia Burbury	Miss Ironside	Mum's Army
Blake Butler	Mr West	A. Wilson Manager
David Butler	Farmhand	Turkey Dinner
Peter Butterworth	Mr Bugden	Face On the Poster
Desmond Cullum-Jones	Regular Extra	In many episodes, (Pte. Desmond)
Andrew Carr	Ops. Officer	Day the Balloon Went Up
John Cater	Pte. Clarke	Two & A Half Feathers
Hugh Cecil	Regular Extra	In many episodes
	Percy the Parrot	The Battle of Godfrey's Cottage
Jonathan Cecil	Cpt. Cadbury	Things That Go Bump In the Night
Timothy Charlton	Lt. Hope Bruce	Lion Has Phones
Geoffrey Chater	Col. Pierce	Round & Round Went the Big Wheel
Erik Chitty	Mr Sedgewick	Boots Boots Boots
	Mr Clerk	Gorilla Warfare
Alec Coleman	Regular Extra.	First & Second series
John Clegg	Radio Operator	Round & Round Went the Great Big Wheel
John D Collins	Naval Officer	Film
Pat Coombs	Mrs Hall	Film
Patrick Connor	Shamus	Absent Friends
Joan Cooper	Miss Baker	No Spring for Frazer
	Miss Fortescue	Time On My Hands
	Dolly	Is There Honey Still For Tea? The Love of Three Oranges, Never Too Old
James Copeland	Cpt. Ogilvy	Operation Kilt
Tina Cornioli	Olive	All Is Safely Gathered In
Leon Cortez	Milkman	Museum Piece
	Small Man	Man Hunt
Deirdre Costello	Buffet Attendant	Mum's Army
Brenda Cowling	Mrs Prentice	All Is Safely Gathered In
Pamela Cundell	**Mrs Fox**	**(13 Shows)**
Amy Dalby	Miss Dolly Godfrey	Battle of Godfrey's Cottage
Colin Daniels	Boy	Lion Has Phones
David Davenport	M/ Police Sgt.	Enemy within the Gates
Janet Davies	**Mrs Pike (Mavis)**	**(30 Shows)**
Paul Dawkins	Nazi General	Film
Gladys Dawson	Mrs Witt	Under Fire

ARTIST	CHARACTER	EPISODE
Andrew Daye	Choir	Bullet is Not for Firing
Roy Denton	Mr Bennett	Big Guns
Jay Denyer	Inspector Blake	Man of Action
J C Devlin	Regan	Absent Friends
Arnold Diamond	Major General	My Brother & I
Maggie Don	Waitress	Brain Versus Brawn
Robert Dorning	Bank Inspector	Something Nasty in the Vault
Sally Douglas	Blodwen	War Dance
Caroline Dowdeswell	**Janet King**	**(5 Shows)**
Vernon Drake	Regular Extra	In many episodes, and as Private Godfrey Number Engaged (long shot)
Clive Dunn	**L/Corp. Jack Jones**	**All 80 TV Shows, Film**
Lindsey Dunn	Small Boy	The Recruit
Freddie Earlle	Henry	Royal Train
	Italian Sergeant	When You've Got To Go
Arthur English	Policeman	Absent Friends
Don Estelle	Pickfords Man	Big Guns
	2nd ARP	Don't Forget the Diver
	Gerald	The Test, Uninvited Guests
Edward Evans	Mr Reed	Loneliness of the Long-Distance Walker
	Mr Rees	Big Guns
	General Monteverdi	Don't Fence Me In
Ewan Evans	Regular Extra	
Rosemary Faith	Ivy Samways	Mum's Army
	Barmaid	Battle of the Giants
	Waitress	Godiva Affair
Blain Fairman	US Sergeant	My British Buddy
Hilda Fenemore	Queenie Beal	Ring Dem Bells
Kate Forge	Choir	Bullet is Not for Firing
Liz Fraser	Mrs Pike	Film
Scott Fredericks	Nazi Photographer	Film
Chris Gannon	Clerk Of Court	Brush with the Law
Jeffrey Gardiner	Mr Wintergreen	Brush with the Law
Rex Garner	Captain Ashley-Jones	Fallen Idol
David Gilchrist	Serviceman	Mum's Army
Robert Gillespie	Charles Boyer	Soldier's Farewell
Jean Gilpin	Sylvia	Making Of Private Pike
Frank Godfrey	Regular Extra	In many episodes
Richard Greene	Sound Engineer	Broadcast to the Empire
Graham Twins	Doris & Dora	War Dance
Carson Green	Boy	Lion Has Phones
Fred Griffiths	Bert King	Film
Jack Haig	Gardener	Day the Balloon Went Up
	Landlord	Ring Dem Bells
Alan Haines	Major Smith	Battle School
	Marine Officer	Film
Miranda Hampton	Sexy Lady	Man Hunt
George Hancock	Pte. Hancock	Godiva Affair and regular Extra in many episodes
Graham Harbord	Young Arthur	Sgt. Wilson's Little Secret
John Hart Dyke	French General	The Captain's Car
Hugh Hastings	Pianist	War Dance
	Pte. Hastings	A. Wilson, Manager?
	Regular Extra	In many episodes
Nigel Hawthorne	Angry Man	Armoured Might of Lance Corporal Jones
Dick Haydon	Raymond	Armoured Might of Lance Corporal Jones
John Henderson	Radio Shop Assistant	Film
Charles Hill	The Butler	Command Decision, Wake-Up Walmington
	Sergeant	Battle of the Giants
Rose Hill	Mrs Cole	Uninvited Guests
Jeffrey Holland	Soldier	Wake-Up Walmington
Frankie Holmes	Fish Fryer	When You've Got To Go
Jonathan Holt	2nd Soldier	Sons of the Sea
Peter Honri	Pte. Day	Godiva Affair
Bob Hornery	City Gent	Royal Train
Tony Hughes	Mr Billings	When Did You Last See Your Money
Neville Hughes	The Soldier	Man and the Hour
Geoffrey Hughes	Bridge Corporal	Brain Versus Brawn
Penny Irving	Chambermaid	My Brother & I

ARTIST	CHARACTER	EPISODE
Richard Jacques	Mr Cheesewright	Lion Has Phones
	Regular Extra	In many episodes
Carl Jaffe	Captain Winogrodzki	Enemy within the Gates
Linda James	Betty	Lion Has Phones, Two & A Half Feathers
Natalie Kent	Miss Twelvetrees	High Finance
Suzanne Kerchiss	Ivy	My British Buddy
Diana King	Chairwoman	Loneliness of the Long-Distance Walker
Richard Kitteridge	Regular Extra	Many Episodes
Michael Knowles	Captain Cutts	Loneliness of the Long-Distance Walker, Bullet is Not for Firing
	Engineering Officer	Sergeant, Save My Boy
	Captain Reed	Fallen Idol
	Captain Stewart	Round & Round went the Big Wheel
	BBC Producer	Broadcast to the Empire (voice only)
	Staff Captain	Film
Sam Kydd	Yokel	Wake-Up Walmington
	Nazi Orderly	Film
Vicki Lane	Girl On Tandem	Day the Balloon Went Up
Robert Lankesheer	Medical Officer	Loneliness of the Long-Distance Walker
John Laurie	**Pte. James Frazer**	**All 80 TV Shows, Film**
Ian Lavender	**Pte. Frank Pike**	**All 80 TV Shows, Film**
John Leeson	1st Soldier	Sons of the Sea
Arthur Lewis	Choir	Bullet is Not for Firing
John Le Mesurier	**Sergeant. Arthur Wilson**	**All 80 TV Shows, Film**
Jack Le White	Porter	Mum's Army
Alvar Lidell	Newsreader	Getting the Bird, Film
Barry Linehan	Van Driver	Wake-Up Walmington
Michael Lomax	2nd ARP	Absent Friends
Eric Longworth	**Mr Gordon Town Clerk**	**(8 Shows)**
Arthur Lowe	**Captain George Mainwaring**	**All 80 TV Shows, Film**
Geoffrey Lumsden	**Colonel Square**	**(7 Shows)**
Jimmy Mac	Regular Extra	In many episodes
Fulton Mackay	Captain Ramsey	We Know Our Onions
	Dr. McCeavedy	Miser's Hoard
Kenneth MacDonald	Army Sergeant	Number Engaged
Philip Madoc	U Boat Captain	Deadly Attachment
Janet Mahoney	Barmaid	Ring Dem Bells
Susan Majolier	Nurse	The Recruit
Melita Manger	Waitress	Mum's Army
	Nora	Making Of Private Pike
Pamela Manson	NAAFI Girl	We Know Our Onions
Larry Martin	Soldier	Loneliness of the Long-Distance Walker
	2nd Sailor	Menace from the Deep
	Italian POW	Don't Fence Me In
	Signals Private	Desperate Drive of Corporal Jones
Roger Maxwell	Peppery Old Gent	Film
Alex McAvoy	Sergeant	If the Cap Fits, We Know our Onions
Parnell McGarry	Elizabeth	Two & A Half Feathers
Stanley McGeagh	Sergeant Waller	Lion Has Phones
Stuart McGugan	Scottish Sergeant	Number Engaged
Therese McMurray	Girl in Window	Showing Up of Corp. Jones, Shooting Pains
	Girl in Haystack	The Day the Balloon Went Up
Eilidh McNab	Choir	Bullet is Not for Firing
Fred McNaughton	Mayor	Royal Train, Honourable Man, The Captain's Car, Knights of Madness
Tom Mennard	Mess Orderly	Fallen Idol
Olive Mercer	**Mrs Yeatman**	**(8 Shows)**
	Fierce Lady	Man Hunt
Robert Mill	Captain Swan	Man of Action
	Army Capt.	Number Engaged
Bernadette Milnes	Lady In Queue	Lion Has Phones
Norman Mitchell	Captain Rogers	Something Nasty in the Vault
Ingo Mogendorf	Nazi Pilot	Film
Michael Moore	Regular Extra	In many episodes
Robert Moore	Large Man	Man Hunt
William Moore	Station Master	Royal Train
Charles Morgan	2nd Member of Parliament	Keep Young & Beautiful
Verne Morgan	Landlord	Don't Forget the Diver, Absent Friends, My British Buddy, Gorilla Warfare
Donald Morley	Glossip	The Captain's Car

ARTIST	CHARACTER	EPISODE
Derek Newark	Regular/Sergeant Major	Film
Leslie Noyes	Regular Extra	In many episodes
Michael Osborne	Boy Scout	Museum Piece
James Ottaway	1st M/Parliament	Keep Young and Beautiful
Robin Parkinson	Lieutenant Wood	Gorilla Warfare
Denys Peek	German Pilot	Enemy within the Gates
Toby Perkins	The Usher	Brush with the Law
Gilda Perry	Blondie	Loneliness of the Long-Distance Walker
	Doreen	Lion Has Phones, Two and a Half Feathers
Jimmy Perry	Charlie Cheeseman	Shooting Pains
Bill Pertwee	**Chief Warden**	**(60 Shows)**
Arnold Peters	Fire Officer	Man of Action
Gordon Peters	The Soldier	Command Decision
	Policeman	A Stripe for Frazer
	Man with Door	Is There Honey Still For Tea
	Lighthouse Keeper	Put That Light Out
June Petersen	Woman	Under Fire
Hana-Maria Pravda	Interpreter	Honourable Man
Mavis Pugh	Lady Maltby	The Captain's Car
Robert Raglan	**The Colonel**	**(17 Shows)**
Harriet Rhys	Girl In Bank	Film
Wendy Richard	Edith Parish	Two & a Half Feathers, Mum's Army
	Shirley	King Was In His Counting House, My British Buddy
Nigel Rideout	German Pilot	Enemy within the Gates
Arnold Ridley	**Pte. Charles Godfrey**	**All 80 TV Shows, Film**
John Ringham	Bracewell	Man and the Hour
	Cpt. Bailey	A Stripe for Frazer, Under Fire, Room at the Bottom, Don't Fence Me In
David Rose	Dump Corporal	Brain Versus Brawn
George Roubicek	Radio Operator	Film
Anthony Roye	Mr Fairbrother	Brain Versus Brawn
Anthony Sagar	Sergeant Gregor	Room at the Bottom
	Sergeant Major	Fallen Idol
	Police Sgt.	Film
Kathleen Saintsbury	Cissy	Is There Honey Still For Tea
Christopher Sandford	Germn Pilot	Time On My Hands
Joan Savage	Greta Garbo	Soldier's Farewell
David Seaforth	Regular Extra	Many Episodes
Jeffrey Segal	The Minister	Round & Round Went the Big Wheel
	Brigadier	Making Of Private Pike
Anthony Sharp	Brigadier War Office	Loneliness of the Long-Distance Walker
	Colonel	Making Of Private Pike
Stuart Sherwin	2nd ARP	Menace from the Deep, Branded, Put That Light Out
	Junior Warden	Brush with the Law
Michael Sharvell-Martin	Lieutenant	Gorilla Warfare
Carmen Silvera	Mrs Gray	Mum's Army
Edward Sinclair	**The Verger**	**(49 Shows)**
Campbell Singer	Maj/Gen. Menzies	If the Cap Fits
	Sir Charles McAllister	Is There Honey Still For Tea
Eleanor Smale	Mrs Prosser	War Dance, Mum's Army
Jean St.Clair	Miss Meadows	Armoured Might of Corporal Jones
Michael Stainton	Frenchy	Wake-Up Walmington
Adele Strong	Lady with Umbrella	Ring Dem Bells
Bill Tasker	Fred	Face On the Poster
James Taylor	Artillery Officer	Desperate Drive of Corporal Jones
Vic Taylor	Regular Extra	In many episodes
Talfryn Thomas	**Pte. Cheeseman**	**(6 Shows)**
Rachel Thomas	Mother Superior	Gorilla Warfare
Alan Tilvern	Cpt. Rodrigues	Battle School
	US. Colonel	My British Buddy
Fred Tomlinson	Choir	Bullet is Not for Firing
Cy Town	Mess Steward	We Know Our Onions
Bill Treacher	1st Sailor	Menace from the Deep
Freddie Trueman	E C Egan	The Test
Patrick Tull	The Suspect	Man Hunt
Ernst Ulman	Sigmund Murphy	Under Fire
Edward Underdown	Major/General Holland	Round & Round Went the Big Wheel

ARTIST	CHARACTER	EPISODE
Gabor Vernon	The Russian,	Honourable Man
	Polish Officer	Face On the Poster
Franz Van Norde	Nazi Co-Pilot	Film
Patrick Waddington	The Brigadier	Showing Up of Corp. Jones, Loneliness of the Long-Distance Walker
April Walker	Judy	All Is Safely Gathered In
Dervis Ward	AA Man	Film
May Warden	Mrs Dowding	Bullet is Not for Firing
Kenneth Watson	RAF Officer	Day the Balloon Went Up
Queenie Watts	Mrs Keen	Under Fire
	Mrs Peters	Armoured Might of Corp. Jones
	Edna	Two & A Half Feathers
Freddie White	Regular Extra	In many episodes
Freddie Wiles	Regular Extra	In many episodes
Marjorie Wilde	Lady Magistrate	Brush with the Law
Frank Williams	**The Vicar**	**(39 Shows)**
Alister Williamson	Bert	Wake-Up Walmington
Seretta Wilson	Wren	Getting the Bird
Barbara Windsor	Laura La Plaz	Shooting Pains
Eric Woodburn	Museum Caretaker	Museum Piece
Martin Wyldeck	Major Regan	Showing Up of Corp. Jones, Shooting Pains

222 Actors in Total

Colin Bean
Battle of Godfrey's Cottage, Battle School, Room at the Bottom, Big Parade, Don't Forget the Diver, A. Wilson, Manager?, Battle of the Giants, Asleep in the Deep, A Soldier's Farewell, The King Was In His Counting House, All Is Safely Gathered In, Time On My Hands, Deadly Attachment, Things That Go Bump In The Night, Everybody's Trucking, Man Of Action, Godiva Affair, When You've Got Go, Come In Your Is Time Up, High Finance, Face On the Poster, My Brother & I, The Love Of Three Oranges, Wake-Up Walmington, Knights Of Madness, Miser's Hoard, Number Engaged, Never Too Old. Also appeared as a regular extra In many other episodes.

Harold Bennett
Armoured Might of Lance Corporal. Jones, The Bullet is Not for Firing, Day the Balloon Went Up, No Spring for Frazer, The Test, When Did You Last See Your Money, Time On My Hands, Everybody's Trucking, A Man of Action, Turkey Dinner, Come In Your Time Is Up, The Face On the Poster, Wake-Up Walmington.

Pamela Cundell
Armoured Might of Corporal Jones, The Lion Has Phones, Big Parade, Mum's Army, Getting the Bird, My British Buddy, Honourable Man, Everybody's Trucking, Godiva Affair, Turkey Dinner, Love Of Three Oranges, Making of Private Pike, Never Too Old.

Janet Davies
Man and the Hour, Museum Piece, Showing Up of Corporal Jones, Shooting Pains, Operation Kilt, Battle of Godfrey's Cottage, Sgt. Wilson's Little Secret, Under Fire, Armoured Might of Lance Corporal Jones, Lion Has Phones, Bullet Is Not for Firing, Something Nasty in the Vault, War Dance, Man Hunt, Big Parade, Boots Boots Boots, Sgt. Save My Boy, Absent Friends, Mum's Army, A Wilson Manager, My British Buddy, Honourable Man, Godiva Affair, Turkey Dinner, When You've Got To Go, High Finance, The Love of Three Oranges, Making of Private Pike, Knights of Madness, Never Too Old.

Caroline Dowdeswell
Man and the Hour, Museum Piece, Command Decision, Enemy within the Gates, Shooting Pains.

Eric Longworth
Time On My Hands, Honourable Man, Man Of Action, Godiva Affair, The Captain's Car, When You've Got To Go, The Love of Three Oranges, Knights of Madness.

Geoffrey Lumsden
A Stripe for Frazer, Under Fire, Command Decision, Don't Forget the Diver, Fallen Idol, Battle of the Giants, Brush with the Law, Wake-Up Walmington.

Olive Mercer
Armoured Might of Lance Corporal Jones, Lion Has Phones, War Dance, Getting the Bird, Everybody's Trucking, Turkey Dinner, The Love of Three Oranges, Knights of Madness, Man Hunt.

Bill Pertwee
Man and the Hour, Enemy within the Gates, Battle of Godfrey's Cottage, Under Fire, The Armoured Might of Lance Corporal Jones,   Lion Has Phones, Something Nasty in the Vault, The Day the Balloon Went Up, Menace from the Deep, Branded, Man Hunt, Big Parade, Don't Forget the Diver, Boots Boots Boots, Sgt. Save My Boy, Absent Friends, Put That Light Out, Two & A Half Feathers, The Test, Uninvited Guests, Battle of the Giants, Asleep In the Deep, Keep Young & Beautiful, A Soldier's Farewell, Getting the Bird, The Desperate Drive Corporal Jones, If the Cap Fits, The King Was in His Counting House, All Is Safely Gathered In, When Did You Last See Your Money, Brain V Brawn, A Brush With the Law, Round Went the Great Big Wheel, Time On My Hands, Deadly Attachment, My British Buddy, The Royal Train, We Know Our Onions, Honourable Man, The Recruit, Everybody's Trucking, A Man of Action, Gorilla Warfare, Godiva Affair, The Captain's Car, Turkey Dinner, Ring Dem Bells, When You've Got To Go, Is There Honey Still For Tea, Come In Your Time

Is Up, High Finance, Face On the Poster, My Brother & I, The Love Of Three Oranges, Wake-Up Walmington, Making Of Private Pike, Knights Of Madness, Miser's Hoard, Number Engaged, Never Too Old, Film.

Robert Raglan
Don't Forget the Diver, A. Wilson Manager, Fallen Idol, Battle of the Giants, Keep Young & Beautiful, Desperate Drive of Corporal Jones, If the Cap Fits, Brain V Brawn, Deadly Attachment, My British Buddy, Honourable Man, Gorilla Warfare, The Captain's Car, Ring Dem Bells, Is There Honey Still For Tea, Wake-Up Walmington, Never Too Old, Film.

Edward Sinclair
Showing Up of Corporal Jones, A Stripe for Frazer, Bullet is Not for Firing, Room at the Bottom, Big Guns, Day the Balloon Went Up, War Dance, No Spring for Frazer, Big Parade, Don't Forget the Diver, Absent Friends, The Test, A Wilson Manager, Uninvited Guests, Battle of the Giants, Getting the Bird, Desperate Drive of Corporal Jones, If the Cap Fits, King Was In His Counting House, All is Safely Gathered In, When Did You Last See Your Money, Brain The V Brawn, Brush with the Law, Time On My Hands, Deadly Attachment, My British Buddy, Royal Train, We Know Our Onions, Honourable Man, The Recruit, Everybody's, Trucking, A Man of Action, Gorilla Warfare, Godiva Affair, The Captain's Car, Turkey Dinner, Ring Dem Bells, When you've Got To Go, Come In Your Time Is Up, High Finance, Face On the Poster, My Brother & I, Love Of Three Oranges, Wake-Up Walmington, Making Of Pte. Pike, Knights Of Madness, Miser's Hoard, Number Engaged, Never Too Old, Film.

Talfryn Thomas
My British Buddy, Man of Action, Gorilla Warfare, Godiva Affair, The Captain's Car, Turkey Dinner.

Frank Williams
Armoured Might of Corporal Jones, The Bullet is Not for Firing, The Day the Balloon Went Up, War Dance, No Spring for Frazer, Don't Forget the Diver, The Test, A. Wilson Manager, Uninvited Guests, Battle of the Giants, A Soldier's Farewell, Getting the Bird, The Desperate Drive of Corporal Jones, The King Was In His Counting House, All Is Safely Gathered In, When Did You Last See Your Money, A Brush with the Law, Time On My Hands, My British Buddy, The Royal Train, Honourable Man, The Recruit, Everybody's Trucking, Man of Action, Godiva Affair, The Captain's Car, Turkey Dinner, Ring Dem Bells, When You've Got To Go, Come In, Your Time Is Up, High Finance, Face On the Poster, My Brother & I, The Love of Three Oranges, Making of Private Pike, Knights of Madness, Miser's Hoard, Number Engaged, Never Too Old, Film.

ARTHUR LOWE as Captain Mainwaring
JOHN LE MESURIER as Sergeant Wilson
CLIVE DUNN as Lance Corporal Jones
JOHN LAURIE (JL) as Private Frazer
JAMES BECK (JB), GRAHAM STARK (GS)
or LARRY MARTYN (LM) as Private Walker
ARNOLD RIDLEY (AR) as Private Godfrey
IAN LAVENDER (IL) as Private Pike

BBC Announcer for all episodes: John Snagge.

series ONE

1. The Man and the Hour
Recorded: Sunday 3rd June 1973
First Broadcast: Monday 28th January 1974, 6.15-6.45pm &
Wednesday 30th January 1974, 12.27-12.57pm
The Man - Mr Mainwaring. The Hour - 11.30am, 14th May
1940, when the Manager of Swallows Bank, Walmington-on-
Sea, answers his country's call and forms a Platoon of Local
Defence Volunteers to defend our island home. With: AR, JB, IL,
JL and Timothy Bateson (Elliott / General Wilkinson / G.H.Q. Driver).
TV: The Man and the Hour, Series 1 (1968)

2. Museum Piece
Recorded: Thursday 7th June 1973
First Broadcast: Monday 4th February 1974, 6.15-6.45pm &
Wednesday 6th February 1974, 12.27-12.57pm
The determination of Captain Mainwaring and his Platoon to
fight to the last man in defence of our island shores is marred
only by one small detail - a total lack of weapons. With: JB, JL,
IL and Eric Woodburn (George Jones).
TV: Museum Piece, Series 1 (1968)

3. Command Decision
Recorded: Thursday 21st June 1973
First Broadcast: Monday 11th February 1974, 6.15-6.45pm &
Wednesday 13th February 1974, 12.27-12.57pm
Mr Mainwaring, self-appointed Commander of his Platoon of
L.D.V., puts the defence of the realm before his own personal
pride - and nearly comes a cropper. With: JL, JB, Geoffrey Lumsden
(Colonel Square) and David Sinclair (the G.H.Q. Driver).
TV: Command Decision, Series 1 (1968)

4. The Enemy Within the Gates
Recorded: Thursday 21st June 1973
First Broadcast: Monday 18th February 1974, 6.15-6.45pm &
Wednesday 20th February 1974, 12.27-12.57pm
Captain Mainwaring and his men triumph over the problems of
security, Fifth Columnists and German parachutists - and make
a profit. With: JB, AR, IL, Carl Jaffe (Captain Winogrodzki) and David
Sinclair (the German Airman).
TV: The Enemy Within the Gates, Series 1 (1968)

5. The Battle of Godfrey's Cottage
Recorded: Friday 6th July 1973
First Broadcast: Monday 25th February 1974, 6.15-6.45pm &
Wednesday 27th February 1974, 12.27-12.57pm
When the bells ring out signalling the invasion, Captain
Mainwaring calls on his men for their supreme effort - only to
find that half of them have gone to the Pictures. With: JL, AR,
IL, Bill Pertwee (the A.R.P. Warden), Nan Braunton (Cissy Godfrey) and Percy
Edwards (Percy the Parrot).
TV: The Battle of Godfrey's Cottage, Series 2 (1968)

6. The Armoured Might of Lance Corporal Jones
Recorded: Friday 6th July 1973
First Broadcast: Monday 4th March 1974, 6.15-6.45pm &
Wednesday 6th March 1974, 12.27-12.57pm
The Walmington-on-Sea Home Guard use their initiative and
convert Corporal Jones' Butchers van into a machine of war.
With: JL, JB, Bill Pertwee (the A.R.P. Warden), Pearl Hackney (Mrs Pike),
Richard Davies (the Volunteer), Elizabeth Morgan (Mrs Lennon) and Diana
Bishop (Miss Meadows).
TV: The Armoured Might of Lance Corporal Jones, Series 3
(1969)

7. Sgt.Wilson's Little Secret
Recorded: Friday 13th July 1973
First Broadcast: Monday 11th March 1974, 6.15-6.45pm &
Wednesday 13th March 1974, 12.27-12.57pm
The freedom of the world pales into insignificance for
Sergeant Wilson when his own freedom is threatened. With: JB,
AR, IL, Bill Pertwee (the A.R.P. Warden) and Pearl Hackney (Mrs Pike).
TV: Sgt Wilson's Little Secret, Series 2 (1969)

8. A Stripe for Frazer
Recorded: Friday 13th July 1973
First Broadcast: Monday 18th March 1974, 6.15-6.45pm &
Wednesday 20th March 1974, 12.27-12.57pm
Captain Mainwaring's promotion of Private Frazer also
promotes a state of none-too-friendly rivalry with Corporal
Jones.   With: JL, JB, IL, Geoffrey Lumsden (Corporal-Colonel Square),
Michael Knowles (Captain Bailey).
TV: A Stripe for Frazer, Series 2 (1969)
N.B. This is the last episode that James Beck recorded, and is
his last work on Dad's Army. The character of Walker does
reappear but not until The Showing Up of Corporal Jones in
which the part is taken over by Graham Stark.

9. Operation Kilt
Recorded: Monday 23rd July 1973
First Broadcast: Monday 25th March 1974, 6.15-6.45pm &
Wednesday 27th March 1974, 12.27-12.57pm
In their efforts to turn themselves into an efficient fighting
force, Mainwaring and his men pit their wits against a
detachment of Highland Infantry. With: JL, IL, AR, Pearl Hackney
(Mrs Pike) and Jack Watson (Captain Ogilvy).
TV: Operation Kilt, Series 2 (1969)

10. Battle School
Recorded: Thursday 28th June 1973
First Broadcast: Monday 1st April 1974, 6.15-6.45pm &Wednesday 3rd April 1974, 12.27-12.57pm
Captain Mainwaring and his men undergo training for guerilla warfare and get their first experience of live ammunition - from the wrong end. With: JL, AR, IL, Jack Watson (Major Smith) and Alan Tilvern (Captain Rodrigues).
TV: Battle School, Series 3 (1969)

11. Under Fire
Recorded: Friday 27th July 1973
First Broadcast: Monday 8th April 1974, 6.15-6.45pm & Wednesday 10th April 1974, 12.27-12.57pm
When German high explosives rain down on Walmington-on-Sea, Captain Mainwaring and his men demonstrate their great resourcefulness and unearth a spy in their midst. With: JL, AR, Pearl Hackney (Mrs Pike), Geoffrey Lumsden (Corporal-Colonel Square), Avril Angers (Mrs Keane) and David Gooderson (Mr Murphy).
TV: Under Fire, Series 2 (1969)

12. Something Nasty in the Vault
Recorded: Monday 23rd July 1973
First Broadcast: Monday 15th April 1974, 6.15-6.45pm & Wednesday 17th April 1974, 12.27-12.57pm
Captain Mainwaring & Sergeant Wilson fall upon an explosive situation when the Bank is broken into. With: JL, IL, Bill Pertwee (the A.R.P. Warden), John Barron (Mr West), Frank Thornton (Captain Rogers) and Elizabeth Morgan (Janet King).
TV: Something Nasty in the Vault, Series 3 (1969)

13. The Showing Up of Corporal Jones
Recorded: Friday 20th July 73
First Broadcast: Monday 22nd April 1974, 6.15-6.45pm & Wednesday 24th April 1974, 12.27-12.57pm
Cpl. Jones must prove his fitness for the Home Guard by completing an assault course in 15 minutes. With: JL, AR, Graham Stark (Private Walker) and Jack Watson (Major Regan).
TV: The Showing Up of Corporal Jones, Series 1 (1968)

14. The Loneliness of the Long Distance Walker
Recorded: Friday 20th July 1973
First Broadcast: Monday 29th April 1974, 6.15-6.45pm & Wednesday 1st May 1974, 12.27-12.57pm
When Private Walker's call up threatens the Platoon's Black Market supplies, Captain Mainwaring and his men scheme to avert this disaster. With: JL, AR, GS, Jack Watson (the Sergeant /Brigadier), Judith Furze (Chairwoman) and Michael Knowles (the Captain / Mr Rees).
TV: The Loneliness of the Long Distance Walker, Series 2 (1969)

15. Sorry, Wrong Number
Recorded: Friday 27th July 1973
First Broadcast: Monday 6th May 1974, 6.15-6.45pm & Wednesday 8th May 1974, 12.27-12.57pm

Captain Mainwaring attempts to instruct the Platoon in the use of telephone boxes, hoping to improve communication between men on patrol and his H.Q. at the Church Hall. But when a German plane crash lands in the reservoir, Corporal Jones causes nothing but confusion! With: JL, IL, GS, Bill Pertwee (the A.R.P. Warden), Pearl Hackney (Mrs Pike), Avril Angers (the Telephone Operator) and John Forest (Lieutenant Hope-Bruce).
TV: The Lion Has Phones, Series 3 (1969)

16. The Bullet is Not for Firing
Recorded: Thursday 26th July 1973
First Broadcast: Monday 13th May 1974, 6.15-6.45pm & Wednesday 15th May 1974, 12.27-12.57pm
When Corporal Jones and his Platoon waste their meagre ration of five rounds of ammunition per man, Captain Mainwaring takes action - a Court of Inquiry. With: AR, GS, Frank Williams (the Vicar), Michael Knowles (Captain Pringle), Timothy Bateson (Captain Marsh) and John Whitehall (all the Choir).
TV: The Bullet is Not for Firing, Series 3 (1969)

17. Room at the Bottom
Recorded: Monday 23rd July 1973
First Broadcast: Monday 20th May 1974, 6.15-6.45pm & Wednesday 22nd May 1974, 12.27-12.57pm
Exactly one year after Captain Mainwaring assumed command of Walmington-on-Sea Home Guard, Brigade Headquarters discover a slight irregularity - he's never had the authority. With: JL, AR, John Ringham (Captain Turner) and Jack Watson (Sergeant Gregory).
TV: Room at the Bottom, Series 3 (1969)

18. The Menace from the Deep
(Recorded: Tuesday 24th July 1973
First Broadcast: Monday 27th May 1974, 6.15-6.45pm & Wednesday 29th May 1974, 12.27-12.57pm
Marooned on the end of the pier with no food, no communication and no means of getting back to dry land, Captain Mainwaring and his doughty men face the horrors of the sea. With: JL, IL, Bill Pertwee (the A.R.P. Warden) and David Sinclair (the 2nd A.R.P. Warden).
TV: Menace from the Deep, Series 3 (1969)

19. No Spring for Frazer
Recorded: Thursday 26th July 1973
First Broadcast: Monday 3rd June 1974, 6.15-6.45pm & Wednesday 5th June 1974, 12.27-12.57pm
When Private Frazer loses a vital part, Captain Mainwaring is prepared to waken the dead at this threat to the security of our island fortress. With: JL, AR, Edward Sinclair (the Verger), Joan Cooper (Miss Baker) and Timothy Bateson (Mr Blewitt / Captain Turner).
TV: No Spring for Frazer, Series 3 (1969)

20. Sons of the Sea
Recorded: Wednesday 25th July 1973
First Broadcast: Monday 10th June 1974, 6.15-6.45pm & Wednesday 12th June 1974, 12.27-12.57pm

When Captain Mainwaring and his men take to the water, their plans go dangerously adrift. With: IL, JL, AR and Timothy Bateson (Mr Maxwell and everybody else).
TV: Sons of the Sea, Series 3 (1969)

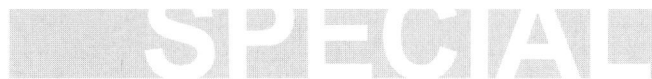

SPECIAL

21. Present Arms
Recorded: Thursday 18th July 1974
First Broadcast: Tuesday 24th December 1974, 1.15-2.15pm & Wednesday 25th December 1974, 7.30-8.30pm
Mainwaring and his men pit their wits against Eastgate Platoon for the honour of guarding a V.I.P. With: JL, IL, AR, Larry Martin (Private Walker), Bill Pertwee (Chief Warden), Pearl Hackney (Mrs Pike), Geoffrey Lumsden (Captain Square), Jack Watson (the Brigadier / Cheerful Charlie Cheeseman) and Norman Bird (Bert Postlethwaite).
TV: Shooting Pains, Series 1 (1968) and Battle of the Giants, One Hour Episode (1971).

series TWO

22. Don't Forget the Diver
Recorded: Tuesday 16th July 1974
First Broadcast: Tuesday 11th February 1975, 12.27-12.57pm & Thursday 13th February 1975, 6.15-6.45pm
Enlisting the additional services of a bird warbler, a scarecrow and a flock of sheep, Captain Mainwaring and his men mount a river attack on Captain Square's H.Q. With: JL, IL, AR, Edward Sinclair (the Verger), Geoffrey Lumsden (Captain Square) and Norman Ettlinger (the Sergeant).
TV: Don't Forget the Diver, Series 4 (1970)

23. If the Cap Fits...
Recorded: Wednesday 17th April 1974
First Broadcast: Tuesday 18th February 1975, 12.27-12.57pm & Thursday 20th February 1975, 6.15-6.45pm
One way to deal with a persistent grumbler is to give him a taste of responsibility. So Captain Mainwaring hands over command to Private Frazer - with unexpected results. With: JL, AR, IL, Edward Sinclair (the Verger) and Fraser Kerr (Major General Menzies / Sergeant MacKenzie).
TV: If the Cap Fits..., Series 5 (1972)

24. Put That Light Out
Recorded: Tuesday 30th April 1974
First Broadcast: Tuesday 25th February 1975, 12.27-12.57pm & Thursday 27th February 1975, 6.15-6.45pm
Put in charge of the observation post in the disused lighthouse, Corporal Jones sets out to prove his qualities of leadership - and ends up endangering the whole town. With: JL, IL, AR, Bill Pertwee (the A.R.P. Warden), Avril Angers (the Telephone Operator) and Stuart Sherwin (the Lighthouse Keeper).
TV: Put that Light Out, Series 4 (1970)

25. Boots, Boots, Boots
Recorded: Tuesday 16th April 1974
First Broadcast: Tuesday 4th March 1975, 12.27-12.57pm & Thursday 6th March 1975, 6.15-6.45pm
The men of Walmington-on-Sea's Home Guard object strongly to Captain Mainwaring's recipe for an efficient fighting force, the three F's - fast feet, functional feet, fit feet. With: JL, AR, IL and Erik Chitty (Mr Sedgewick).
TV: Boots, Boots, Boots, Series 4 (1970)

26. Sgt... - Save My Boy!
Recorded: Tuesday 16th April 1974
First Broadcast: Tuesday 11th March 1975, 12.27-12.57pm & Thursday 13th March 1975, 6.15-6.45pm
When Pike gets the seat of his pants caught by barbed wire in a minefield, Captain Mainwaring springs to his rescue - treading very, very carefully. With: JL, AR, IL and Pearl Hackney (Mrs Pike).
TV: Sgt - Save My Boy!, Series 4 (1970)

27. Branded
Recorded: Wednesday 17th July 1974
First Broadcast: Tuesday 18th March 1975, 12.27-12.57pm & Thursday 20th March 1975, 6.15-6.45pm
Thrown out of the Platoon by Captain Mainwaring for being a conscientious objector, spurned by his friends, Godfrey has to prove himself - and does! With: JL, AR, IL, Bill Pertwee (Chief Warden Hodges), Nan Braunton (Cissy Godfrey), Michael Segal (the 2nd Warden) and Norman Ettlinger (the Doctor).
TV: Branded, Series 3 (1969)

28. Uninvited Guests
Recorded: Thursday 18th April 1974
First Broadcast: Tuesday 25th March 1975, 12.27-12.57pm & Thursday 27th March 1975, 6.15-6.45pm
When Chief Warden Hodges and his men try to take over the Church Hall, Captain Mainwaring is determined to make things hot for them... With: JL, AR, IL, Bill Pertwee (the A.R.P. Warden), Frank Williams (the Vicar) and Edward Sinclair (the Verger).
TV: Uninvited Guests, Series 4 (1970)

29. A Brush with the Law
Recorded: Wednesday 17th July 1974
First Broadcast: Tuesday 1st April 1975, 12.27-12.57pm & Thursday 3rd April 1975, 6.15-6.45pm
When a light is left switched on in the Church Hall, the Chief Warden achieves his burning ambition - to haul Captain Mainwaring into Court. With: JL, AR, IL, LM, Bill Pertwee (Chief Warden Hodges), Geoffrey Lumsden (Captain Square), Edward Sinclair (the Verger), Michael Segal (the 2nd Warden), Michael Knowles (Mr Wintergreen) and Norman Ettlinger (the Clerk of the Court).
TV: A Brush with the Law, Series 5 (1972)

30. A Soldier's Farewell
Recorded: Wednesday 15th May 1974
First Broadcast: Tuesday 8th April 1975, 12.27-12.57pm &

Thursday 10th April 1975, 6.15-6.45pm
A visit to the Cinema and an off-the-ration toasted-cheese supper set the scene for Captain Mainwaring at the Battle of Waterloo. With: JL, AR, IL, LM, Bill Pertwee (the A.R.P. Warden) and Pat Coombs (the Clippie / Marie).
TV: A Soldier's Farewell, Series 5 (1972)

31. Brain Versus Brawn
Recorded: Tuesday 30th April 1974
First Broadcast: Tuesday 15th April 1975, 12.27-12.57pm & Thursday 17th April 1975, 6.15-6.45pm
During an initiative test, Captain Mainwaring and his men disguise themselves as Firemen complete with Fire Engine, but get diverted to tackle a real blaze. With: JL, AR, IL, LM, Avril Angers (the Waitress / the Policewoman), Robert Raglan (Colonel Pritchard) and Stuart Sherwin (Mr Fairbrother / the Corporal).
TV: Brain Versus Brawn, Series 5 (1972)

32. War Dance
Recorded: Sunday 12th May 1974
First Broadcast: Tuesday 22nd April 1975, 12.27-12.57pm & Thursday 24th April 1975, 6.15-6.45pm
The enjoyment of a Platoon Dance - arranged by Captain Mainwaring to boost the morale of his men - is spoiled when Pike announces his engagement. With: JL, AR, IL, LM, Pearl Hackney (Mrs Pike) and Wendy Richard (Violet Gibbons).
TV: War Dance, Series 3 (1969)

33. Mum's Army
Recorded: Sunday 12th May 1974
First Broadcast: Tuesday 29th April 1975, 12.27-12.57pm & Thursday 1st May 1975, 6.15-6.45pm
When Captain Mainwaring opens the ranks of his Home Guard Platoon to the ladies of Walmington, he discovers to his sorrow that the problems are not only physical, but emotional as well. With: JL, AR, IL, LM, Carmen Silvera (Mrs Gray), Mollie Sugden (Mrs Fox / the Waitress) and Wendy Richard (Edith Parrish).
TV: Mum's Army, Series 4 (1970)

34. Getting the Bird
Recorded: Monday 15th July 1974
First Broadcast: Tuesday 6th May 1975, 12.27-12.57pm & Thursday 8th May 1975, 6.15-6.45pm
Private Walker arranges to supply Corporal Jones with some off-the-ration pigeons. But the question is not where they come from, but where to store them. With: JL, AR, IL, LM, Frank Williams (the Vicar) and Diana Bishop (Sgt Wilson's Daughter).
TV: Getting the Bird, Series 5 (1972)

35. Don't Fence Me In
Recorded: Thursday 16th May 1974
First Broadcast: Tuesday 13th May 1975, 12.27-12.57pm & Thursday 15th May 1975, 6.15-6.45pm
While the Walmington-on-Sea Platoon are in charge of a P.O.W. Camp, the prisoners escape and a traitor is unearthed in their midst - Private Walker. With: JL, AR, IL, LM, Cyril Shaps (General Monteverdi), John Ringham (Captain Turner) and Sion Probert (the P.O.W. / the Sentry).
TV: Don't Fence Me In, Series 4 (1970)

36. The King was in His Counting House
Recorded: Wednesday 15th May 1974
First Broadcast: Tuesday 20th May 1975, 12.27-12.57pm & Thursday 22nd May 1975, 6.15-6.45pm
When a bomb falls on the strong-room of Mainwaring's Bank, the Platoon are set to guard the money. But first they must count it - every penny. With: JL, AR, IL, LM, Bill Pertwee (the A.R.P. Warden) and Wendy Richard (Shirley).
TV: The King was in His Counting House, Series 5 (1972)

37. When Did You Last See Your Money?
Recorded: Wednesday 15th May 1974
First Broadcast: Tuesday 27th May 1975, 12.27-12.57pm & Thursday 29th May 1975, 6.15-6.45pm
Corporal Jones can't remember how he lost £500, so the Platoon try to jog his memory and Private Frazer reveals himself as a hypnotist. With: JL, AR, IL and Timothy Bateson (Mr Blewitt / Mr Billings).
TV: When Did You Last See Your Money?, Series 5 (1972)

38. Fallen Idol
Recorded: Tuesday 16th July 1974
First Broadcast: Tuesday 3rd June 1975, 12.27-12.57pm & Thursday 5th June 1975, 6.15-6.45pm
On a weekend exercise, Captain Mainwaring's maxim that he and his men eat together, sleep together and fight together comes badly unstuck - and so does his sobriety. With: JL, AR, IL, Geoffrey Lumsden (Captain Square), Jack Watson (Captain Reed), Michael Brennan (the Sergeant-Major) and Norman Ettlinger (Pritchard).
TV: Fallen Idol, Series 4 (1970)

39. A. Wilson (Manager) ?
Recorded: Wednesday 17th April 1974
First Broadcast: Tuesday 10th June 1975, 12.27-12.57pm & Thursday 12th June 1975, 6.15-6.45pm
Captain Mainwaring's complacency is rudely shaken when Wilson, his Chief Clerk at the Bank, is given his own Branch - and promoted to Second Lieutenant. With: JL, AR, IL, Edward Sinclair (the Verger), Michael Knowles (Captain Bailey) and Fraser Kerr (Mr West).
TV: A. Wilson (Manager) ?, Series 4 (1970)

40. All is Safely Gathered In
Recorded: Monday 15th July 1974
First Broadcast: Tuesday 17th June 1975, 12.27-12.57pm & Thursday 19th June 1975, 6.15-6.45pm
Captain Mainwaring and his men try to work alongside the Warden to bring in the harvest, but not even the presence of the Vicar can ensure peaceful co-existence. With: JL, AR, IL, Bill Pertwee (the A.R.P. Warden), Frank Williams (the Vicar) and Nan Kenway (Mrs Prentice).
TV: All is Safely Gathered In, Series 5 (1972)

41. The Day the Balloon Went Up
Recorded: Thursday 18th April 1975
First Broadcast: Tuesday 24th June 1975, 12.27-12.57pm &
Thursday 26th June 1975, 6.15-6.45pm
Captain Mainwaring and Corporal Jones get carried away in their efforts to secure a runaway barrage balloon. With: JL, AR, IL, Bill Pertwee (the A.R.P. Warden), Frank Williams (the Vicar), Edward Sinclair (the Verger) and Michael Knowles (Squadron Leader Horsfall).
TV: The Day the Balloon Went Up, Series 3 (1969)

series THREE

42. A Man of Action
Recorded: Monday 28th April 1975
First Broadcast: Tuesday 16th March 1976, 12.27-12.57pm &
Thursday 18th March 1976, 6.15-6.45pm
For the benefit of a reporter from the Eastbourne Gazette, Captain Mainwaring tries to portray himself as a dynamic, efficient leader in the true Churchill mould, only to come a shade unstuck when Private Pike gets up to his ears in trouble. With: JL, AR, IL, LM, Bill Pertwee (Chief Warden Hodges), Julian Orchard (Mr Upton - the Town Clerk), Jonathan Cecil (Mr Norris) and Fraser Kerr (Captain Swan / the Inspector).
TV: A Man of Action, Series 7 (1974)

43. The Honourable Man
Recorded: Monday 28th April 1975
First Broadcast: Tuesday 23rd March 1976, 12.27-12.57pm &
Thursday 25th March 1976, 6.15-6.45pm
On the occasion of the goodwill visit by a distinguished Russian, the Town Council of Walmington-on-Sea decides to offer him the Freedom of the Town. With: JL, AR, IL, LM, Bill Pertwee (the A.R.P. Warden), Julian Orchard (Mr Upton - the Town Clerk) and Fraser Kerr (the Visiting Russian).
TV: The Honourable Man, Series 6 (1973)

44. The Godiva Affair
Recorded: Monday 5th May 1975
First Broadcast: Tuesday 30th March 1976, 12.27-12.57pm &
Thursday 1st April 1976, 6.15-6.45pm
The choosing of a local lady to play the part of Lady Godiva in Walmington's Carnival Procession in aid of the Spitfire Fund strikes a discordant note for Captain Mainwaring and his men, who were planning their own musical surprise. With: JL, AR, IL, LM, Bill Pertwee (A.R.P. Warden), Frank Williams (the Vicar), Julian Orchard (Mr Upton) and Mollie Sugden (Mrs Fox).
TV: The Godiva Affair, Series 7 (1974)

45. Keep Young and Beautiful
Recorded: Monday 12th May 1975
First Broadcast: Tuesday 6th April 1976, 12.27-12.57pm &
Thursday 8th April 1976, 6.15-6.45pm
When the War Office notifies all Home Guard Units that in future only the younger and healthier members will be retained, while those older and less fit will be exchanged with A.R.P. personnel - Captain Mainwaring and the veteran members of his Platoon are driven to adopt drastic measures. With: JL, AR, IL, LM and Michael Burlington (the Wig Maker).
TV: Keep Young and Beautiful, Series 5 (1972)

46. Absent Friends
Recorded: Tuesday 6th May 1975
First Broadcast: Tuesday 13th April 1976, 12.27-12.57pm &
Thursday 15th April 1976, 6.15-6.45pm
With mutiny on his hands from within the ranks of his Home Guard Platoon, Captain Mainwaring, battling to regain his authority, receives unexpected help - from an escaped convict. With: JL, AR, IL, LM, Bill Pertwee (Chief Warden Hodges), Pearl Hackney (Mrs Pike), Michael Brennan (Tom / George Pearson) and Stuart Sherwin (the Policeman).
TV: Absent Friends, Series 4 (1970)

47. Round and Round Went the Great Big Wheel
Recorded: Wednesday 7th May 1975
First Broadcast: Tuesday 20th April 1976, 12.27-12.57pm &
Thursday 22nd April 1976, 6.15-6.45pm
When, during its testing at Walmington-on-Sea, a new secret weapon runs amok, Captain Mainwaring and his Home Guard Platoon turn the humiliation of spud-bashing into the glory of saving the town. With: JL, AR, IL, LM, Bill Pertwee (the A.R.P. Warden), John Barron (Colonel Pierce) and Michael Knowles (Captain Stewart).
TV: Round and Round Went the Great Big Wheel, Series 5 (1972)

48. The Great White Hunter
Recorded: Friday 30th May 1975
First Broadcast: Tuesday 27th April 1976, 12.27-12.57pm &
Thursday 29th April 1976, 6.15-6.45pm
Private Walker converts an open parachute he's found into several pairs of ladies underwear and in the process, causes Captain Mainwaring and his men some embarrassment. With: JL, AR, IL, LM, Pearl Hackney (Mrs Pike), Elizabeth Morgan (Housewife) and Fraser Kerr (the Policeman).
TV: Man Hunt, Series 3 (1969)

49. The Deadly Attachment
Recorded: Wednesday 30th April 1975
First Broadcast: Tuesday 4th May 1976, 12.27-12.57pm &
Thursday 6th May 1976, 6.15-6.45pm
Corporal Jones' life is put in jeopardy when the crew of a German U Boat and their cunning Commander turn the tables on Captain Mainwaring and his men, who are supposed to be guarding them. With: JL, AR, IL, LM, Frank Williams (the Vicar), Philip Madoc (Captain Muller) and Fraser Kerr (Colonel Winters).
TV: The Deadly Attachment, Series 6 (1973)

50. Things That Go Bump in the Night
Recorded: Wednesday 7th May 1975
First Broadcast: Tuesday 11th May 1976, 12.27-12.57pm &
Thursday 13th May 1976, 6.15-6.45pm

A storm forces Captain Mainwaring and his men to take shelter for the night in a deserted country mansion, but when they begin to hear weird noises, everyone is convinced that the hounds of Hell are after them. With: JL, AR, IL, LM and John Barron (Captain Cadbury).
TV: Things That Go Bump in the Night, Series 6 (1973)

51. My British Buddy
Recorded: Tuesday 6th May 1975
First Broadcast: Tuesday 18th May 1976, 12.27-12.57pm & Thursday 20th May 1976, 6.15-6.45pm
Captain Mainwaring arranges a Welcome to England party for the first contingent of American troops to arrive in Walmington, but his hopes to cement Anglo-U.S. relations come somewhat unstuck when a brawl develops between the visitors and his Platoon. With: JL, AR, IL, LM, Bill Pertwee (Chief Warden Hodges), Jack Watson (Colonel Schultz), Pearl Hackney (Mrs Pike), Mollie Sugden (Mrs Fox), Wendy Richard (Shirley), Suzanne Lavender nee Kerchiss (Ivy) and Michael Middleton (the American Sergeant).
TV: My British Buddy, Series 6 (1973)

52. Big Guns
Recorded: Monday 5th May 1975
First Broadcast: Tuesday 25th May 1976, 12.27-12.57pm & Thursday 27th May 1976, 6.15-6.45pm
Captain Mainwaring and his men set their sights on total dominance of Walmington-on-Sea. With: JL, AR, IL, LM, Julian Orchard (Mr Upton - the Town Clerk) and Michael Middleton (the Pickfords Man).
TV: Big Guns, Series 3 (1969)

53. The Big Parade
Recorded: Friday 2nd May 1975
First Broadcast: Tuesday 1st June 1976, 12.27-12.57pm & Thursday 3rd June 1976, 6.15-6.45pm
When Private Walker offers to provide the Walmington-on-Sea Home Guard Platoon with a suitable mascot to lead them on parade, Captain Mainwaring, to his dismay, discovers that the cheapest is not necessarily the best. With: JL, AR, IL, LM, Bill Pertwee (Chief Warden Hodges), Edward Sinclair (the Verger) and Pearl Hackney (Mrs Pike).
TV: The Big Parade, Series 4 (1970)

54. Asleep in the Deep
Recorded: Friday 9th May 1975
First Broadcast: Tuesday 8th June 1976, 12.27-12.57pm & Thursday 19th June 1976, 6.15-6.45pm
While attempting to rescue Privates Walker and Godfrey from the bombed Water Works, Captain Mainwaring and his men themselves become trapped - with the water rapidly rising about them. With: JL, AR, IL, LM and Bill Pertwee (the A.R.P. Warden).
TV: Asleep in the Deep, Series 5 (1972)

55. We Know Our Onions
Recorded: Thursday 8th May 1975
First Broadcast: Tuesday 15th June 1976, 12.27-12.57pm &

Thursday 17th June 1976, 6.15-6.45pm
With Captain Mainwaring and his men facing the humiliation of failure in the Home Guard Efficiency Tests and Private Pike on the verge of tears, it takes a shady deal by Joe Walker to save the day. With: JL, AR, IL, LM, Bill Pertwee (the A.R.P. Warden), Alan Tilvern (Captain Ramsay) and Michael Middleton (Sgt Baxter).
TV: We Know Our Onions, Series 6 (1973)

56. The Royal Train
Recorded: Tuesday 29th April 1975
First Broadcast: Tuesday 22nd June 1976, 12.27-12.57pm & Thursday 24th June 1976, 6.15-6.45pm
With the main line at Walmington Station blocked and H.M. King George VI due any moment, Captain Mainwaring and his men take charge, only to find they are on a runaway train. With: JL, AR, IL, Bill Pertwee (the A.R.P. Warden), Frank Williams (the Vicar), Stuart Sherwin (the Station Master), Fraser Kerr (the Train Driver) and Michael Middleton (the Driver's Mate).
TV: The Royal Train, Series 6 (1973)

57. A Question of Reference
Recorded: Monday 12th May 1975
First Broadcast: Tuesday 29th June 1976, 12.27-12.57pm & Thursday 1st July 1976, 6.15-6.45pm
Having sent Captain Mainwaring and his Home Guard Platoon into the target area by mistake, it's up to Corporal Jones and Private Godfrey to save them being blown to pieces by the 25-pounders. With: JL, AR, IL, LM, Peter Williams (the Colonel) and Michael Burlington (the Signaller).
TV: The Desperate Drive of Corporal Jones, Series 5 (1972)

58. High Finance
Recorded: Friday 27th June 1975
First Broadcast: Tuesday 6th July 1976, 12.27-12.57pm & Thursday 8th July 1976, 6.15-6.45pm
When Mr Mainwaring refuses any longer to extend Jones's credit at the Bank, the rest of the Platoon try to find the £50 to save him from bankruptcy. With: JL, AR, IL, LM, Bill Pertwee (Chief Warden Hodges), Pearl Hackney (Mrs Pike) and Frank Williams (the Vicar).
TV: High Finance, Series 8 (1975)

59. The Recruit
Recorded: Thursday 1st May 1975
First Broadcast: Tuesday 13th July 1976, 12.27-12.57pm & Thursday 15th July 1976, 6.15-6.45pm
Sergeant Wilson takes over command of the Home Guard Platoon during Captain Mainwaring's enforced absence and makes the most unusual addition to their strength. With: JL, AR, IL, LM, Bill Pertwee (Chief Warden Hodges), Frank Williams (the Vicar), Edward Sinclair (the Verger) and Elizabeth Morgan (the Nurse and the Small Boy).
TV: The Recruit, Series 6 (1973)

60. A Jumbo-Sized Problem
Recorded: Wednesday 18th June 1975
First Broadcast: Tuesday 20th July 1976, 12.27-12.57pm &

Thursday 22nd July 1976, 6.15-6.45pm
Travelling in Jones's van to a vitally important assignment, Captain Mainwaring and his men get bogged down, and it takes two pairs of feet and a trunk to get them out. With: JL, AR, IL, LM and Bill Pertwee (Chief Warden Hodges).
TV: Everybody's Trucking, Series 7 (1974)

61. The Cricket Match
Recorded: Thursday 1st May 1975
First Broadcast: Tuesday 27th July 1976, 12.27-12.57pm & Thursday 29th July 1976, 6.15-6.45pm
As a relief from their accustomed role as defenders of these island shores against the common foe - Adolf Hitler - Captain Mainwaring and his men propose to do battle with their local adversary, Chief Warden Hodges, on the playing field. With: JL, AR, IL, LM, Bill Pertwee (Chief Warden Hodges), Frank Williams (the Vicar), Edward Sinclair (the Verger), and Anthony Smee (G.C. Egan).
TV: The Test, Series 4 (1970)

62. Time On My Hands
Recorded: Tuesday 29th April 1975
First Broadcast: Tuesday 3rd August 1976, 12.27-12.57pm & Thursday 5th August 1976, 6.15-6.45pm
When a German pilot bales out over Walmington, his parachute gets entangled with the Town Hall clock and so does Captain Mainwaring's Platoon when they attempt to rescue him. With: JL, AR, IL, LM, Bill Pertwee (Chief Warden Hodges), Frank Williams (the Vicar), Erik Chitty (Mr Parsons) and Fraser Kerr (the German Pilot).
TV: Time On My Hands, Series 5 (1972)

63. Turkey Dinner
Recorded: Friday 2nd May 1975
First Broadcast: Tuesday 10th August 1976, 12.27-12.57pm & Thursday 12th August 1976, 6.15-6.45pm
When Captain Mainwaring is due to be guest speaker at the local Rotary Club, he and his dress suit have to run the gauntlet of some sloppy work by the men of his own Platoon. With: JL, AR, IL, LM, Bill Pertwee (Chief Warden Hodges), Frank Williams (the Vicar), Pearl Hackney (Mrs Pike) and Harold Bennett (Mr Blewitt).
TV: Turkey Dinner, Series 7 (1974)

64. The Captain's Car
Recorded: Friday 9th May 1975
First Broadcast: Tuesday 17th August 1976, 12.27-12.57pm & Thursday 19th August 1976, 6.15-6.45pm
The running feud between the Wardens and the Home Guard of Walmington-on-Sea is sorely aggravated, when Captain Mainwaring is offered the use of a Rolls-Royce for the duration. With: JL, AR, IL, LM, Bill Pertwee (Chief Warden Hodges), Betty Marsden (Lady Maltby) and Gerard Green (Colonel).
TV: The Captain's Car, Series 7 (1974)

65. The Two and a Half Feathers
Recorded: Thursday 8th May 1975
First Broadcast: Tuesday 24th August 1976, 12.27-12.57pm &

Thursday 26th August 1976, 6.15-6.45pm
The bemedalled military career of Lance-Corporal Jones comes under grave suspicion when an old comrade-in-arms dredges up their past service in the Sudan. With: JL, AR, IL, LM, Bill Pertwee (Chief Warden Hodges), Michael Bates (Pte Clarke) and Avril Angers (Edna).
TV: The Two and a Half Feathers, Series 4 (1970)

66. Is There Honey Still for Tea?
Recorded: Friday 11th July 1975
First Broadcast: Tuesday 31st August 1976, 12.27-12.57pm & Thursday 2nd September 1976, 6.15-6.45pm
When plans for building a new airfield in the neighbourhood are announced, Captain Mainwaring and his men engage bureaucracy in a rearguard action to save Godfrey's cottage from demolition. With: JL, AR, IL, Joan Cooper (Cissy Godfrey) and Fraser Kerr (Sir Charles Renfrew-McAllister / the Colonel).
TV: Is There Honey Still for Tea?, Series 8 (1975)

67. Ten Seconds from Now
Recorded: Wednesday 18th June 1975
First Broadcast: Tuesday 7th September 1976, 12.27-12.57pm & Thursday 9th Sept 1976, 6.15-6.45pm
The climax to Captain Mainwarings role as O.C. Walmington-on-Sea Home Guard comes when his Platoon is chosen to take part in a world-wide radio broadcast that culminates in a speech from H.M. King George VI. With: JL, AR, IL, LM, Frank Thornton (the BBC Producer) and Roger Gartland (Bert - the BBC Engineer).
TV: Christmas Night with the Stars: Broadcast to the Empire, (1972), see Related Appearances section.

Arthur Lowe, John Le Mesurier and Clive Dunn appeared in all 67 episodes, the other main members of the cast appeared as listed

Television Episodes not adapted for radio:-

SERIES 7 (1974):
63.Gorilla Warfare.

SERIES 8 (1975):
67.Ring Dem Bells, 68.When You've Got to Go, 70.Come In, Your Time is Up, 72.The Face on the Poster.

SPECIAL EPISODE FOR CHRISTMAS (1975):
73.My Brother and I.

SPECIAL EPISODE FOR CHRISTMAS (1976):
74.The Love of Three Oranges.

SERIES 9 (1977):
75.Wake Up Walmington, 76.The Making of Private Pike, 77.Knights of Madness, 78.The Miser's Hoard, 79.Number Engaged, 80.Never Too Old.

Of the Christmas Night with the Stars mini-episodes, the 1972 sketch -'Broadcast to the Empire' - was adapted for radio. The Choir Practice (Floral dance) from 'Christmas Night with the Stars' 1970 was used to replace the Morris Dance in the radio version The Godiva Affair. This item was also adapted for the Stage Show, scene five.

N.B. On first broadcast of Series 1, all episodes were given numbers in their introduction by John Snagge, eg Episode 19: No Spring for Frazer. These were frequently omitted from subsequent broadcasts and from several of the BBC Enterprises L.P. and cassette releases.

Radio Production Credits

Adapted by Michael Knowles and Harold Snoad from TV Scripts written by Jimmy Perry and David Croft.

Produced by John Dyas.

Recorded at The Playhouse Theatre, Northumberland Avenue, London and at Paris Studios, Lower Regent Street, London. Recorded in Mono.

All 67 episodes exist on magnetic tape at the BBC Sound Archive.

Dad's Army
A Norcon Production (Released: 1971)
Copyright MCMLXXI Columbia (British) Productions Ltd.

Starring:
ARTHUR LOWE as Captain Mainwaring
JOHN LE MESURIER as Sergeant Wilson
CLIVE DUNN as Lance Corporal Jones
JOHN LAURIE as Private Frazer
JAMES BECK as Private Walker
ARNOLD RIDLEY as Private Godfrey
IAN LAVENDER as Private Pike

Plot Synopsis

Britain 1939, Walmington-on-Sea on the south coast of England... George Mainwaring, Manager of Martins Bank, has to refuse credit to a customer who wants to cash a cheque. The man, a Major-General Fullard, is angered by this and storms off.

Later that morning, Mainwaring and his two subordinates - Arthur Wilson and Frank Pike - hear the Rt. Hon. Anthony Edens call for a national network of Local Defence Volunteers. They go to the Police Station to sign on, only to find chaos. Mainwaring decides to take charge and reconvenes the meeting at the Church Hall, where he forms the Walmington-on-Sea Platoon of the L.D.V. appointing himself as Captain, Wilson as his Sergeant and Jack Jones, the town Butcher, as Lance Corporal - but only after Jones bribes him with a pound of sausages! The men meet again that evening and as Mainwaring gives a lecture on their aims - despite virtually no means of defence - the Germans across the English Channel are drawing up plans to invade our island shores. They feel that their Operation Sealion cannot fail to succeed...

After a week, the first pieces of L.D.V. equipment arrive - armbands and ammunition, but no guns! One evening, as Mainwaring demonstrates the construction of petrol bombs, two workmen arrive at the Church to remove all but one of the Church Bells, so that they can be melted down for the war effort. The Vicar, an enthusiastic campanologist, cannot resist one last ringing of his beloved bells before they are taken away. Unfortunately, Mainwaring and his L.D.V.s misinterpret this as a warning of imminent invasion by the Germans and proceed to blockade the High Street with all manner of household items - including beds, wardrobes, and even a large pot-plant care of Private Godfrey! - and shortly hear the sounds of gunshots coming from the town. Expecting Germans, they instead discover that the shots are caused by the faulty exhaust of the bell workers van, and feel rather foolish...

Time passes and the Dunkirk Evacuation takes place. Frank Pike notices that Wilson is spending more and more time with Frank's widowed mother, Mavis. Meanwhile, Lance Corporal Jones comes up with various ingenious weapons for the now re-named Home Guard. These include a dive bomber rocket gun (which blows up a barn housing the Platoon), a one-man bullet proof tank, constructed from an old bath (which nearly ends up causing the drowning of the operator, Private Walker!) and finally Frazer presents his anti-vehicle device, which, in the event of invasion, could flood roads with oil, making them unpassable. However, due to gross negligence on the part of Jones, the machine is activated prematurely, floods the road and causes the Staff Car of Major General Fullard to skid wildly and is almost written off. Fullard is furious - in fact, even more so when he recognises Mainwaring as the bloody Bank Clerk who would not cash his cheque. A bad omen!

Feature Film Supporting Cast

Liz Fraser (Mrs Pike), Bernard Archard (Major General Fullard), Derek Newark (Regimental Sergeant Major), Bill Pertwee (Hodges), Frank Williams (the Vicar), Edward Sinclair (the Verger), Anthony Sagar (Police Sergeant), Pat Coombs (Mrs Hall), Roger Maxwell (Peppery Old Gent), Paul Dawkins (Nazi General), Sam Kydd (Nazi Orderly), Michael Knowles (Staff Captain), Fred Griffiths (Bert King), John Baskcomb (Mayor), Alvar Lidell (Newsreader), George Roubicek (German Radio Operator), Scott Fredericks (Nazi Photographer), Ingo Mogendorf (Nazi Pilot), Franz van Norde (Nazi Co-Pilot), John Henderson (Radio Shop Assistant), Harriet Rhys (Girl in Bank), Dervis Ward (A.A. Man), Robert Raglan (Inspector Hardcastle), John D. Collins (Naval Officer), Alan Haines (Marine Officer).

The Platoon:
Desmond Cullum-Jones, Colin Bean, Frank Godfrey, Freddie Wiles, Freddie White, Leslie Noyes, David Fennell, Hugh Hastings, George Hancock, Bernard Severn.

Finally, the Platoon are issued with proper uniforms and guns and go on their first weekend manoeuvres in Jones' armoured Butchers van - which has recently been converted to run on gas. Jones manages to burst the gas bag during a false alarm, which results in Mainwaring's men arriving five hours late at Camp. They use a traction engine to get them to the site but lose control of it destroying tents they were to have been using that night...

After sleeping in the open, they all miss breakfast (except Wilson). They are especially upset about this as they had already missed dinner the previous evening. However, they get on with their exercise, which is to guard a pontoon bridge on the river. Unbeknown to the Platoon, part of the pontoon has been sabotaged by another group. Private Walker notices the cut rope and Jones and the others try to hold the structure together. Just at this point, Major General Fullard rides his horse, unawares, onto the loose section of the bridge and insists on a salute from Jones and his men. Jones tries to explain to his superior that it really isn't advisable, but Fullard is adamant and they reluctantly let go of the rope to oblige his order. The Major General receives the salute as he and his horse drift off slowly downstream. Mainwaring and the Platoon manage to lift Fullard off the horse onto an overhanging bridge, but in the process Jones falls onto the horse and pontoon section himself. He, in turn, is rescued by Mainwaring, Wilson and Frazer, who unwittingly become stranded themselves until later that evening when they run aground in the shallows. It is therefore unsurprising when, the next morning, Fullard informs Mainwaring that his position as leader of the Platoon is in serious doubt after the weekends mishaps.

A dejected Platoon travel home to Walmington whilst, at the same time, a German observer plane crew have to bail out over the town. They land near the Church Hall, where the Mayor is fronting a meeting, and shortly the townspeople present are taken hostage. Chief A.R.P. Warden Hodges manages to escape and warn Major General Fullard of the situation. The Home Guard arrive back in the Church grounds at this time, and Hodges informs them of the events. Fullard tells Mainwaring and his men to go home as this is a job for the regular Army. However, Jones has the idea that the Platoon could enter the Church via the crypt and surprise the Germans. They do so and once in the Church, disguise themselves as choir members, enter the room and force the Germans to surrender their weapons. By the time Fullard and the others enter, the situation is under control.

Mainwaring later reveals to Wilson that his gun was unloaded when he threatened one of the German airmen (as was the airman's own weapon). However, the whole Platoon are now heroes in the town and his position as Captain of the Walmington-on-Sea Home Guard is secure. Now they must follow through the course of the War with courage and determination as theirs is a just cause...

DAD'S ARMY (BBFC Certification: U)
A Norcon Production 1970/1. Premiered March 1971.
Film Running Time: approx. 94 minutes (Cinema), 90 minutes (TV/ Video)
(The running times vary because cinema film runs at 24 frames per second, whereas, for technical reasons, film is transferred for television at 25 frames per second.)

Dads Army (ISBN 0 340 15027 0), a novelisation of the feature film, written by John Burke, was published by Hodder Paperbacks (UK/Australia/NZ/Canada) in 1971.

Feature Film Production Credits

Based upon an idea by Jimmy Perry.

Screenplay by Jimmy Perry and David Croft, utilising, in part, many sequences from The Man and the Hour (Series 1, 1968) and minor sections of several other episodes.

The recording of Rt. Hon. Anthony Eden's radio speech and the recording of the signature tune by kind permission of the British Broadcasting Corporation.

Music Composed and Conducted by Wilfred Burns.

Who Do You Think You Are Kidding, Mr Hitler:-
Words by JIMMY PERRY,
Music by JIMMY PERRY and DEREK TAVERNER,
Sung by BUD FLANAGAN.

Art Director: TERRY KNIGHT.
Director of Photography: TERRY MAHER.
Camera Operator: GERRY ANSTISS.
Film Editor: WILLY KEMPLEN, G.B.F.E.
Sound Recordists: KEN RITCHIE, BOB JONES.
Sound Editor: DINO DI CAMPO, G.B.F.E.

Production Manager: LEONARD C. RUDKIN.
Location Manager: BOB SIMMONDS.
Assistant Director: DOUGLAS HERMES.

Set Dresser: DIMITY COLLINS.
Wardrobe Supervisor: BRIDGET SELLERS.
Make Up: JIM EVANS.
Hairdressing: MERVYN MEDALIE.
Casting: HARVEY WOODS.
Continuity: ZELDA BARRON.

Produced by: JOHN R. SLOAN.
Directed by: NORMAN COHEN.

Made in Technicolor.
Sound: Westrex Recording System.

Studio Sequences Filmed at:-
Shepperton Studios, Shepperton, Middlesex.

Location Sequences Filmed at:-
Chalfont St. Giles, Buckinghamshire (Walmington-on-Sea), Chobham, Surrey, Seaford, Sussex, and various streets around Shepperton, Middlesex.

At last! Their epic story invades the Big Screen!

DAD'S ARMY

DAD'S ARMY ARTHUR LOWE · JOHN LE MESURIER · CLIVE DUNN · JOHN LAURIE JAMES BECK · ARNOLD RIDLEY IAN LAVENDER · LIZ FRASER
JIMMY PERRY · DAVID CROFT · JOHN R. SLOAN · NORMAN COHEN TECHNICOLOR

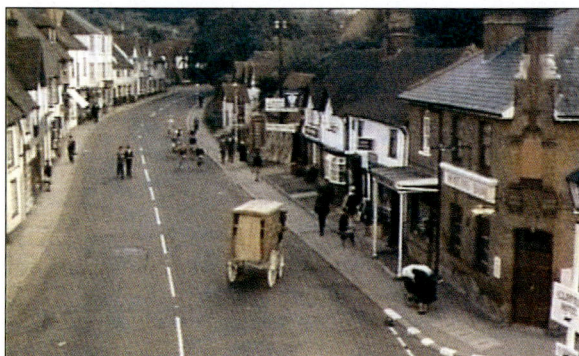

Top: The Dad's Army Film poster, which rather strangely depicts the platoon on the camera platform attached to the steam roller.

Above: Main publicity picture used to promote the film.

Right: Filming a scene at Chalfont St Giles. The whole village seems to have turned out to watch.

Below right: How the scene looks in the film.

THIS IS IMPORTANT AND SHOULD BE READ AT ONCE

O.D.A.S

This arm-band enrolls you into

DAD'S ARMY

It is your official pass to the Columbia Theatre
on Sunday, March 14, at 7 for 7.30 p.m.
1971.

(No printed tickets will be issued — the arm-band
will secure your admission — please be sure to
have it with you)

Officer Commanding Dad's Army

MINISTRY OF ENTERTAINMENT

ENLISTMENT NOTICE

ALL RANKS

"REMEMBER – never discuss military,
naval or air matters in public or with any
stranger, no matter to what nationality he
or she may belong.

The enemy wants information about
you, your unit, your destination. He will
do his utmost to discover it.

Keep him in the dark. Gossip on
military subjects is highly dangerous to
the country, whereas secrecy leads to
success.

BE ON YOUR GUARD and report
any suspicious individuals."

Dear Sir,
In accordance with the National Entertainment Act
you are called upon to join

DAD'S ARMY

and you are requested to present yourself on

SUNDAY, MARCH 14

between 7 p.m. and 7.30 p.m. to:

RECRUITING OFFICE,
COLUMBIA THEATRE,
SHAFTESBURY AVENUE, W.1.

for: **ATTENDANCE AT PREMIERE
OF FILM 'DAD'S ARMY'.**

DRESS: 1940's style, come-as-you-please, or *uniforms* which
may be obtained from Bermans, 18 Irving Street, W.C.2
with the compliments of Columbia (please mention DAD'S
ARMY when enquiring or attending for a fitting).

R.S.V.P. Commanding Officer,
O.D.A.S. Operations,
c/o Columbia Pictures Corporation Limited,
142 Wardour Street, London W1V 4AH

BUT DUE TO POSTAL DISPUTE PLEASE TELEPHONE YOUR
ACCEPTANCE TO SPECIAL SERVICES OFFICE, 01-437 4321, Ext. 211

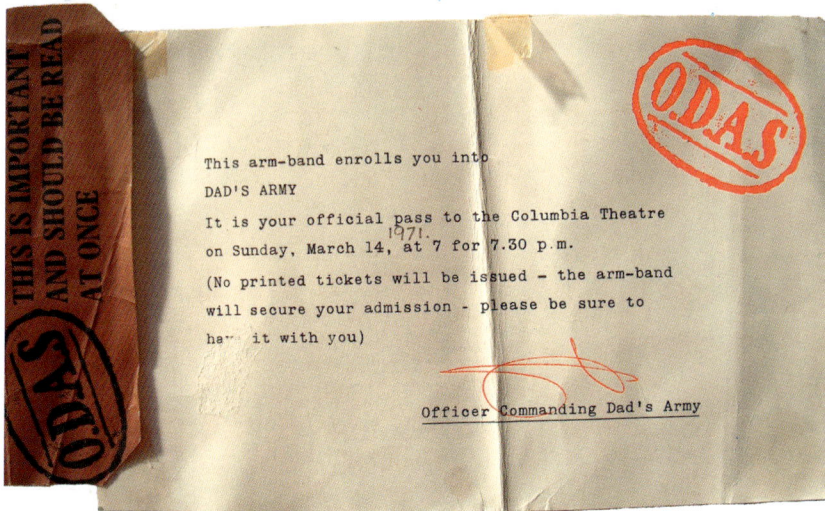

Invitations to the opening night of the Dad's Army feature film were distributed to Chalfont St Giles villagers.
The invitation arrived in a formal envelope, with the following wording printed on it - "O.D.A.S. This is important and should be read at once.". Inside the envelope was a mock enlistment notice (from the Ministry of Entertainment) and a yellow canvas armband with 'DAD'S ARMY' boldly printed on it in capital letters.
The accompanying letter, again headed by the O.D.A.S stamp (Official Dad's Army Staff?), Stated "This armband enrolls you into Dad's Army.
It is your official pass to the Columbia Theatre on Sunday, March 14, at 7 for 7.30pm.
(No printed tickets will be issued - the arm-band will secure your admission - please be sure to have it with you)"
The letter was signed:
'Officer Commanding Dad's Army'.

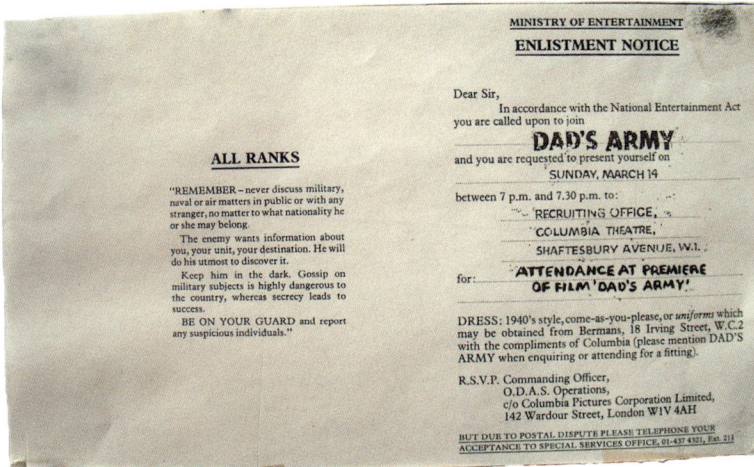

The above mock Enlistment Notice was also enclosed with the armband.
It invited guests to dress up in 1940s period costume, even going so far as pointing them to Bermans, the theatrical outfitters.
It would be the equivalent of today dressing in 70's outfits - both were 30 years ago.
Guests were asked to RSVP to Columbia Pictures at Wardour Street, but due to the postal strike it may be advisable to telephone instead - well it was the 70s after all!

Thanks to Mrs Warner (whose late husband ran the butchers used in the film) for supplying these very rare items.

DAD'S ARMY

▲ Chalfont St Giles High Street

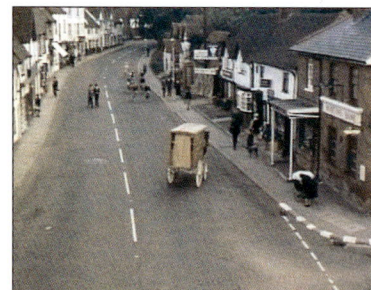

Walmington on Sea ▲

OS Sheet: 175 Map ref: 990 936:
Additional notes: Location unchanged since filming.

▲ Secret Oil Weapon demonstration.

OS Sheet: 175 Map ref: 976 656
Additional notes: The small concrete bollards are still in situ.

▲ Burma Road, Chobham Common, Surrey.

▲ Burma Road, Chobham Common, Surrey.

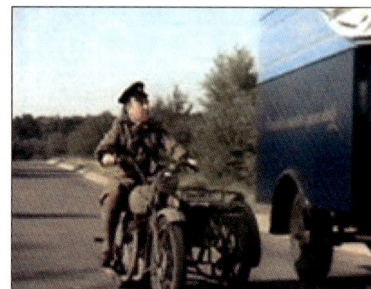

Jones' van runs out of gas. ▲

OS Sheet: 175 Map ref: 976 656
Additional notes: A few yards up the road from the above location.

Rifle Training.

OS Sheet:175 Map ref: 972 648
Additional notes: Such has been the rate
of growth of the trees etc, the only
reference point remaining is the
monument itself.

Monument Car Park, Chobham Common.

Staple Hill, Chobham Common, Surrey.

Marching in Long Johns. ▲

OS Sheet: 175 Map ref: 972 648
Additional notes: During this scene the
shadow cast by the vehicle and the
cameraman filming from the roof can
clearly be seen.

Footbridge over river

OS Sheet: 175 Map ref: 904 856
Additional notes:Location unchanged
since filming.

Cookham Lock Footbridge, Bucks (River Thames).

Seaford Cliffs, East Sussex.

Toilet Hut on Cliff ▲

OS Sheet: 199 Map ref: 509 973
Additional notes: It is still just possible to discern where the hut was positioned.

▲ Platoon display Union Flag

OS Sheet 199 Map ref: 495 978
Additional notes: A fence now stands between the cliff face and edge.

▲ Seaford Cliffs, East Sussex.

Road to Seaford Cliffs, East Sussex.

France, German Staff Car. ▲

OS Sheet: 199 Map ref: 510 977

▲ Listening for burrowing.

OS Sheet: 199 Map ref: 508 974
Additional notes: All the cliff top filming was performed at the same location due to the cost of transporting all the equipment.

▲ Seaford Cliffs, East Sussex.

▲ Old Charlton Road, Shepperton, Middlesex.

Street barricade ▲

OS Sheet: 176 Map ref: 081 680
Additional notes: The public house in the background still houses an interesting collection of photographs. 'Genevieve' was also filmed in this street.

▲ Army Training Camp.

OS Sheet: 176 Map ref: 066 689
Additional notes: This is the location where the 'running to camera' and other publicity shots were taken.

▲ Shepperton Reservoir grounds, Middlesex.

St Aldhelms Church ▲

OS Sheet: 176 Map ref: 071 687
Additional notes: The angel looks like a prop - it isn't!

▲ St Mary Magdelen Church, Shepperton, Middlesex.

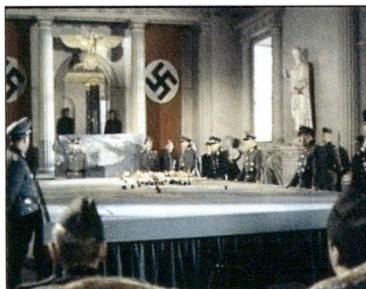

▲ German HQ

OS Sheet: 176 Map ref: 173 767
Additional notes: Syon House is open to the public

▲ The Great Hall, Syon House, Brentford, Middlesex.

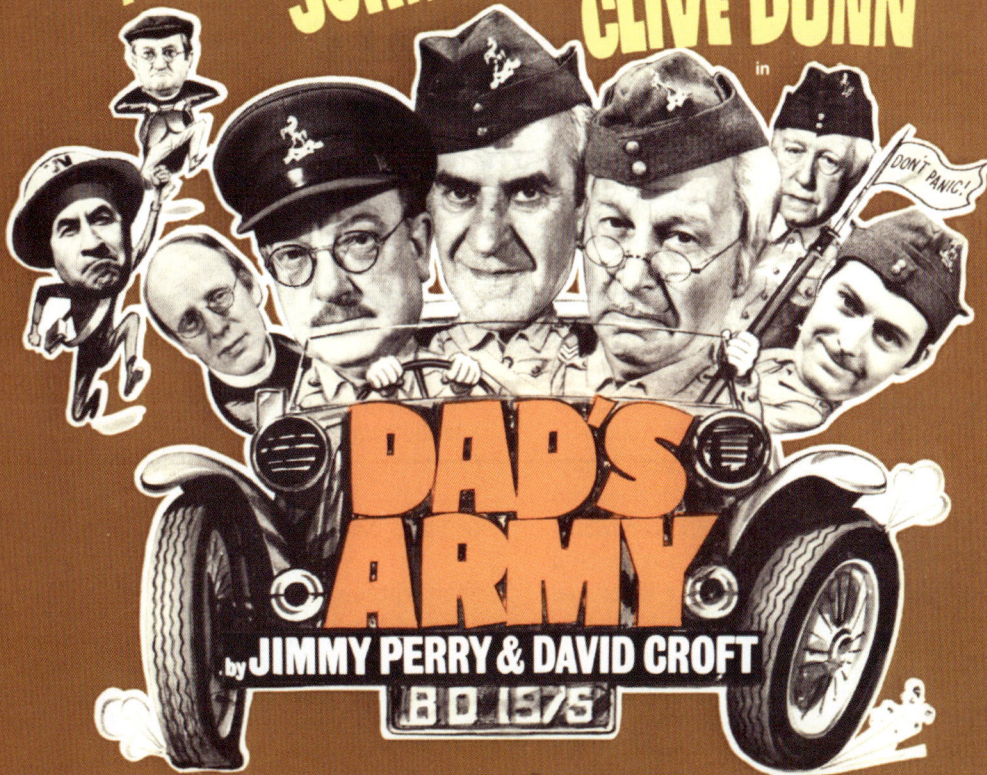

In his book 'Dad's Army, The Making of a Television Legend', Bill Pertwee tells the tale of Jimmy Perry enthusiastically acting out his idea for a Dad's Army stage play in a room at the Bell Hotel, Thetford.

His ideas came to fruition, and following rehearsals at the Richmond Theatre, Surrey, the Stage Play premiered at the Forum Theatre, Billingham. Certain alterations were made prior to the transition to the West End. These were made either to keep the running time down, or at the request of Bernard Delfont, who financed the production.

All the then current cast apart from John Laurie (who decided against appearing in the show) and Clive Dunn (who opted out later due to other commitments) performed for the show's entire run, taking on other roles in addition to their Dad's Army characters.

The stage show was never filmed for posterity and photographic images of the production are also few and far between.

Cast for Billingham & Shaftesbury Theatres

Captain Mainwaring	Arthur Lowe	Britannia	Peggy Ann Jones
Sergeant Wilson	John Le Mesurier	Soldier	Graham Hamilton*
Lance Corporal Jones	Clive Dunn	Izzy Bonn	David Wheldon Williams*
Private Godfrey	Arnold Ridley	Happidrome Announcer $	Eric Longworth
Private Pike	Ian Lavender	Mr. Lovejoy $	Arthur Lowe
Private Frazer	Hamish Roughead	Ramsbottom $	Michael Bevis
Private Walker	John Bardon	Enoch $	Ian Lavender
Private Meadow	Graham Hamilton	Max Miller $	Bill Pertwee
Private Woods	Eric Longworth	Gert and Daisy $	Joan Cooper
Private Maple	Norman Macleod		Pamela Cundell
Chief ARP Warden Hodges	Bill Pertwee	Robb Wilton $	Arthur Lowe
Rev. Timothy Farthing	Frank Williams	The Andrews Sisters	Debbie Blackett
Mr. Yeatman (Verger)	Edward Sinclair		June Shand
Mrs. Pike	Jan Davies	Flanagan and Alan $	Arthur Lowe
Mrs. Holdane Hart (WVS)	Joan Cooper		John Le Mesurier
Mrs. Fox	Pamela Cundell	Girls on the Beach $	Bernice Adams
BBC Announcer	Michael Bevis		Debbie Blackett
The Town Clerk	Eric Longworth		June Shand
British Restaurant Lady	Pamela Cundell	Man on the Beach	Graham Hamilton
Carmen Caramba	Bernice Adams		
General von Seltz	Bill Pertwee	The Home Front Company	
German Inventor	Jeffrey Holland		
Hermann Goering	David Wheldon Williams		
Dolly (Godfrey's sister)	Joan Cooper		
Newspaper Boy	Ronnie Grainge		
Raymond	Graham Hamilton*		
Dave (songwriter)	John Bardon		
Jim (songwriter)	Jeffrey Holland		
General Gordon	Michael Bevis*		
	John Conroy		
General Wolsey	Norman Macleod		
Dervishes	Barrie Stevens*		
	Ronnie Grainge*		
	Kevin Hubbard*		

The Home Front Company
Bernice Adams, Michael Bevis, Debbie Blackett, Ronnie Grainge, Graham Hamilton, Jeffery Holland, Kevin Hubbard, Peggy Anne Jones, Eric Longworth, Norman Macleod, Vivien Pearman, June Shand, Michele Summers, Barrie Stevens, Jan Todd, David Wheldon Williams, Alan Woodhouse.

Standbys:
for Arthur Lowe Eric Longworth
for John Le Mesurier Michael Bevis
for Clive Dunn Norman Macleod

* - Character/actor only appeared at Billingham
$ - Character first appeared at The Shaftesbury

Cast for Tour

Captain Mainwaring	Arthur Lowe
Sergeant Wilson	John Le Mesurier
L/Cpl Jones	Clive Dunn#
	Jack Haig
Private Godfrey	Arnold Ridley
Private Pike	Ian Lavender
Private Staines	Michael Bevis†
Private Walker	Jeffery Holland
Chief ARP Warden Hodges	Bill Pertwee
Rev. Timothy Farthing	Frank Williams
Mr. Yeatman (Verger)	Edward Sinclair
Mrs. Holdane Hart WVS	Joan Cooper
Mrs. Pike	Bernice Adams
Mrs. Fox	Peggy Ashby
BBC Announcer	Michael Bevis
Carmen Caramba	Bernice Adams
General von Seltz	Bill Pertwee
General Gordon	John Conroy
German Inventor	Jeffrey Holland
Hermann Goering	David Wheldon Williams
General Wolsey	Bill Pertwee
Brittannia	Peggy Ashby
Dolly (Godfrey's sister)	Joan Cooper
Newspaper Boy	Ronnie Grainge
Dave (songwriter)	Ronnie Grainge
Jim (songwriter)	Michael Bevis
Happidrome Announcer	Bill Pearson
Mr. Lovejoy	Arthur Lowe
Ramsbottom	Michael Bevis
Enoch	Ian Lavender
Max Miller	Bill Pertwee
Gert and Daisy	Joan Cooper
	Peggy Ashby
Robb Wilton	Arthur Lowe
The Andrews Sisters	Bernice Adams
	Pauline Stork
	Marsha Harris
Flanagan and Alan	Arthur Lowe
	John Le Mesurier
Girls on the Beach	Elizabeth Suggers
	Marianne Parnell
Man on Beach	Bill Pearson

Home Front Company
Bernice Adams, Peggy Ashby, Gina Ball, Michael Bevis, John Conroy, Ronnie Grainge, Marsha Harris, Jeffery Holland, Kevin Hubbard, Marianne Parnell, Bill Pearson, Pauline Stork, Elizabeth Suggars, David Wheldon Williams, Alan Woodhouse.

Clive Dunn only appeared at Billingham, The Shaftesbury, Manchester, Nottingham, Bradford, Birmingham and Bournemouth.
† Character first seen at the Opera House, Manchester.

Production Credits:
Designer: TERRY PARSONS
Choreography: SHEILA O'NEILL
Costumes: MARY HUSBAND
Musical Director: ED COLEMAN
Musical Assistant to Perry and Croft: JO STEWART
Orchestration by:
DON SAVAGE, DENNIS WALTON & ED COLEMAN
Lighting: ROBERT ORNBO
Sound: DAVID COLLISON

Props and supplies (for whole run):
Light & Sound Equipment:
THEATRE PRODUCTION SERVICES
Costumes: BERMAN'S / NATHAN'S
Wigs: SIMONWIGS
Watches: TIMEX
Binoculars: DIXON'S
Head Dresses: PAT DAWSON & MARK EMBLETON*
South American Costumes: NATASHA KORNITOFF*
Fur Coats: RICHARD CATERMOLE
Chesney Allen Hats: MOSS BROS.
Chesney Allen Suits: CARNABY CAVERN
Miner's Helmet and Lamp: NATIONAL COAL BOARD
Poster Transparencies: IMPERIAL WAR MUSEUM**
Hair Styling: DEREK EASTON
*For 'When Can I Have a Banana Again' dream sequence.
** Projected onto the stage backdrop at the opening of the show (see Bill Pertwee's 'Dad's Army TV Legend' book, 1989 edition, p116)

Written by Jimmy Perry & David Croft
Directed by DAVID CROFT & JIMMY PERRY
Staged by ROGER REDFARN

Scene Breakdown:
Act One
Scene 1:
Who Do You Think You're Kidding, Mr Hitler?
Orchestra & Company
The show opens with black and white back-projected World War II news footage. The cast slowly descend a flight of stairs to the strains of Who Do You Think You Are Kidding Mr Hitler? (an orchestral version with accompanying vocals).

Scene 2:
Put That Light Out
Bill Pertwee, Frank Williams, Edward Sinclair & Ensemble
Hodges, making his entrance from the audience, warns the Vicar and the Verger that they are showing a light. He then leads them in a song, performed in a chanting fashion, explaining blackout regulations. The Vicar and the Verger's input highlights how awkward it is to blackout a church!

Scene 3:
Carry On on the Home Front
Bill Pertwee, Frank Williams, Edward Sinclair,
Pamela Cundell, Janet Davies, Joan Cooper & Ensemble
A musical number which leads into a scene in Walmington-on-Sea's British Restaurant, where Mainwaring and the platoon have gone to eat. Scene taken from 'The Two and a Half Feathers'.

Scene 4:
Command Post
Arthur Lowe & John Le Mesurier
Mainwaring and Wilson keep watch on the waters of the English Channel from their cliff top command post. Scene similar to cliff top scene in the Feature Film.

Scene 5:
Private Pike's Dream
Ian Lavender, John Bardon, Bernice Adams & Ensemble
Aided by John Bardon as Walker, Ian Lavender as Private Pike sings a big production number entitled When Can I Have a Banana Again?, whilst zipped into a huge plastic banana (due to a government import ban, bananas were not available in Britain during the War).

Scene 6:
Lance Corporal Jones Stands Guard
Clive Dunn, Bill Pertwee & Ensemble
Jones stands guard on the English Coast, while the German General (a dual role for Bill Pertwee) and the Mad Inventor look across the English Channel from occupied France.

Scene 7:
Lords of the Air
Arnold Ridley & Ensemble
Private Godfrey and his sister Dolly sit outside their cottage, drinking tea, whilst across the Channel, Field Marshall Goering is extolling the virtues of the Luftwaffe, pronouncing that they will blast the British Squadrons from the skies. The scene culminates in a moving reading, by Arnold Ridley, of the poem Lords of the Air, backed by a choir of girls and boys.

Scene 8:
Choir Practice
Arthur Lowe & Company
Rounding off the first Act, this scene depicts a rehearsal for the Platoon and the people of Walmington-on-Sea of a planned Choir Concert they are to give in aid of wounded soldiers. The scene closes with the cast performing the Floral Dance. Similar to a scene from the 1969 Christmas Special.

AN INTERVAL OF FIFTEEN MINUTES

Scene Breakdown:
Act TWO

Scene 1:
The Song We Would Rather Forget
Bill Pertwee, Frank Williams, Edward Sinclair,
Pamela Cundell, Janet Davies, Joan Cooper & Ensemble
A rendition of "We're Going to Hang Out the Washing on the Siegfried Line" which leads into "We'll Meet Again".

Scene 2:
Unarmed Combat (*)
Captain Mainwaring gives a lecture to the Platoon on unarmed combat. Jones volunteers to be the man with the knife, they only have a cudgel on account of the accident the previous night. They then discuss how to tackle the enemy when he is wearing a gas mask. (similar to scene from 'Command Decision'). This scene comes to a close with all singing ' Don't sit under the apple tree with anyone else but me'.

Scene 3:
Tin Pan Alley Goes to War
Dave (John Bardon) seated at the piano
Jim (Jeffrey Holland) standing behind
Jim and Dave are songwriters, Jim has written some lyrics and Dave declares he "can't put music to that, there's a war on. The public want ordinary songs with ordinary words". After some discussion they hit on the idea of a song while

watching a man painting a white line down the middle of the road. The scene moves into the Verger, Vicar, Warden and Mrs Fox singing a song about Goodnight.
(In the Thetford amateur production, this scene is replaced by the ladies of Walmington singing a song believed to be 'He's Only a Working Man'.

Scene 4:
A Nightingale Sang in Berkeley Square
John Le Mesurier & Ian Lavender
After discussing women with Private Pike, Sergeant Wilson, nostalgically recalling a past acquaintance - who was completely different from his current love - performs A Nightingale Sang in Berkeley Square.

Scene 5:
Morris Dance (*)
The Platoon rehearse, in secret, their version of the Morris Dance. This they intend to perform at the carnival which is to raise money for the Spitfire fund. (Very similar to scene from 'The Godiva Affair').

Scene 6:
Radio Personalities of 1940
Arthur Lowe, John Le Mesurier, Ian Lavender, Bill Pertwee, Pamela Cundell, Joan Cooper, Michael Bevis & Company
This scene is composed of several set pieces and involves the cast impersonating the radio stars of the day. Arthur Lowe portrays Robb Wilton, while Pamela Cundell and Joan Cooper showcase their talents as the Elsie and Doris Waters creations Gert and Daisy. Three young female members of the company join in the fun as the Andrews Sisters, and Bill Pertwee becomes the cheeky chappie - Max Miller. The tribute concludes with a rendition of Hometown, featuring Arthur Lowe and John Le Mesurier as Flanagan and Allen.

Scene 7:
The Beach
Arthur Lowe, John Le Mesurier, Clive Dunn & Graham Hamilton
We end up on the beach, saying goodbye, rolling up the barbed wire, the War is over and we're going back to our business. At the end, the beach is deserted, Mainwaring goes down to the floats and delivers the epilogue and we get through to the truth of the man - all the fooling is over, all the pomposity is pricked - and we get a flash again of the truth about Mainwaring and what he really believes. And he says:- "The Home Guard never went into battle, but the two million men - shop assistants, factory workers, doctors, lawyers, men from every walk of life - gave of their spare time, and, in some cases, their lives, to defend their homeland. And if ever this island were in danger again, men like those would be there once more - standing ready."
Arthur Lowe, interviewed c. 1975-6.

Scene 8:
Finale
Orchestra
Leading on from Mainwaring's speech, a strident, upbeat orchestral version of the Dad's Army theme brings the show to its conclusion.

*This information was taken from a copy of the original script

DAD'S ARMY, The Stage Show performed at:
The Forum Theatre, Billingham, 4 Sept to 20 Sept 1975.
The Shaftesbury Theatre, London, 2 Oct 1975 until Feb 1976.
On Tour:
Manchester Opera House, 23 March 1976 to 10 April 1976.
Nottingham Theatre Royal, 12 April 1976 to 1 May 1976.
Bradford Alhambra, 3 May 1976 to 15 May 1976.
Birmingham Hippodrome, 17 May 1976 to 22 May 1976.
Bournemouth Pavillion, 24 May 1976 to 5 June 1976.
Blackpool Winter Gardens, 7 June 1976 to 19 June 1976.
Newcastle Theatre Royal, 22 June 1976 to 3 July 1976.
Richmond Theatre, Surrey, 12 July 1976 to 24 July 1976.
Brighton Theatre Royal, 26 July 1976 to 21 August 1976.
Bath Theatre Royal, 23 August 1976 to 4 September 1976.
Tour finished September 4 1976
Februrary - August 1976 Jeffrey Holland took over as Walker, and from Blackpool onwards, Jack Haig as L/Cpl Jones.

STAGE SHOW RUNNING ORDER

Original running order at Billingham:

Act One
Scene 1   Who Do You Think You Are Kidding, Mr Hitler?
Scene 2   Put That Light Out
Scene 3   When Can I Have a Banana Again?
Scene 4   Command Post
Scene 5   Carry On on the Home Front
               Butchers Shop
               British Restaurant
Scene 6   Cliff Top / Don't Panic
Scene 7   Battle of Britain (Lords of the Air)
Scene 8   The Choir
Interval
Act Two
Scene 9   The Song We Would Rather Forget / Rumour
Scene 10 Unarmed Combat
Scene 11 Tin Pan Alley
Scene 12 Too Late / Rumour
Scene 13 A Nightingale Sang in Berkeley Square
Scene 14 The Floral Dance
Scene 15 Radio Personalities of 1941
Scene 16 The Beach
Scene 17 Finale

After various alterations, the following order applied to shows at The Shaftesbury Theatre and was the basis for the subsequent tour:

Act One
Scene 1   Who Do You Think You Are Kidding, Mr Hitler?
Scene 2   Put That Light Out
Scene 3   Carry On on the Home Front
               Butchers Shop
               British Restaurant
Scene 4   Command Post
Scene 5   Private Pike's Dream
Scene 6   Lance Corporal Jones Stands Guard
Scene 7   Lords of the Air
Scene 8   Choir Practice
Interval
Act Two
Scene 9   The Song We Would Rather Forget
Scene 10 Unarmed Combat
Scene 11 Tin Pan Alley Goes to War
Scene 12 Morris Dance
Scene 13 A Nightingale Sang in Berkeley Square
Scene 14 Radio Personalities of 1940
Scene 16 The Beach
Scene 17 Finale

Billingham Scene 12 (Too Late) was dropped. this had Jones tell the story in full dress uniform of the 43rd reunion of the Battle of Omdurman. Finishes with the song 'Too Late'.

STAGE SHOW NOTES

Stage Show Production Notes

* Other Songs included:-
Follow the White Line, which served to advise people of how to get home safely in the black-out. Too Late, a production number with Clive Dunn recalling the killing of General Gordon at Khartoum and his experiences as a young soldier.

* The production was rehearsed at the Richmond Theatre, Surrey, for a period of three weeks in the Summer of 1975. This was followed by a short pre-West End run at the Forum Theatre, Billingham, Cleveland, which was effectively a technical run-through, where problems with the production were sorted out.

* Clive Dunn was unable to remain with the company for the full tour period due to prior commitments and was replaced by Jack Haig. Additionally, at Newcastle's Theatre Royal, Jeffrey Holland played Private Walker, Bernice Adams was Mrs Pike, with Peggy Ashby taking the role of Mrs Fox. This was also one of the venues at which Jack Haig deputised for Clive Dunn.

* John Bardon portrayed Walker, James Beck having died two years before this production.

* John Laurie declined to appear, as he felt that a performance of the show every night coupled with commuting daily from his Buckinghamshire home after the show left London and started to tour would be too tiring for him.

* On several occasions in the West End run of the show, at the Shaftesbury Theatre, the performance was interrupted by bomb scares, which would invariably prompt Arthur Lowe, in true Mainwaring style, to say "Right, follow me, men!" and march the cast up to the pub to await the call to return to the building...

* The sets that were designed to represent the sides of the English Channel and Godfrey's Cottage were constructed on electronically controlled trucks that move on to the stage from the wings.

* Shortly after the West End run commenced, the cast were asked to perform an item at the 1975 Royal Variety Performance, to be staged at the London Palladium. The Dad's Army cast accepted the invitation and elected to perform the Floral Dance scene from the show.

* Some sequences were adapted from television episodes for example The Morris Dance which was from the 1974 episode.

REAR GUARD
Starring:-
Lou Jacobi as Sgt Raskin (Wilson)
Cliff Norton as Capt Rosatti (Mainwaring)
Eddie Foy Jnr as Bert Wagner (Jones/Godfrey)
Jim Connell as Father Fitzgerald (Rev T Farthing)
Ronda Copland as Marsha
Dennis Kort as Henderson (Pike)
John McCook as Crawford (Frazer/Walker)
Arthur Peterson as Mr Muldoon (the Verger)
Special Guest:-
Conrad Janis as the 'U' Boat Captain
**with: James McCallon, Dave Morlick, Don Diamond &
Claude Sone**
Created by Arthur Julian
Written and Produced by Arthur Julian
Executive Producer Herman Rush

Directed by Hal Cooper, Assistant Producer: Dee Baker, Music: Pete Rugolo, Lyrics: Solomon Burke, Herman Rush, Vocals: Willow Sisters, Art Director: Edward Stephenson, Costumes; Ed Smith, Assistant to Producer: Lorraine Severe Kenney, Casting: Martha Kleinman & Pat Harris, Assistant Director: Anthony Chickey, Post Production Assistant Director: Hal Collins, Unit Manager: Robert M Furiga, Engineering Supervisor: Gerry Bobian, Studio Supervisor: Darrell Gentry, Technical Director: Jim Doll, Lighting Director: Jack Denton, Senior Video: Bad Hendricks, Audio: Art Du Pont, Stage Managers: Jerry Blumenthal & James Woodworth, Production Adminisrator: Ron Von Schimmelmann, Production Coordinator: Bryant Henry, Production Supervisor: Conrad Holzgang.
Video taped at ABC Television Center, Hollywood, California.
Herman Rush Associates in association with Wolper Productions

Left: Jimmy Perry and David Croft join the cast on the set of Rear Guard.

Screened as part of the ABC 'Tuesday Night Pilot Film' series on channels 7 & 8, 10 - 10.30pm on Tuesday 10 August 1976.
Not repeated
A pilot episode based on the plot for Dad's Army episode 'The Deadly Attachment' was produced by ABC in 1975. Jimmy Perry and David Croft went over to Los Angeles, America to assist in its production.
Thanks to the efforts of Dave Homewood of the NZ DAAS who has researched and contacted some of the actors who took part in the episode and after obtaining a video copy of the show, most of the details we need to know are now available to us.
After viewing the episode, if you were not aware that this was based on a well loved and popular British sitcom, you could easily dismiss it as an average America comedy of the time.
Recorded twice in front of two different audiences, the first took place at 5pm, then after a break and taking notes from the director, recorded again at 8pm. This is the way most American shows were and are still made - some even record the dress rehearsal in case they need to use any part of it. The basic plot synopsis is the same as the UK version albeit completely studio bound. Characterisations seemed to have been changed, in that Wagner is a combination of Jones and Godfrey, and the Sergeant is more prominent than the Captain. Some of the lines spoken have been swapped between different characters, and, being America, a woman was introduced into the cast. All but one of the main cast members were Jewish.

Rear Guard was set on Long Island, New York. The characters were members of the Civilian Defense, a veterans organisation set up in 1944 who took it upon themselves to defend their homes from the threat of a Nazi attack during WWII.

NOTES:

* In the famous 'soggy chips' exchange the emphasis is turned to the provision of 'deli' food. The 'U' Boat captain is offered salami, but he insists on corned beef - lean! Henderson, who is taking the order, suggests going to Greenblats Kosher Deli, to which the unflappable 'U' Boat Captain then orders "pastrami on rye, mit plenty of mustard". On hearing this Raskin tells him that "as prisoner of war, I say you will get pastrami... on white bread....and with mayonnaise!" The combination would, of course, be an improbable order at a New York deli!

* The machine gun was not used until the actual recording, which ended up deafening a number of actors for several minutes.

* The Godfrey character (Wagner) is most impressed when told he had only left the room four times in one hour!

* The Captain (Rosatti) had the grenade put down his trousers, as Perry and Croft had originally intended for Mainwaring,until Arthur Lowe refused to do anything that involved removing his trousers.

* The grenades were fitted with dummy detonators by Henderson (Pike) and Crawford (Walker).

The only known photograph showing the cast of 'It Sticks Out Half A Mile'. It originally appeared in the Radio Times.

A RADIO SERIES
"A Seaside Saga of Post-War Pier Perpetuation."

ARTHUR LOWE as George Mainwaring (1st Pilot)
JOHN LE MESURIER as Arthur Wilson
IAN LAVENDER as Frank Pike (2nd Pilot onwards)
BILL PERTWEE as Bert Hodges (2nd Pilot onwards)

All episodes broadcast on BBC Radio 2.

first PILOT

It Sticks Out Half a Mile Studio Recording Date: early 1982.
Not Broadcast (see below)
This programme starts with a solo version of the signature
tune slightly longer than that of the following broadcast
episodes. It is 1948 and George Mainwaring after leaving the
bank and spending some time abroad returns to England,
apparently being abroad did not suit Elizabeth. He has
arranged to see the manager of 'Swallow Bank' in the hope
of securing a loan to buy Frambourne Pier, the bank manager
turns out to be a certain Arthur Wilson. Mainwaring's plan is
to renovate the pier and make it the town's centre of
attraction, so he takes Wilson along to see the pier and the
Town Council. The Town Council had been trying to raise the
money to dismantle the pier and were delighted that
Mainwaring wanted to buy it. Mainwaring gets his loan and
toasts himself as the new proud owner of the pier. Wilson
points out that actually the real owner is Swallow Bank!
This pilot episode for It Sticks Out Half A Mile was recorded
with Arthur Lowe as George Mainwaring, but was shelved
due to his sudden death (15/4/82) shortly after the
recording. Apparently it was Joan Cooper (Arthur's wife) who
convinced Harold Snoad and Michael Knowles to carry on as
Arthur had liked it so much. Naturally, this caused the
writers a considerable rethink and the character Hodges was
brought in to replace Mainwaring.
Sadly to date this episode was never broadcast although the
BBC do possess a copy.
This programme featured Arthur Lowe (George Mainwaring),
John Le Mesurier (Arthur Wilson), Josephine Tewson (Miss
Baines), Dougie Brown (Stephen Rawlings), Timothy Weston
(Guthrie), Anthony Sharp (Charles Hunter), Sidney Bronty
(Percy Short) and Hayden Wood (The Man).
The programme was produced by Jonathan James Moore.

second pilot - series ONE

1. Episode One
Recorded: Saturday 11th September 1982
First Broadcast Sunday 13th November 1983, 1.30-2.00pm
Rpts. Friday 18th November 1983, 10.00-10.30pm and
Tuesday 17th July 1984, 10.30-11.00pm
(Broadcast as Episode One of the series.)
The War has been over three years. Arthur Wilson is now
Manager of Swallows Bank in Frambourne-on-Sea. Frank Pike
has moved there too, but their peacetime lives are shattered
when Bert Hodges suddenly appears with a business
proposition for Frank. With: Vivienne Martin (Miss Perkins), Robin
Parkinson (Mr Hunter), Edward Burnham (Mr Short), Gordon Peters (Mr
Rawlings) and Spencer Banks (Council Employee).
Episode sometimes referred to as 'The Business Proposition'.

series ONE

2. Episode Two
Recorded: Saturday 19th February 1983
First Broadcast: Sunday 20th November 1983, 1.30-2.00pm
Rpts. Friday 25th November 1983, 10.00-10.30pm and
Tuesday 24th July 1984, 10.30-11.00pm
Bert Hodges and Frank Pike have persuaded Arthur Wilson
reluctantly to loan them £5000, from Swallows Bank to
renovate the pier at Frambourne-on-Sea, but on the pier
they meet resistance from its Caretaker, Guthrie, and Hodges
almost goes to a watery grave. With: Vivienne Martin (Miss Perkins),
Glynn Edwards (Fred Guthrie) and Michael Bilton (Mr Johnson).
Episode sometimes referred to as 'The Bank Loan.'

3. Episode Three
Recorded: Wednesday 23rd February 1983
First Broadcast: Sunday 27th November 1983, 1.30-2.00pm
Rpts. Friday 2nd December 1983, 10.00-10.30pm and
Tuesday 31st July 1984, 10.30-11.00pm
Hodges, Pike and Wilson continue their renovations of the
pier at Frambourne-on-Sea and visit the local library to do
some research on the previous pre-War owners. With: Vivienne
Martin (Miss Perkins), Glynn Edwards (Fred Guthrie), Barry Gosney (Mr
Watkins / the Electrician), James Bryce (the Bank Cashier / the Librarian)
and Stuart Sherwin (Electricity Showroom Assistant).
Episode sometimes referred to as 'Who Owned the Pier?'

4. Episode Four
Recorded: Wednesday 23rd February 1983
First Broadcast: Sunday 4th December 1983, 1.30-2.00pm
Rpts. Friday 9th December 1983, 10.00-10.30pm and
Tuesday 7th August 1984, 10.30-11.00pm
In an effort to save money Hodges, Pike and Wilson decide

to inspect the foundations of Frambourne Pier themselves and put to sea at night in an inflatable rubber dinghy. With: Vivienne Martin (Miss Perkins).
Episode sometimes referred to as 'Inspecting the Piles.'

5. Episode Five

Recorded: Saturday 19th February 1983
First Broadcast: Sunday 11th December 1983, 1.30-2.00pm
Rpts. Friday 16th December 1983, 10.00-10.30pm and Tuesday 14th August 1984, 10.30-11.00pm
This episode is a mono recording - reason unknown.
Pike is unable to concentrate on the pier renovations, because he is in love. Mrs Pike is worried and calls in Mr Wilson to lecture her son on the birds and the bees. With: Vivienne Martin (Miss Perkins), Carol Hawkins (Avril), Janet Davies (Mavis Pike) and Gordon Salkild (the Telephone Engineer).
Episode sometimes referred to as 'Pike in Love'.

6. Episode Six

Recorded: Saturday 26th February 1983
First Broadcast: Sunday 18th December 1983, 1.30-2.00pm
Rpts. Friday 23rd December 1983, 10.00-10.30pm and Tuesday 28th August 1984, 10.30-11.00pm
Pike and Hodges decide to launch a campaign asking for volunteers to save the pier. And so the Friends of Frambourne Pier Association (F.O.F.P.A.) is born. With: Vivienne Martin (Miss Perkins), Glynn Edwards (Fred Guthrie), Michael Knowles (Ernest Woolcot) and Hilda Braid (Olive Briggs).
Episode sometimes referred to as 'The Friends of Frambourne Pier.'

7. Episode Seven

Recorded: Saturday 5th March 1983
First Broadcast: Sunday 1st January 1984, 1.30-2.00pm
Rpts. Friday 6th January 1984, 10.00-10.30pm and Tuesday 11th September 1984, 10.30-11.00pm
The first meeting of the Friends of Frambourne Pier Association is convened. Arthur Wilson attends but has to explain his evening out to a suspicious Mrs Pike. With: Glynn Edwards (Fred Guthrie), Michael Knowles (Ernest Woolcot), Hilda Braid (Olive Briggs), Michael Bilton (the Elderly Man), Madi Hedd (the Woman) and Jill Lidstone (the Young Lady).
Episode sometimes referred to as 'The First Meeting'

8. Episode Eight

Recorded: Tuesday 8th March 1983
First Broadcast: Sunday 8th January 1984, 1.30-2.00pm
Rpts. Friday 13th January 1984, 10.00-10.30pm and Tuesday 25th September 1984, 10.30-11.00pm
A visit to the Pier Theatre, which can only be reached by Bosun's Chair, ends in disaster when Arthur Wilson and romantically inclined Miss Perkins are marooned together.
With: Vivienne Martin (Miss Perkins) and Paul Russell (Derek).
Episode sometimes referred to as 'Marooned.'

9. Episode Nine

Recorded: Saturday 5th March 1983
First Broadcast: Sunday 15th January 1984, 1.30-2.00pm
Rpts. Friday 20th January 1984, 10.00-10.30pm and Tuesday 2nd October 1984, 10.30-11.00pm
The Friends of Frambourne Pier Association arrange a Fancy Dress Night on the Pier to raise money, but problems arise for Arthur Wilson when Miss Perkins and Mrs Pike choose the same costumes. With: Janet Davies (Mavis Pike), Vivienne Martin (Miss Perkins), Michael Knowles (Ernest Woolcot), Hilda Braid (Olive Briggs), Gordon Clyde (Willoughby Smallpiece) and Miranda Forbes (the Waitress).
Episode sometimes referred to as 'The Fancy Dress Night.'

10. Episode Ten

Recorded: Saturday 26th February 1983
First Broadcast: Tuesday 21st August 1984, 10.30-11.00pm
Pike and Hodges find a builder to repair the Pier, but old hostilities are renewed when they discover his nationality.
With: Vivienne Martin (Miss Perkins), Glynn Edwards (Fred Guthrie), Stella Tanner (Myrte Spivy), Gordon Clyde (Mr Fisher), Carole Harrison (the Builders Receptionist) and Katherine Parr (the Irish Nun).
Episode sometimes referred to as 'The Builder'.

11. Episode Eleven

Recorded: Tuesday 8th March 1983
First Broadcast: Tuesday 4th September 1984, 10.30-11.00pm
Wilson, Pike and Hodges go to London to claim War Damage Compensation for the Pier. With: Vivienne Martin (Miss Perkins), Reginald Marsh (Sir Wensley Smithers), Gordon Clyde (Civil Servants 1 & 5), Jon Glover (Civil Servants 2 & 4) and Michael Bilton (Mr Thornedyke / Civil Servant 3).
Episode sometimes referred to as 'War Damage.'

12. Episode Twelve

Recorded: Tuesday 15th March 1983
First Broadcast: Tuesday 18th September 1984, 10.30-11.00pm
Pike and Hodges decide to update the photographs in the Pier's What the Butler Saw machine and persuade Miss Perkins to pose as their pin-up girl. With: Vivienne Martin (Miss Perkins), Christopher Biggins (Dudley Watkins) and Robin Parkinson (Mr Hunter).
Episode sometimes referred to as 'The Pin Up Girl.'

13. Episode Thirteen

Recorded: Tuesday 15th March 1983
First Broadcast: Tuesday 9th October 1984, 10.30-11.00pm
Pike and Hodges discover that there may be hidden treasure on the Pier and clairvoyant Madame Zara is called in to help them.
With: Vivienne Martin (Miss Perkins), Glynn Edwards (Fred Guthrie) and Betty Marsden (Madame Zara).
Episode sometimes referred to as 'Hidden Treasure.'

Production Credits:

Written by Harold Snoad and Michael Knowles
The characters of Wilson, Pike and Hodges were originally created by Jimmy Perry and David Croft.

Recorded in Stereo.

Producers: Jonathon James Moore (1st Pilot) & Martin Fisher (2nd Pilot and series)
Episodes were originally not preserved by the BBC Transcription Service as the series was thought to be of little interest to an international audience. However, with the introduction of BBC7, a digital radio station, the series has been broadcast to a new (younger?) audience.
In the closing months of 2003, Harold Snoad submitted his copy of the original pilot, starring Arthur Lowe, to the BBC as part of their Treasure Hunt initiative.
This episode is now available on the Collector's Edition Series Three CD.
There have been no plans to broadcast the entire episode, but tantilising snippets have been aired on several

TV VERSIONS OF THE SERIES

It is not widely known that 'It Sticks Out Half A Mile' spawned two TV outings based on the same premise, one was a pilot, the other a seven part series.

Walking the Planks (1985)
A BBC 30 min pilot set in 1946 starring Michael Elphick as Ron Archer (Hodges' role) and Richard Wilson as Richard Talbot (Wilson's role) joined by Gary Raynsford as Ron's gormless son, Trevor Archer (Pike's role).
Written by Michael Knowles and Harold Snoad, Produced by Harold Snoad.

High and Dry (1987)
A Yorkshire TV production which ran for 7 x 30min episodes.
Starring Bernard Cribbins as Ron Archer and Richard Wilson as Richard Talbot. This time Archer's son, Trevor, was played by Angus Barnett in the Pike role.
The setting was Midbourne set just before 1946 and it was entirely studio bound. It was networked but to little response.
Written by Alan Sherwood (a Harold Snoad pseudonym due to his contract with the BBC) & Michael Knowles. Produced by Ronnie Baxter.

IT STICKS OUT HALF A MILE ACTORS LIST

ACTOR	CHARACTER	EPISODE
Spencer Banks	Council Employee	Episode 1
Christopher Biggins	Dudley Watkins	Episode 12
Michael Bilton	Mr Johnson	Episode 3
	Mr Thornedyke	Episode 11
	Elderly Man	Episode 7
Hilda Braid	Olive Briggs	Episode 6, 7, & 9
Sidney Bronty	Percy Short & Hayden	1st pilot
Dougie Brown	Stephens Rawlings	1st pilot
James Bryce	Bank Cashier	Episode 3
Edward Burnham	Mr Short	Episode 1
Gordon Clyde	Willoughby Smallpiece	Episode 9
	Mr Fisher	Episode 10
	Civil Servant	Episode 11
Janet Davies	Mrs Pike	Episodes 5, 9
Glynn Edwards	Fred Guthrie	Episodes 2, 3, 6, 7, 10 & 13
Miranda Forbes	The Waitress	Episode 9
Jon Glover	Civil Servant	Episode 11
Barry Gosney	Mr Watkins	Episode 3
Carole Harrison	Builder's Receptionist	Episode 10
Carol Hawkins	Avril	Episode 5
Madi Hedd	The Woman	Episode 7
Michael Knowles	Ernest Woolcot	Episodes 6, 7, & 9
Ian Lavender	Frank Pike	All 13 episodes
John Le Mesurier	Arthur Wilson	1st pilot & all 13 episodes
Jill Lidstone	Young Lady	Episode 7
Arthur Lowe	George Mainwaring	1st pilot
Betty Marsden	Madame Zara	Episode 13
Reginald Marsh	Sir Wensley Smithers	Episode 11
Vivienne Martin	Miss Perkins	All 13 episodes
Robin Parkinson	Mr Hunter	Episodes 1 & 12
Katherine Parr	Irish Nun	Episode 10
Gordon Peters	Mr Rawlings	Episode 1
Bill Pertwee	Bert Hodges	All 13 episodes
Paul Russell	Derek	Episode 8
Gordon Salkilid	Telephone Engineer	Episode 5
Anthony Sharp	Charles Hunter	1st pilot
Stuart Sherwin	Showroom Assistant	Episode 3
Stella Tanner	Myrte Spivy	Episode 10
Josephine Tewson	Miss Baines	1st pilot
Timothy Weston	Guthrie	1st pilot

THE COWARD REVUE

Recorded 27 November 1969
Broadcast Friday 26 December 1969 BBC2 7.35-8.30pm
A Musical Tribute to Noel Coward, produced by James Gilbert.
Performances were staged and choreographed by Alfred Rodrigues.
This programme included a 4 minute performance from Arthur Lowe, John Le Mesurier and Clive Dunn singing the Noel Coward song 'Can You Please Oblige Us With A Bren Gun'. The trio are seen in Army uniform sorting out their various weapons and composing a letter requesting more weapons. The scene closes with the group marching around the desk holding Union Jack flags.
A short extract appeared in the 'Telly Addicts' quiz programme.

This programme also featured amongst others Ian Carmichael, Ronnie Barker, Dora Bryan, Ronnie Corbett, Danny LaRue, Kenneth More and Vanessa Redgrave.
This item exists in the BBC Archive.

THIS IS YOUR LIFE: CLIVE DUNN

Broadcast Wednesday 24 March 1971, ITV Colour.
Clive Dunn was the featured guest in this edition, which was hosted by Eamonn Andrews.
This programme no longer exists in the Thames TV archive, though two short clips are known to exist on audio tape in a private collection.

THE MORECAMBE AND WISE SHOW

Broadcast Thursday 22 April 1971, BBC2 Colour.
Rpts. 09/02/97 BBC 1
'Monty on the Bonty'
Arthur Lowe was the featured guest and appeared in several sequences featuring Janet Webb. Later, in one of Ernie's plays, based upon Mutiny on the Bounty, he portrayed Captain Bligh, while members of the Platoon (John Le Mesurier, John Laurie, James Beck, Arnold Ridley and Ian Lavender) made a cameo appearance as a few of the ship's crew still loyal to Bligh.
This item exists in the BBC Archive.

BBC 24 Hours

Broadcast 1971
Shepperton Studios. This documentary show the cast of Dad's Army while working on the Columbia Pictures film and the decline in British film industry, approximately 4 minutes. Switching on Blackpool Lights, the Dad's Army cast are invited to switch on the illuminations. Approximately 4 minutes

AN HOUR WITH CLIVE DUNN

Broadcast Wednesday 18 August 1971 BBC 1 9.20 pm.
This 60 minute programme was an extensive interview with the actor. It also included a showing of 'The Armoured Might of Lance Corporal Jones'.

SOUNDS FAMILIAR

Broadcast Thursday 19 October 1972, BBC Radio 1 & 2, 8.02-8.30pm
Arthur Lowe, John Le Mesurier, John Laurie and Bill Pertwee were special guests on the showbiz history game show. Chaired by Jack Watson.

ASK ASPEL

Broadcast Sunday 22 October 1972, BBC1 Colour.
Arthur Lowe was interviewed as Michael Aspel's guest.

SMOOTH OPERATOR

Barclays Bank Training Film 1974
This training film features Arthur Lowe and Ian Lavender, Arthur as Mr Mainwaring the manager and Ian as the trainee and the story revolves around answering the telephone. This film was produced by Paul Ellis Associates, for Barclays Bank PLC approximately 15 minutes.

BARCLAYS BANK

Television Commercials 1974
Two ITV commercials featuring Arthur Lowe and Ian Lavender as Mainwaring and Pike, Mainwaring is reluctant to retire and want to ensure Pike understands all the benefits from Barclays. Pike is keen to take over as manager.

THE BLACK AND WHITE MINSTREL SHOW

Recorded 11 May 1975, BBC 1 Colour.
Broadcast June 1975
This musical show featured Arthur Lowe, as Captain Mainwaring, in 7 minute song and dance routines with other members of the show. Arthur sings a medley of wartime songs including 'We're going to hang out the washing on the Siegfried line, Run Rabbit, White Cliffs of Dover and Kiss me goodnight Mr Mainwaring.
This must be one of the rare times where we clearly see Captain Mainwaring but hear Arthur Lowe!
This programme exists in the BBC archive.

THIS IS YOUR LIFE: ARNOLD RIDLEY

Broadcast Wednesday 10 March 1976, ITV Colour.
Eamonn Andrews is dressed as a ticket collector at Marylebone Station, Dad's Army regulars Ian Lavender, Frank Williams, Edward Sinclair, John Le Mesurier and Arthur Lowe led by Bill Pertwee march along the platform, Arnold comes running along dragging his kit bag.
Arnold believes they are there to make a promotional film for the coming Stage Show tour.
Other celebrities paying tribute are David Croft, Jimmy Perry, Dirk Bogarde, Noel Gordon, Gerad Fairley and James Mills.
This programme exists in the Thames TV archive.

THE MORECAMBE AND WISE CHRISTMAS SHOW

Sunday 25 December 1977, BBC1 Colour.
Rpt. 25/12/93
Produced several months after the completion of work on the final series of Dad's Army, Arthur Lowe, John Le Mesurier and John Laurie reprised their roles in a brief sequence with Elton John, who asked them to direct him to the TV studio where The Morecambe and Wise Show was being recorded.
This item exists in the BBC Archive.

A NIGHT OF ONE HUNDRED STARS

Broadcast 21 December 1980. ITV's charity gala at the National Theatre to celebrate 50 years of equity, compere Terry Wogan featured in costume John Le Mesurier, Ian Lavender, Arnold Ridley, Bill Pertwee and Frank Williams. LWT Productions.

THE BRITISH ACADEMY OF FILM & TELEVISION ARTS (BAFTA)

Broadcast Thursday 18 March 1982 from the Top of The Town, Thames TV.
Compered by Denis Norden
Arthur Lowe is invited to make the Desmond Davies Award to David Croft for his outstanding creative contribution to television. Arthur gives a hilarious 7 minute introduction, making fun of his own legendary foibles.
Clips from Keep Young and Beautiful, Hugh & I, It Ain't Half Hot Mum, Are You Being Served? and Hi Di Hi! Arthur and David are joined on stage by Terry Scott, Frank Thornton, Windsor Davies, Ruth Madoc, Jimmy Perry and Jeremy Lloyd.
This part of the programme is 12 minutes long.

BBC 1 PEBBLE MILL AT ONE

ARTHUR LOWE INTERVIEW Pebble Mill at One.
Broadcast Thursday 15 April 1982 1.00pm BBC1 Colour.
Running time 10 minutes.
Arthur Lowe was appearing in 'Home at Seven' at the Alexandra Theatre Birmingham. Arthur is asked about some of the very successful programmes he has been involved with: 'Coronation Street, Dad's Army, Potter and Bless Me Father'.
Clips are shown from Number Engaged and Potter.
This programme was broadcast live and was the last interview Arthur made, as sadly that same day, he was taken ill and died in hospital.
This item does not exist in the BBC archive, however and thankfully a private copy exists in the Dad's Army Appreciation Society's video library.

GOOD MORNING

BBC 1, 22nd March 1994. Ian Lavender goes to Kent and meets the Barmy Army, approximately 4 minutes, recorded 13/3/1994.

JIM DAVIDSON SPECIAL

Broadcast Wednesday 6 June 1984 8pm Thames.
Part of the D Day 40th anniversary.
Featured Clive Dunn, Bill Pertwee, Windsor Davies, Melvyn Hayes & Tony Selby who all appeared as their respective television characters.
Produced by Dennis Kirkland.

THE GENERATION GAME

Broadcast 1994
Bill Pertwee makes a guest appearance as Warden Hodges.

WOGAN
Monday 1 August 1988, BBC1 Colour.
Running time 16 minutes.
Clive Dunn, Ian Lavender, Bill Pertwee, David Croft and Jimmy Perry were interviewed by Terry Wogan to mark the twentieth anniversary of the first 'Dad's Army' episode. Clips taken from 'The Man and the Hour' and 'Battle of the Giants'. This item exists in the BBC Archive.

DEFINITELY DUNN
1. Pubs and Parents
2. Flat Feet and Concert Parties
3. Relieving General Gordon
4. Glamorous Nights in a Prison Camp
5. Grandad and the Elephant
6. The Men from Walmington
Wednesday 6 July to Wednesday 1 August 1988,
BBC Radio 2, 10.00-10.15pm.
In a series of six 15-minute programmes, Clive Dunn recalled some highlights from his 50 years in entertainment. In front of a studio audience, Clive told anecdotes and sang songs, accompanied by Ronnie Bridges on piano.

DAYTIME LIVE
Tuesday 24th October 1989, BBC1 Colour
Running time 17 minutes.
Bill Pertwee, Clive Dunn, Ian Lavender and Frank Williams were interviewed by Judy Spiers to celebrate twenty-one years of the programme and to promote Bill Pertwee's book "Dad's Army: The Making of a Television Legend". David Croft and Jimmy Perry were also interviewed via a video link to the North Acton Rehearsal Rooms, where they were supervising rehearsals for their up coming series, 'You Rang M'Lord'. A clip from 'The Face on the Poster' was featured. This item exists in the BBC Archive.

OPEN AIR
Broadcast 6 December 1989
Ian Lavender, Bill Pertwee and Jimmy Perry are interviewed.

NOEL'S HOUSE PARTY
Broadcast Saturday 27 November 1993.
Featured Clive Dunn as Corporal Jones in a three minute sketch.

THE ARTHUR LOWE STORY
Broadcast 28 December 1993, BBC Radio 2.
This 60 minute programme was written and narrated by Bill Pertwee.

THIS MORNING
Recorded 13 March 1994.
Broadcast Tuesday 22 March 1994.
Hosted by Anne Diamond and Nick Owen.

Ian Lavender, one time Private Pike, pays a visit to the Barmy Army Film Club as he thinks there might be a part in their new film for him.
Many of the club members are interviewed about the film club's activities.
This 4 minute programme finishes with the Barmy Army members and Ian marching in a field towards the camera. This item is held by the Barmy Army Film Club and a copy exists in the DAAS video library.

FAREWELL TO THE PARIS
Compared by Bob Holness.
Recorded 26 February 1995.
Broadcast 11 March 1995 7.33pm BBC Radio 2.
A celebration and tribute of six decades of comedy, music and light entertainment and to all the stars who performed there. This programme featured Betty Marsden interviewing Bill Pertwee. Other stars included June Whitfield, Frank Muir, Denis Norden, Leslie Philips, Jon Pertwee and Roy Hudd. Announcer Alan Dedicoat. Produced by Richard Wilcox and Aled Evans.

OMNIBUS: PERRY & CROFT; THE SITCOMS
Broadcast Tuesday 18 April 1995, BBC1 Colour.
This long-overdue fifty minute documentary celebrated the collaborative works of Jimmy Perry and David Croft. Concentrating on their three main successes - 'Dad's Army', 'It Ain't Half Hot Mum' and 'Hi-De-Hi!' - the programme boasted interviews with Perry and Croft, contributions from the regular artistes who appeared in each series, plus comments from celebrity admirers and from representatives of academia and the media. 'Dad's Army' received much praise from those interviewed, many citing it as a masterpiece of television comedy. Of the surviving personnel from 'Dad's Army', only Clive Dunn, Bill Pertwee and Ian Lavender were interviewed for this tribute, with Frank Williams, Colin Bean and Pamela Cundell sadly not appearing. The main 'Dad's Army' section of the documentary lasted some fifteen minutes in total, and featured clips from many episodes. The closing credit sequence featured the wonderful scene from 'A Soldier's Farewell' where Mainwaring is trampled under the feet of the platoon as they leave the cinema. It is interesting to note that the documentary ignored completely their most recent collaboration - "You Rang M'Lord' - which featured several of the actors interviewed.
Programmes repeated on consecutive Tuesdays (BBC1) to accompany this documentary were: 'It Ain't Half Hot Mum': The Road to Bannu (18th April 1995), 'Dad's Army': The Deadly Attachment (25th April 1995) and 'Hi-De-Hi!': A Night Not to Remember (2nd May 1995).
This item exists in the BBC Archive.

FULL STEAM A-HUDD
Recorded at The BBC Theatre Broadcasting House on 30 April 1995 7pm.
Broadcast 3 June 1995 7.30pm BBC Radio 2.
Featuring Roy Hudd with Barry Forgie and the BBC Big Band. A Dad's Army sketch (written by Jimmy Perry) called 'The Boy Who Saved England' featured Ian Lavender, Frank Williams, Bill Pertwee and Jimmy Perry.
This programme also featured, amongst others, Ken Bruce, Barry Cryer, June Whitfield, Peter Goodwright and Frankie Vaughan.
Produced Richard Wilcox, Phil Clarke and Phil Bowker.

THIS IS YOUR LIFE: DAVID CROFT
Broadcast Wednesday 20th December 1995 BBC 1.
Clive Dunn, Bill Pertwee, Frank Williams and Michael Aspel, complete with Jones's Butchers van meet David Croft in the car park at the television studios to spring the surprise.
In this programme David Croft's contribution to television and to the lives of his friends, colleagues and family was recognized.
Co-writers and actors from his many television productions included:
Jimmy Perry, Jeremy Lloyd, Gorden Kaye, Carmen Silvera, Wendy Richard and Molly Sugden also paid a tribute.
Scenes from The Desperate Drive of L/corp Jones and The Armoured Might of L/corp Jones.

THE JAMESON'S
Broadcast Tuesday 14 January 1997 BBC Radio 2.
An interview with Bill Pertwee and Ian Lavender. Running time approximately 30 minutes.

DAD'S ARMY SELECTION BOX
Broadcast Wednesday 5 February 1997 BBC 1.
This 30 minute programme featured various celebrities from the world of entertainment describing their favourite programme or character. All the main characters, starting with Capt. Mainwaring, were featured along with clips from many of the Dad's Army series, which supported the relationships and foibles of the characters, in particular Mainwaring and Wilson, Wilson and Mrs. Pike and Mainwaring and Elizabeth.
TV celebrates included Nicholas Parsons, Chris Tarrant, Wendy Richard, and Roy Hudd.

CROFT ORIGINALS
Broadcast Tuesday 29th April 1997 BBC Radio 2.
This celebration programme of David Croft was presented by Ian Lavender and featured an interview with David Croft. Ian talks about the early days in David's acting, singing and writing career and features several songs by David. They then discuss David's move into television and the start and history of his writing and directing career, which produce

some interesting facts about the casting of the actors. There are also contributions from Jimmy Perry and Jeremy Lloyd.

THIS MORNING
Broadcast Tuesday 7th October 1997 ITV.
Interviewed by Richard Madeley featured Jimmy Perry, Bill Pertwee, Frank Williams, Ian Lavender and a telephone call from Clive Dunn.
This part of the programme was designed to promote Bill Pertwee's revised edition of his book 'Dad's Army The Making of a Television Legend'. It was broadcast live at 10.45am and is 12 minutes long.

JOHN DUNN SHOW
BBC RADIO 2 30th October 1997.
Interview with Bill Pertwee who launched the revised edition of 'Dad's Army, The Making of a Television Legend' This part of the programme was broadcast live at 6pm and is 10 minutes long.

THIS IS YOUR LIFE: BILL PERTWEE
Broadcast Monday 1 February 1999, BBC 1 7pm.
Michael Aspel and Ian Lavender surprise Bill Pertwee who was lured to the Imperial War Museum London on the pretext of a real ARP warden reunion, on Tuesday 23 January 1999. They are then taken to the Teddington Studios where the programme was recorded.
Dad's Army members introduced were Clive Dunn, Ian Lavender, Pamela Cundell, Hugh Hastings, Frank Williams, David Croft and Jimmy Perry.
Clips were shown from The Man and the Hour, Two and a Half Feathers, Asleep In the Deep and The Royal Train.
Celebrities paying tribute included Bill Maynard, Roy Hudd, Bernard Cribbins, Lisa Goddard and Spike Milligan.

THAT REMINDS ME
Bill Pertwee
Broadcast 22 April 1999. Radio 4
Bill Pertwee recalls his memories of getting into 'The Business'

ARTHUR LOWE, A LIFE ON THE BOX
Broadcast Sunday 21 February 1999. 1.45pm. BBC 1
This 45 minute programme, presented by Terry Wogan, was a tribute to the varied career of Arthur Lowe. The programme started with the famous scene 'Don't tell him Pike' from Deadly Attachment.
Several clips were shown from Dad's Army, his most celebrated role, with others being Coronation Street, Potter, Bless Me Father, Car Along the Pass, A Voyage Round My Father, Z Cars and David Copperfield.
Interviewed celebrities were Clive Dunn, Bill Pertwee, William Roache, David Croft, Jimmy Perry, Wendy Richard and Roy Hattersley.

THE ARTHUR LOWE STORY
Radio 2.
Bill Pertwee tells the story of Arthur Lowe.

LAUGHTER IN THE HOUSE: The Story of British Sitcom
Broadcast Wednesday 24 March 1999 BBC 1, 10pm.
This 50 minute Omnibus programme explores the history of British Television Comedy.
The Dad's Army section of 7 minutes featured an interview with Jimmy Perry and David Croft, where Jimmy explained that while watching 'Oh Mister Porter' with Will Hay he got the idea of the Old Man, The Young Boy and the Pompus Man for the programme he was working on.
Clips from 'The Man and the Hour, Enemy Within the Gates, A Wilson (Manager)? and Deadly Attachment. The clip comes to a close with an interview with Ian Lavender.

DON'T PANIC
The Dad's Army Story BBC1 28 May 2000
Repeated 27/12/01
Introduced by Victoria Wood who was trying to be funny and knowledgeable about the programme tells the story of Dad's Army, with contributions by David Croft, Jimmy Perry, Clive Dunn, Bill Pertwee, Ian Lavender, Frank Williams, Pamela Cundell, Wendy Richard, Philip Madoc and Carmen Silvera.

THE UNFORGETTABLE ARTHUR LOWE
Recorded 4 July 2000, Broadcast 18 September 2000
A tribute to the acting talent of Arthur Lowe tells the story of Arthur's beginning during the war to the success on television, with contributions from Jimmy Perry, Bill Pertwee and Pamela Cundell. Includes clips from Coronation Street, Bless Me Father, Pardon the Expression and several from Dad's Army. Watchmakers Productions, 30 minutes.

THE UNFORGETTABLE JOHN LE MESURIER
Broadcast ITV, 9 September 2001
Another in the series telling the story of John Le Mesurier's acting career. Contributions from Clive Dunn, Jimmy Perry and Joan Le Mesurier with a liberal sprinkling of Dad's Army clips.

TOP TEN LOSERS
Channel 4, 21 September 2001
Series of programmes featuring different subjects this programme looks at the top ten television comedy losers, Captain Mainwaring weighing at number 10. Contributions from David Croft, Bill Pertwee, Jimmy Perry and Ian Lavender.

MISSING PRESUMED WIPED
First Broadcast 28 December 2001 BBC2
Following a nationwide public appeal by David Croft as a part of the BBC's campaign to recover missing programmes and to the delight of Dad's Army fans, two missing episodes Operation Kilt and The Battle of Godfrey's Cottage were discovered and handed in to the BBC. The programme unfolds the story of how they were lost and their eventual discovery. This still leaves three episodes undiscovered (The Loneliness of the Long Distance Walker, A Stripe for Frazer & Under Fire). Introduced by Terry Wogan.

IAN LAVENDER THIS YOUR LIFE
Broadcast BBC1 6 March 2002
This long running programme tells the story of Ian Lavender's career. A healthy collection of clips from Dad's Army and a chance for Bill Pertwee to return the favour. Contributions from David Croft, Jimmy Perry, Michael Knowles, Wendy Richard and Bill Pertwee.

REPUTATIONS
First Broadcast BBC2 21 September 2002
This programme takes a close look at the at the life of Arthur Lowe often a personal view of his private life although his comic genius was well established. Based largely on Stephen Lowe's book 'Arthur Lowe a Life' and contributions from friends, family and colleagues.

AFTER THEY WERE FAMOUS
First Broadcast ITV 3 December 2002
Bill Pertwee is filmed while at Sherringham during the 1940s weekend on the North Norfolk Railway. Clips shown from Uninvited Guests, Put That Light Out and Battle of the Giants, approximately 5 minutes.

ITV BRITISH COMEDY AWARDS
First Broadcast 10 December 2003
Presented by Jonathan Ross, Jimmy Perry and David Croft receive a LifeTime Award.

BBC 2 BRITAIN'S BEST SITCOM, THE LAUNCH.
Presented by Jonathan Ross television's comedies have been categorised and the 'Top Ten have been selected, which includes 'Dad's Army'.

BBC 2 TOP TEN BRITAIN'S COMEDY
First Broadcast 20 March 2004.
Repeated 27 March 2004 as part of the final programme. Comedian Phil Jupitus makes the case why the viewers should vote for Dad's Army.

BBC 2 TOP TEN BRITAIN'S COMEDY FINAL
First Broadcast 27 March 2004
Viewers voted for their favourite sitcom, 'Only Fools And Horses' came first with Dad's Army coming fourth. Hosted by Jonathan Ross.

Big Guns
A few minutes of cine film in the car park at London Transport's Wood Lane Training Centre where the main cast practice the scene of putting the net over the big gun.
Source: Harold Snoad 1969.

The Big Parade
Five minutes of cine film showing the platoon rehearsing marching past the Warden and Verger in Nether Row, Thetford.
Source: Jacelton Video, Thetford 1970.

All Is Safely Gathered In
This eight minute cine film captures the rehearsals at Walnut Tree Farm, Bressingham. It features the platoon marching into the meadow and while under the influence of potato wine leaving the farmhouse.
Source: Filmed and owned by Brian Woods, Diss 1972.

Brain Versus Brawn
A few minutes of cine film footage outside the farmhouse at Walnut Tree Farm, Bressingham showing the Warden getting a full-face exposure to the water hose.
Source: Filmed and owned by Brian Woods, Diss 1972.

The Captain's Car
A few minutes of cine film outside the Guildhall, Thetford rehearsing the French General leaving and featuring Talfryn Thomas.
Source: Jacelton Video, Thetford 1974

On Tour with the Stage Show
This 20 minute cine film records the cast and crew during the 1976 Stage Show tour. It features rare glimpses of the stage show. Narration added in 2003, edited by Tony Pritchard.
Source: Frank Williams 1976

Knights of Madness
A few minutes of cine film footage at Sapiston, featuring Edward Sinclair.
Source: Filmed and owned by Frank Williams 1977.

The Dad's Army Stage Show
The Thetford Music and Drama Society perform the Dad's Army Stage Show at the Theatre Royal Bury St Edmunds, May 1981, with David Croft and Jimmy Perry in the audience. The only known recording of the amateur production of the full stage show.
SYNOPSIS OF SCENES
ACT 1
Walmington-on-Sea
The Black Out
A British Restaurant
Outside Private Pike's Home
Command Post
Outside Private Pike's Home
Cliff Top
Battle of Britain
A Street
Church Hall
INTERVAL of 15 Minutes
ACT 2
Siegfried Line
Church Hall
Church Hall
Outside Private Pike's Home
Happidrome
Radio Personalities of 1943
Walmington-on-Sea
Finale
PRODUCTION
Director: Fred Calvert
Production Coordinator: Derek Mortimer
Music Direction: Jean Bishop & Thelma Ely
Source:Thetford Music and Drama Society Programme.

DAAS York Convention
The first York Dad's Army Appreciation Society convention at the Bonding Warehouse 19 October 1996. Bill Pertwee, Frank Williams, Colin Bean & Eric Longworth in attendance. Amateur video filmed in low light, but tells the story of a very successful event.
Source: Filmed and owned by Tony Pritchard (DAAS) 1996.

Colin Bean Interview
A ninety seven minute interview with Colin Bean who recalls his time with the Dad's Army cast.
Source: The Barmy Army Film Club 1997.

DAAS 30th Anniversary Convention
Held in the Banqueting Suite of the Oval Cricket Ground on 18 April 1998. This 120 minute video recalls the reunion between all of the surviving cast members.
Source: Filmed and owned by Tony Pritchard (DAAS) 1998

DAAS York Convention
This thirty six minute video taken on 12 September at the Society's second York Convention. Featuring Frank Williams and Alec Coleman.
Source: Filmed and owned by Tony Pritchard (DAAS) 1998

Dad's Army Day & Collection opening
This video features the events surrounding Thetford's Dad's Army Day on 13 May 2000, including the cavalcade, led by the Fire Engine from Bressingham carrying some of the cast including Clive Dunn, and including Jones' Van.
The events of the following day - the opening of the

— THETFORD MUSIC AND DRAMA SOCIETY —
Proudly presents the   first amateur showing of
DAD'S ARMY
Written by David Croft   Directed by
Jimmy Perry   Fred Calvert
A Nostalgic Evening of Sketch, Comedy and Songs
**** *Gala Evening* ****
Monday, 11th May, 1981
Tickets £3.00 – Proceeds of the evening to two local charities
**Tuesday 12th -
Saturday 16th May, 1981**
DOORS OPEN 7.15 p.m.   CURTAIN UP 8 p.m.
Carnegie Room, Thetford
Tickets: Adults £2.00 – Children and Senior Citizens £1.00
BOOKING OFFICE:
PREMIER TRAVEL, 18 WELL STREET, THETFORD—Tel. 4771
By kind permission of David Croft and Jimmy Perry

Bressingham Dad's Army Collection - are also captured.
Source: Jacelton Video, Thetford 2000.

Dad's Army at Bressingham
This thirty eight minute documentary tells the story of the
design and construction of the Dad's Army Museum during
early 2000.
Source: Eastern Associates MM, 2000.

The Jimmy Perry Interview
Over one hour of conversation with Jimmy Perry talking to
John Simpson of the Barmy Army Film Club. Jimmy covers a
wide range of subjects including the history of Dad's Army.
Source: The Barmy Army film Club 2000.

A Tribute to Dad's Army
Performed by the Tring Festival Company, it features two
Dad's Army episodes adapted for the stage by Ian Gower 'The
Godiva Affair' and 'The Deadly Attachment'. Saturday night
performance on 27 April 2002 in the presence of Bill
Pertwee, Frank Williams, Pamela Cundell, Eric Longworth and
Philip Madoc.
Source: The Tring Festival Company 2002.

We Are The Boys
A stage play by Nick Scovell at the New Theatre, Portsmouth.
on 27 July 2002. Using existing material and new scripts by
Nick Scovell, the story of the start and demob of the Home
Guard is seamlessly joined together.
Source: Nick Scovell 2002.

The Lost Episodes & DAAS 10th Anniversary Convention
Performed by the Tring Festival Company it features two lost
episodes adapted for the stage by Ian Gower and Paul
Carpenter, 'The Loneliness of the Long Distance Walker' and
'Under Fire'. Features rehearsal footage and the 10th DAAS
Anniversary Convention at the Court Theatre with a number
of the surviving cast members attending including writer
Jimmy Perry.

Below is a selection of related programmes which have used or featured Dad's Army in an individual way.

GOODNIGHT SWEETHEART
'Don't Get Around Much Any More'
Broadcast BBC1 Mon 20 February 1995.
Although not featuring any original Dad's Army cast
members, this episode featured an affectionate tribute to
its comic precursor. The series, written by Laurence Marks
and Maurice Gran, concerns a TV repair man, Gary Sparrow
(Nicholas Lyndhurst), who, having discovered a way to
travel back in time to wartime Britain, finds himself
romantically entangled with two women fifty years apart.
Don't Get Around Much Any More opened the second
series of this light-hearted comedy and saw Gary
depositing money at the Stepney branch of the Provincial
Bank in 1940, planning to pick it up with interest in the
present. However, when the bank manager and his chief
clerk reveal themselves to be Mainwaring and Wilson, Gary
is quite dumbstruck. He soon recovers enough to sing a
particularly tuneless rendition of 'Who Do You Think You
Are Kidding, Mr Hitler' and discovers that they are,
indeed, Home Guard members, too. When a gangly youth
brings in the tea in a most clumsy fashion, Lyndhurst's
character is sure it must be Frank Pike, but some sanity is
restored to the proceedings, when it transpires that he is
called Major. The sequence ends with Gary Sparrow
delighting in referring to him as a stupid boy!
The part of Mainwaring was played by Alec Linstead,
Terrence Hardiman played Wilson and Max Digby played
Major. The sequence featuring the Dad's Army characters
lasts for four minutes and forty seconds.
Directed by Robin Nash.

BEADLES HOT SHOTS
Broadcast Tuesday 19 August 1997 8pm ITV Colour.
An amateur group produced a 3 minute video spoof on the
main 'Dad's Army' characters and featured an interview by
satellite link with Clive Dunn from his home in Portugal.

COLLECTORS LOT
Broadcast Friday 2 April 1999 3pm C4 Colour
This programme featured the Society's 1998 Dad's Army
tour of locations.
Presenter Ken Snowdon and a film crew followed the tour
around on Sunday 27th September 1998. In the broadcast
five minute section the locations of Eleveden Water Tower,
Sapiston, Ixworth Flour Mill, Oxburgh Hall and Honington
were clearly visible. The programme came to a close at
Bressingham Museum with a march past by members of
the Appreciation Society and featured interviews with
Jack Wheeler and Tony Pritchard

NOTE: ONLY BOOKS COVERING DAD'S ARMY OR ITS CAST MEMBERS HAVE BEEN INCLUDED.

Dad's Army (the book of the film)
by John Burke.
160pp. Hodder Paperbacks, 1971.
ISBN 0340 15027 0

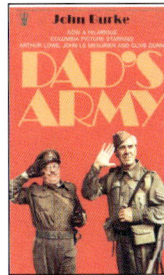

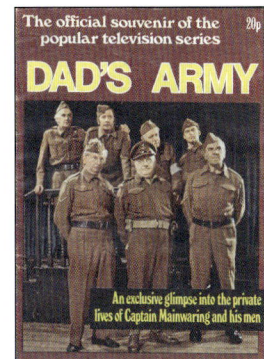

Dad's Army
The official souvenir of the popular TV Series.
Edited by Ted Hart
48pp. A Peter Way Magazine Special, 1972.

Dad's Army Annual
Six editions produced each year between 1973 and 1978.
World Distributors, Manchester 1973 - 1978.

1973 78pp SBN 7235 01424

1974 78pp SBN 7235 0209 9

1975 76pp SBN 7235 0233 1

1976 62pp SBN 7235 0319 2

1977 76pp SBN 7235 0350 8

1978 62pp SBN 7235 0438 0

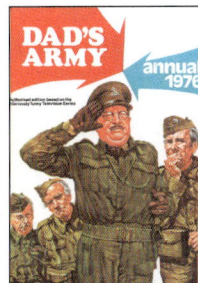

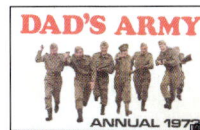

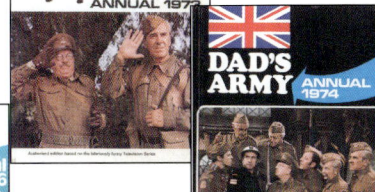

Dad's Army
by Jimmy Perry and David Croft.
Contains five scripts:- 'Asleep in the Deep', 'The Deadly Attachment', The Godiva Affair', 'Everybody's Trucking' and 'Keep Young and Beautiful'. Includes a brief history of the Home Guard by Norman Longmate and character profiles.
122pp Elm Tree Books, 1975.
SBN 241 89251 1
Also in paperback, Sphere Books, 1976.(126pp)
SBN 0 7221 0406 5

A Jobbing Actor
by John Le Mesurier.
160pp Elm Tree Books/Hamish Hamilton, 1984.
Also in paperback (156pp)
ISBN 0 7221 6032 1

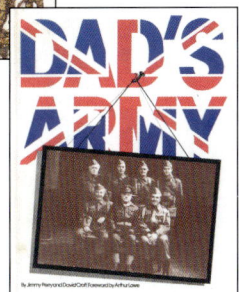

Permission to Speak, An Autobiography
by Clive Dunn.
250pp Century Books, 1986.
SBN 0 7126 1216 5

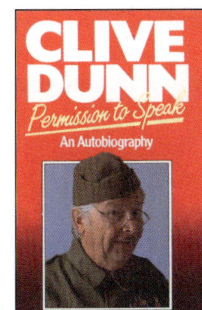

Dad's Army
The Defence of a Front Line English Village
by Paul Ableman, edited by A. Wilson MA.
Contains novelisations based on four Perry and Croft scripts:
'The Battle of Godfrey's Cottage', 'Getting the Bird', 'Mum's Army' and 'My British Buddy'.
130pp BBC Books 1989.
SBN 0 563 20850 3

Dad's Army
The Making of a Television Legend
by Bill Pertwee.
144pp David & Charles 1989
SBN 0 7153 9489
(also available in paperback, Richard Joseph 1989.)
Fully revised and extended by Pavilion Books 1997.
210pp (Hardback) SBN 1 86205 17 3
206pp (Softback 1998) ISBN 1 86205 212 3

Dad's Army Song Book
Wise Publications, distributed by Music Sales Ltd 1995.
48pp SBN 0 7119 5141 1

Dad's Army
A Guide to TV, Radio and Stage
by David Hamilton, Alan and Alys Hayes.
34pp Homefront Publication 1996.
Revised, extended and renamed as:
Dad's Army Handbook.
D.A.A.S. Publication 1998 (80pp).
Extended Second Edition
D.A.A.S Publication 1999 (118pp).

Arthur Lowe A Life.
by Stephen Lowe.
214pp Nick Hern Books, 1996.
SBN 1 85459 279 3

A Funny Way To Make A Living
by Bill Pertwee.
320pp Sunburst Books, 1996.
SBN 1 85778 268 2

Walmington Town Plan & Guide.
by Paul Carpenter.
D.A.A.S Publication,1996. Revised 1999.

Dad's Army - A Celebration
by Richard Webber.
192pp Virgin Books, 1997.
SBN 1 85227 694 0

Dad's Army, The Lost Episodes
by Jimmy Perry & David Croft.
160pp Virgin Books 1998.
SBN 1 85227 757 2

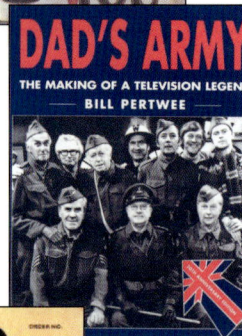

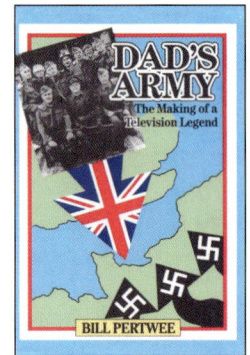

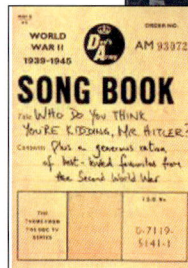

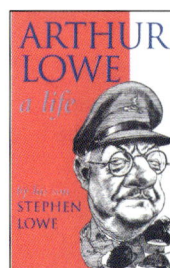

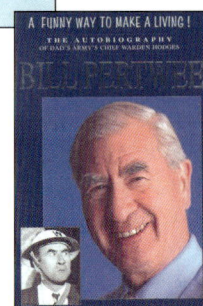

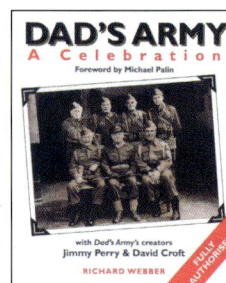

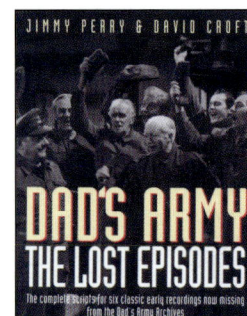

Who Do You Think YOU ARE KIDDING!
by Colin Bean
372pp Minerva Press 1998
SBN 0 75410 499 0
Re-published in 2004 by Edward & George Publishers.

The Complete A-Z of Dad's Army
by Richard Webber
288pp Orion Books 2000
SBN 0 75281 838 4

Dear John
by Joan Le Mesurier
276pp Sidgwick & Jackson
SBN 0 28306 272 6

You Have Been Watching
by Graham McCann
292pp Fourth Estate 2001
SBN 1 84115 308 7

Dad's Army - Walmington Goes to War
by Perry & Croft
Edited & Coordinated by Richard Webber
456pp Orion Books 2001
SBN 0 75284 153 X

Arthur Lowe
by Graham Lord
258pp Orion Books 2002
SBN 0 75284 184 X

Dad's Army - The Home Front
by Perry & Croft
Edited & Coordinated by Richard Webber
432pp Orion Books 2002
SBN 0 75284 743 0

Vicar to Dad's Army
by Frank Williams
238pp Canterbury Press 2002
SBN 1 85311 4944

A Stupid Boy
by Jimmy Perry
294pp Century Books 2002
SBN 0 7126 2338 8

You Have Been Watching
by David Croft
256pp BBC Books 2004
ISBN 0563487399

Other books featuring Dad's Army:

Look In (TV Comic)
Dad's Army strips, 1970/80.

Dad's Army Activity Book.
62pp World Books Manchester, 1973.
SBN 7235 17401

Dad's Army Colouring Book
48pp World Distributors, Manchester, 1971.
SBN72353289 3.

Dad's Army Comic Strips.
by H A G Clarke & B Titcombe
94pp Piccolo 1973.
BSN 0330 23759 4

Permission To Speak, Sir!
The Dad's Army Appreciation Society(DAAS)
(Quarterly)

Platoon Attention!
The D.A.A.S NZ (Quarterly)

Hello Campers.
Celebrating the work of Perry & Croft.
(last published late 1998)

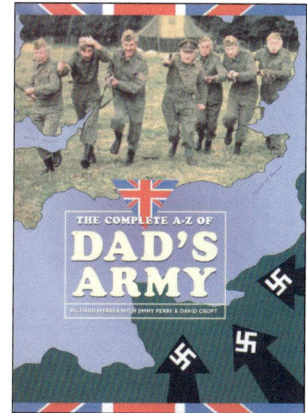

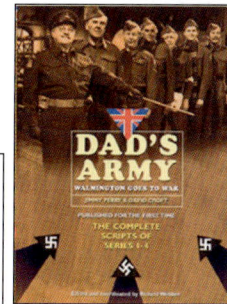

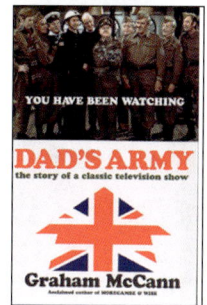

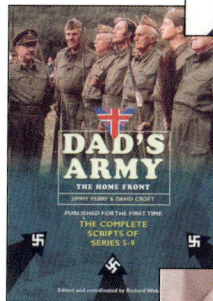

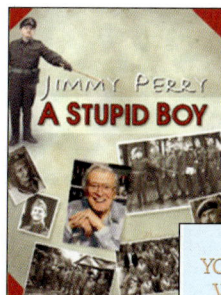

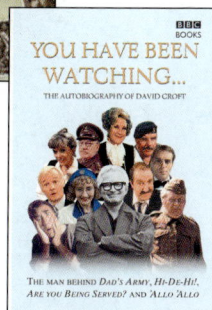

ONLY DAD'S ARMY RELATED RECORDINGS APPEAR HERE. THIS LIST DOES NOT CONTAIN THE MANY OTHER RECORDINGS MADE BY CAST MEMBERS DURING THEIR LONG CAREERS.

"Sgt. Wilson's Little Secret' c/w 'Something Nasty in the Vault'.
DA BBC Records (LP)

'Dad's Army March' c/w 'What Did You Do in the War?' - Dad's Army Platoon.
1971 Columbia DB8766

'We Stood Alone' c/w 'Down Our Way' - Dad's Army Platoon.
1972 Columbia DB8952

'Dad's Army Stage Show. Original Cast Recording'.
Warner Brothers (LP) K56196

'Hooligans' c/w 'Get out and Get Under the Moon' - Bill Pertwee & Norman MacLeod.
EMI 1975

'Permission to Sing' - Clive Dunn.
Music for Pleasure (LP)

'Bless'em All' - Arthur Lowe.
World Record Club Ltd

'A Nightingale Sang in Berkeley Square' John Le Mesurier c/w 'Home Town' Arthur Lowe & Company.
Warner Bros 1975 K16670

'The Story of Dad's Army' - Bill Pertwee.
1995 Speaking Volumes No5266804.
Re-issued on Cassette and CD in 2003

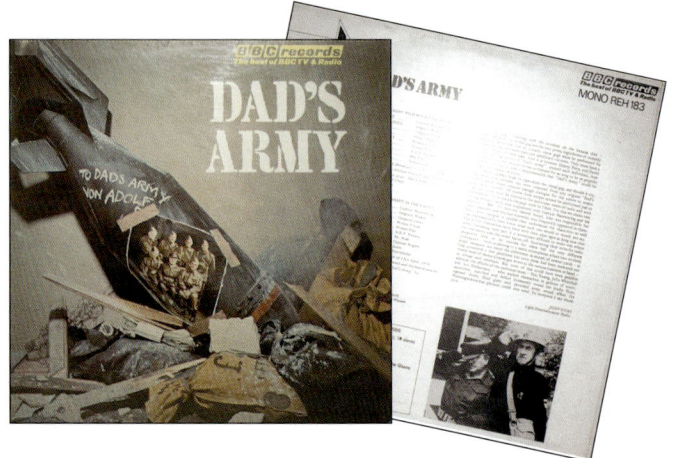

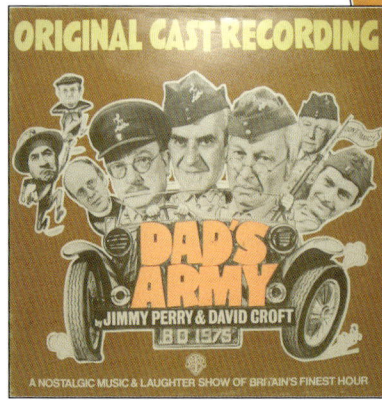

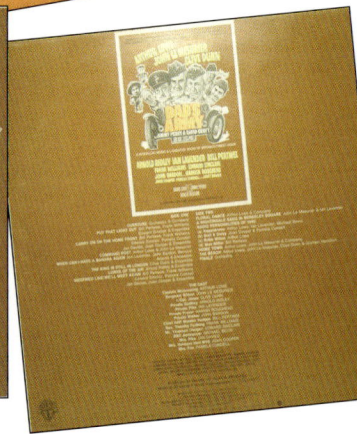

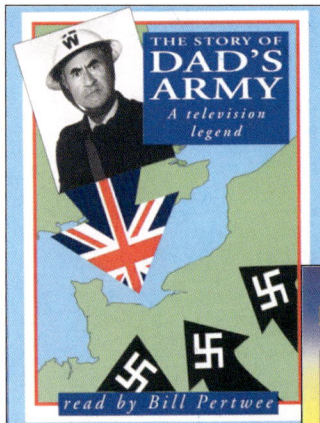

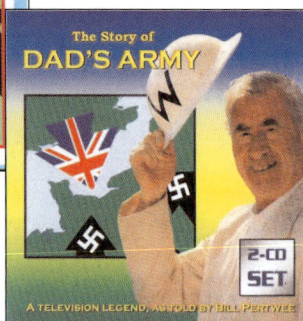

BBC Video Releases

Date	No.	Col 1	Col 2	Col 3
Apr-97	4088	The Day The Balloon Went Up	Sons Of The Sea	Don't Forget The Diver
Oct-87	4089	Asleep In The Deep	Boots Boots Boots	A Soldier's Farewell
Jun-90	4320	The Two & A Half Feathers	The Test	Fallen Idol
Sep-90	4400	The Deadly Attachment	If The Cap Fits	The Honourable Man
Jun-91	4489	Big Guns	Menace from the Deep	The Bullet Is Not For Firing
Jun-91	4490	Mum's Army	The Armoured Might L/Cpl Jones	Put That Light Out
Aug-91	4660	When Did You Last See Your Money	Battle School	Branded
Aug-95	4661	Man Hunt	Sgt. Save My Boy	Don't Fence Me In
Jun-92	4763	No Spring For Frazer	Absent Friends	A Wilson (Manager)
Apr-97	4764	Uninvited Guests	The Desperate Drive Corporal Jones	The King Was In His Counting House
Feb-93	4892	The Man & The Hour	Museum Piece	Command Decision
Jul-93	4992	Enemy within the Gates	Showing Up Of Corporal Jones	Shooting Pains
Oct-93	5120	The Day The Balloon Went Up	Sons Of The Sea	The Two & A Half Feathers
		Asleep In The Deep	The Deadly Attachment	
Aug-94	5372	A Brush with the Law	Brain Versus Brawn	Keep Young & Beautiful
Jun-94	5442	My British Buddy	The Royal Train	All Is Safely Gathered In
Apr-95	5572	The Recruit	A Man of Action	The Captain's Car
Aug-95	5643	Knights of Madness	The Making of Private Pike	The Miser's Hoard
Oct-94	5396	No Spring For Frazer	Mum's Army	Menace From The Deep
Oct-94	5396	When Did You Last See Your Money	The Honourable Man	
Feb-96	5784	Morecombe & Wise	The Liver Birds	Battle Of The Giants
Mar-96	5857	The Armoured Might of L/Cpl Jones	Something Nasty In The Vault	The Lion Has Phones
Oct-96	5932	Round Went The Great Big Wheel	Time On My Hands	We Know Our Onions
Mar-97	5967	Room At The Bottom	War Dance	Getting The Bird
Sep-97	6162	Sergeant Wilson's Little Secret	Everybody's Trucking	Things That Go Bump In The Night
Aug-98	6266	The Big Parade	The Godiva Affair	Gorilla Warfare
Sep-98	6583	Turkey Dinner	Ring Dem Bells	When You've Got To Go
Jan-99	6711	Is There Honey Still For Tea?	Come In Your Time Is Up	High Finance
Jun-99	6715	The Face On The Poster	My Brother and I	The Love Of Three Oranges
Sep-99	6810	Wake Up Walmington	Number Engaged	Never Too Old

BBC DVD Releases

BBC GOLD PRODUCTION

No.	Col 1	Col 2	Col 3
BFS 30072-D	The Day the Balloon Went Up	Sons of the Sea	Don't Forget the Diver
	Asleep In The Deep	Boot, Boots, Boots	A Soldier's Farewell
BFS 30073-D	Big Guns	Menace From The Deep	The Bullet Is Not For Firing
	Mum's Army	The Armoured Might of L/Cpl Jones	Put That Light Out
BFS 30074-D	The Two and A Half Feathers	The Test	Fallen Idol
	The Deadly Attachment	If The Cap Fits	The Honourable Man
BBCDVD 1057	The Deadly Attachment	Keep Young and Beautiful	Never Too Old
	Asleep In The Deep	Sons of The Sea	
BBCDVD 1121	No Spring For Frazer	Mum's Army	Menace From The Deep
	When Did You Last See Your Money	The Honourable Man	

Columbia Pictures Release

CC7142   The Movie

The changing face of the Dad's Army video box is illustrated here.

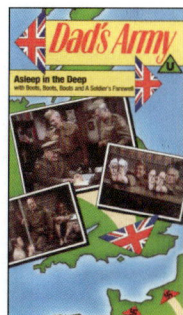

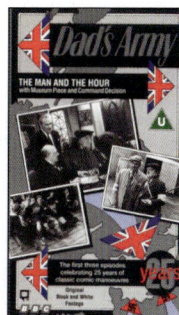

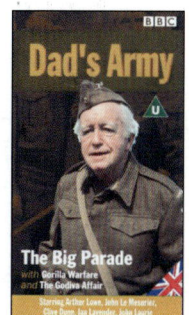

The popular radio series was made available on the BBC Audio Collection series from 1990. Each collection contained four episodes on two cassette tapes.

Recently BBC Wordwide have released three Collector's Edition CD box sets containing the complete radio series, plus on volume three the additional bonus of the pilot episode of 'It Sticks Out Half a Mile' with Arthur Lowe as George Mainwaring and John LeMesurier as Sergeant Wilson.

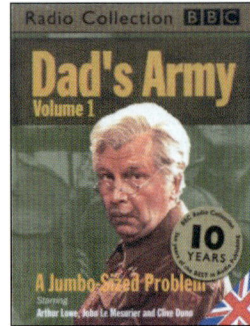

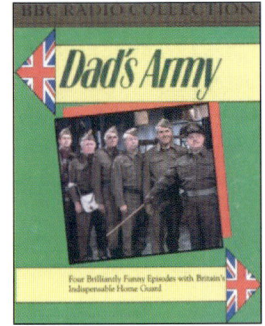

Audio Cassettes
Vol 1 ISBN 0563 411201
When Did You Last See Your Money - A Jumbo Sized Problem - Time On My Hands - Ten Seconds From Now
Vol 2 ISBN 0563 365803
The Man and the Hour - Museum Piece - Command Decision - The Enemy Within the Gates
Vol 3 ISBN 0563 401044
The Honourable Man - High Finance - The Battle of Godfrey's Cottage - A Stripe For Frazer
Vol 4 ISBN 0563 394404
Armoured Might Of L/Cp Jones - Sergeant Wilson's Little Secret - Operation Kilt - Battle School
Vol 5 ISBN 0563 390581
Something Nasty In The Vault - Showing Up Of Corporal Jones - Loneliness of the Long Distance Walker - Sorry Wrong Number
Vol 6 ISBN 0563 388781
Under Fire - The Bullet Is Not For Firing - Room At The Bottom - The Menace From The Deep
Vol 7 ISBN 0563 381175
Don't Forget the Diver - If the Cap Fits - A Brush with the Law - Getting the Bird
Vol 8 ISBN 0563 557451
My British Buddy - The King Was In His Counting House - Deadly Attachment - The Godiva Affair
Vol 9 ISBN 0563 558873
The Day the Balloon Went Up - Branded - Round & Round Went the Great Big Wheel - A Man of Action
Vol 10 ISBN 0563 553472
A Soldier's Farewell - All Is Safely Gathered In - The Big Parade - Asleep In the Deep
Vol 11 ISBN 0563 478160
Put That Light Out - Sergeant,- Save My Boy - Uninvited Guests - Fallen Idol
Vol 12 ISBN 0563 528060
No Spring For Frazer - Sons of The Sea - Brain Versus Brawn - Absent Friends
Vol 13 ISBN 0563 529261
Boots, Boots, Boots - War Dance - Mum's Army - Don't Fence Me In
Vol 14 ISBN 0563494905
A. Wilson Manager - The Great White Hunter - Things That Go Bump In The Night - Big Guns
The Story Of Dad's Army
by Bill Pertwee (Cassette) Bill Pertwee & Barry-Mour Productions 1995 ISBN 1 85849 8430
The Story Of Dad's Army
by Bill Pertwee (CD) Bill Pertwee & Barry-Mour Productions 2001

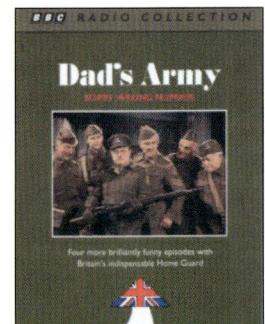

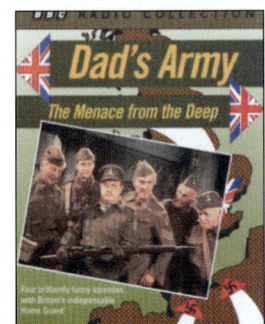

Collectors Edition Box Sets (CD)
Each box set features full track listings, cast biographies and a history of the series
Vol 1 ISBN 0563 528575
Containing the first 21 episodes including 'The Battle of the Giants'.
Vol 2 ISBN 0563 496614
Containing the first 20 episodes from the second series.
Vol 3 ISBN 0563 496622
Containing the remaining 26 episodes plus the pilot edition of 'It Sticks Out Half A Mile'.

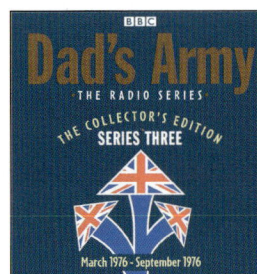

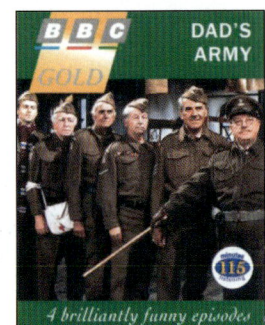

In late 1998 Britannia Music Company promoted the release of the entire Dad's Army series as a Collectors Edition, each tape being released at monthly intervals (in fact they arrived quicker towards the end). It was disappointing to discover that the set did not include series one and two, nor any of the special editions, although Battle of the Giants was included on tape 10.

1	BBCV6207	The Armoured Might Of Lance Corporal Jones / Battle School / The Lion Has Phones
2	BBCV6208	The Bullet Is Not For Firing / Something Nasty In The Vault / Room At The Bottom
3	BBCV6209	Big Guns / The Day The Balloon Went Up / War Dance
4	BBCV6210	Menace From The Deep / Branded / Man Hunt
5	BBCV6414	No Spring For Frazer / Sons Of The Sea / The Big Parade
6	BBCV6415	Don't Forget The Diver / Boots,Boots,Boots / Sergeant, - Save My Boy!
7	BBCV6416	Don't Fence Me In / Absent Friends / Put That Light Out!
8	BBCV6417	The Two And A Half Feathers / Mum's Army / The Test
9	BBCV6418	A.Wilson(Manager) / Uninvited Guests / Fallen Idol
10	BBCV6419	Battle Of The Giants! / Asleep In The Deep / Keep Young And Beautiful
11	BBCV6420	A Soldiers Farewell / Getting The Bird / The Desperate Drive Of Corporal Jones
12	BBCV6421	If The Cap Fits / The King Was In His Counting House / All Is Safely Gathered In
13	BBCV6422	When Did You Last See Your Money? / Brain Versus Brawn/ A Brush With The Law
14	BBCV6423	Round And Round Went The Great Wheel / Time On My Hands / The Deadly Attachment
15	BBCV6424	My British Buddy / The Royal Train / We Know Our Onions
16	BBCV6425	The Honourable Man / Things That Go Bump In The Night / The Recruit
17	BBCV6426	Everybody's Trucking / A Man Of Action / Gorilla Warfare
18	BBCV6427	The Godiva Affair / The Captain's Car / Turkey Dinner
19	BBCV6428	Ring Dem Bells / When You've Got To Go / Is There Honey Still For Tea ?
20	BBCV6429	Come In, Your Time Is Up / High Finance / The Face On The Poster
21	BBCV6430	My Brother And I / The Love Of Three Oranges / Wake Up Walmington
22	BBCV6431	The Making Of Private Pike / Knights Of Madness / The Miser's Hoard
23	BBCV6432	Number Engaged / Never Too Old

Episodes not included are : **Series One:** The Man and the Hour / Museum Piece / Command Decision / The Enemy Within the Gates / The Showing Up of Lance Corporal Jones / Shooting Pains. **Series Two:** Operation Kilt / The Battle of Godfrey's Cottage / The Loneliness of the Long Distance Walker / Sgt Wilson's Little Secret / A Stripe for Frazer / Under Fire.

When displayed as a complete set (right),an error in the video box design is evident at tapes 9 & 10, which spoils the overall effect somewhat.

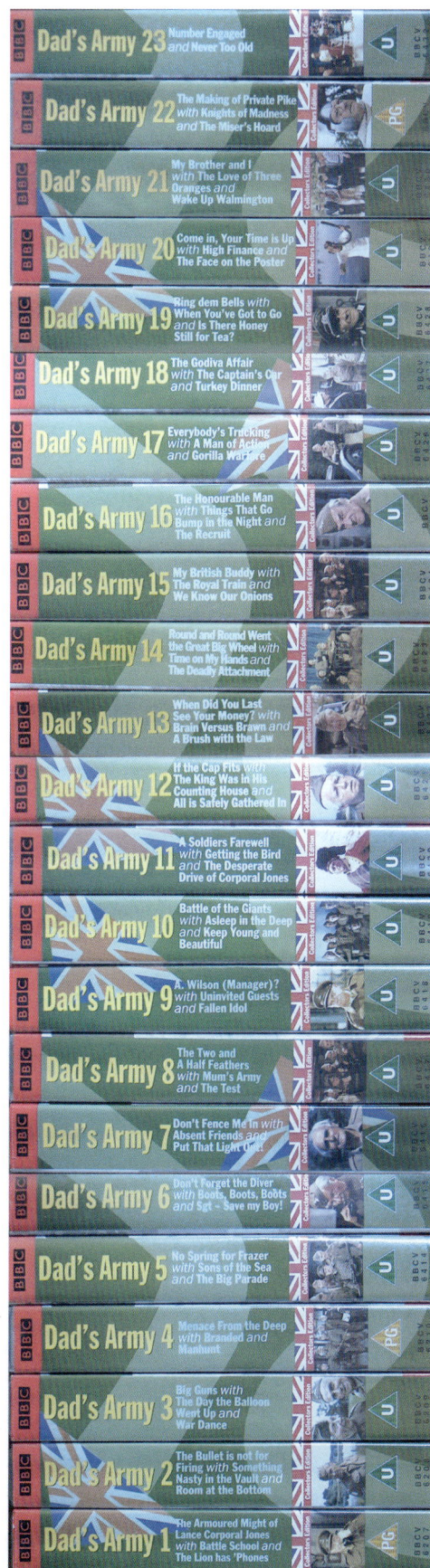

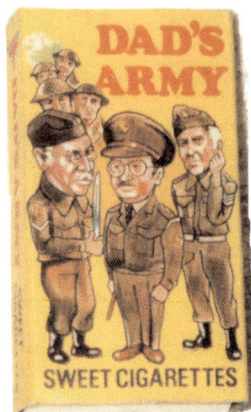

Produced by Primrose Confectionary using images from the 1971 feature film on all 25 cards. The main body text of each has been reproduced on this page exactly as it appeared on the reverse of each card.

No. 2
Lance Corporal Jones and Captain Mainwaring planning how they will capture some German airmen. The Corporal's opinion is that they should rush in and give them a piece of cold steel, maintaining "they don't like it up them, sir."

No. 3
The churchbells have sounded the invasion alarm so the Land Defence Volunteers start building their defences. The barricade across the main street is one of the key defence points.

No. 1
One of the German airmen who was shot down over England threatens the verger with his Luger.

No. 5
Captain Mainwaring, in his typical fashion, thinks he ought to have the only shotgun. However, its owner, General Wilkinson has another opinion.

No. 7
The crew of a shot down bomber holding everybody at gunpoint. They want a boat, so that they can escape back to Germany.

No. 8
While Captain Mainwaring is forming the Warmington-on-Sea Land Defence Volunteers the German High Command are planning the invasion of England.

No. 4
Mr Frazer, the local undertaker, is a Scotsman who served in the Roayal Navy during the 1914/18 War. Despite his grumbling and muttering he is an enthusiastic and popular member of the Warmington-on-Sea Home Guard.

No. 6
Captain Mainwaring and Lance Corporal Jones on the footplate of a steam road roller. Despite the trouble they both get into on occassions the two men like and respect each other.

No. 12
Lance Corporal Jones and the Captain cannot control the steam road roller and it ploughs its way straight across the men's kit and demolishes half the camp.

No. 13
Jonesy in trouble as usual. This time his "I'd like to volunteer, sir" has landed him in an awful jam. It seems he'll never learn to keep quiet and let someone else volunteer for a change.

No. 9
Mr. Frazer and Joe Walker doing some private business. Somehow Joe has the ability of getting almost anything despite wartime rationing and shortages. Usually he manges to satisfy his customers, but sometimes he gets into terrible trouble.

No. 10
Jonesy (Lance Corporal Jones) trying to rescue General Fuller from the middle of the river. As usual he has volunteered and as usual this has led to chaos and disaster.

No. 11
Captain Mainwaring and his Land Defence Volunteers, dressed as choirboys, finally capture an enemy airman.

No. 15
Panic strikes the platoon as the Captain sights an enemy dive bomber. His aircraft spotting, however, is not very good for the plane turns out to be a Spitfire.

No. 17
Three of the platoon setting sail to rescue Lance Corporal Jones. Little did they know that before long they, too, would need rescueing. Somehow things never seem to work out properly for the Warmington-on-Sea Home Guard.

No. 16
Jonesy shows off his homemade anti-dive bomber rocket gun. Needless to say, it puts the spectators in grave danger - as usual Jonesy's invention misfires.

No.18
General Fuller congratulating Captain Mainwaring and his platoon for capturing 3 enemy airmen. It is the first action the Warmington-on-Sea Home Guard have seen and they have come through it with flying colours.

No. 14
The local vicar, whose life is being continually upset by the Home Guard, rings the church bells. He has forgotten that this is the invasion warning and that Captain Mainwaring and his men will spring into immediate action.

No. 20
Jonesy demonstrating his new invention, a one man bullet proof tank. The armament is a double barrelled shot gun poking through the overflow hole. Visibility is through a periscope sticking out of the plug hole.

No. 21
Major General Fuller inspects the Warmington-on-Sea Land Defence Volunteers. Although the men have uniforms, they have not yet received their rifles or ammunition. Their only weapons are homemade bayonets, old swords, pitchfolks and other items which would be useless against a well armed enemy.

No. 19
Mr. Jones, the local butcher, is Lance Corporal in the Warmington-on-Sea Home Guard. This is partly due to his past experience as a regular soldier and partly to the "little extras" he sometimes finds in his shop for Captain Mainwaring.

No. 24
Godfrey on patrol. A retired gentleman who is by far the most gentle member of the platoon. Godfrey nevertheless tries to pull his weight for King and Country.

No.25
Arthur Wilson, the Chief Clerk at Captain Mainwaring's Bank. He is Second-in-Command of the platoon as Seargeant, but is always under the watchful eye of his boss.

No.22
The Warmington-on-Sea Land Defence Volunteers trying on their new army issue underwear. Although there are all types of men in the platoon Captain Mainwaring has welded them into a happy and enthusiastic bunch - only their efficiency is in doubt.

No. 23
Arthur (Sergeant) Wilson having dinner with his old friends Mrs. Pike and her son Frank. Sergeant Wilson and Frank are rather dominated by Mrs. Pike who is very bossy, and Frank is often embarrassed by her in front of the rest of the platoon.

▲ Currently owned by Mr A Hodgson, Ipswich.

REG No: JJ 1813
MAKE: 1932 Hillman Minx.
EPISODE: Time on my Hands.
Brief appearance in road scene. ▲

REG No: NF 3226 ▲
MAKE: Vauxhall 14/40
EPISODE: The Desperate Drive of L/Cpl
Jones.
Colonel Pritchard's car.

▲ Origin unknown. Vehicle destroyed in a film (driven over a cliff).

▲ Currently owned by Mr K Robinson, Basingstoke.

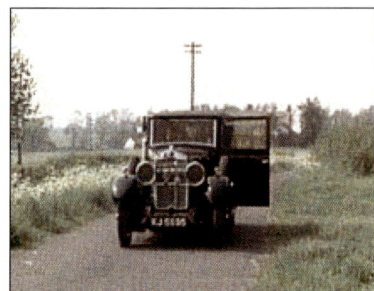

REG No: KJ 5595 ▲
MAKE: 1929 Lanchester Straight 8,
Laudaulet 30hp.
EPISODE: The Honourable Man.
The Russian Visitor's car.

REG No:VG 1002
MAKE: Unknown
EPISODE: Face on the Poster
Parked car. Also used as Mr
Clerk's car in 'Gorilla Warfare'.

REG No:55 807
MAKE: Unknown
EPISODE: Wake Up Walmington.

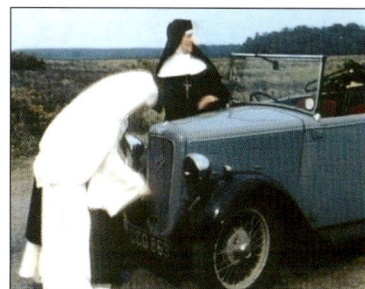

REG No:CCG 853
MAKE: Ford
EPISODE: Gorilla Warfare
Nuns' car.

REG No:34 YY 02
MAKE: Unknown
EPISODE: Number Engaged.
Troop Transport.

REG No:RAF 7121
MAKE: Unknown
EPISODE: The Day the
Balloon Went Up.

REG No:ANR 480
MAKE: Bedford KD
EPISODE: Number Engaged.

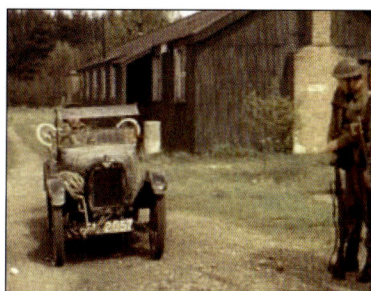

REG No: EU 2657
MAKE: Austin 7 Convertible.
EPISODE: The Desperate Drive of L/Cpl
Jones.
Walkers '£10' car.
Originally supplied by Mr A Hodgson.

Currently owned by Alistair Pringle, Kent.

▲ Currently owned by Roger Miles, Warwickshire.

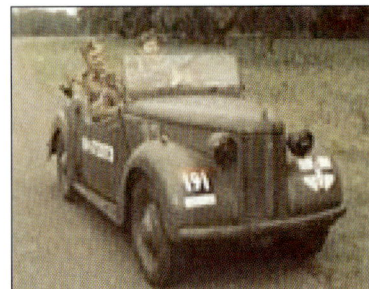

REG No: M4672973a (KHT 568) ▲
MAKE: Austin 8, Military Type 2 seater.
EPISODE: The Making of Private Pike
Mainwaring's Staff car. Currently on
loan at the Bressingham Steam
Museum for the Dad's Army Collection.

REG No: GLA 719 ▲
MAKE: 1939 Rolls Royce.
EPISODE: The Captain's Car.
Lady Maltby's Rolls.

▲ Currently owned by Sandra Cottingham, Leicestershire.

▲ Currently owned by Brian Saunders, Enfield, Middlesex

REG No: BMG 443 ▲
MAKE: 1934 Rolls Royce
EPISODE: The Captain's Car.
The Mayor's Rolls.

REG No:GJ 789

MAKE: 1930 Rolls Royce Phantom 2 Barrel Tourer

EPISODE: Is There Honey Still For Tea? Frazer's Hearse. Vehicle has changed significantly since filming the episode.

Currently owned by Richard Burning, Haywards Heath.

Currently awaiting restoration, owned by Jeff Helmdon, Northhants.

REG No: DX 9547

MAKE: Gilford AS6 20 seat coach.

EPISODE: Everybody's Trucking. Coach was in regular use at Jack Mulley's Coaches at Ixworth, the picture on the left taken in 1965.

REG No: JL 2323

MAKE: 1935 Leyland 6 Cylinder Cub

EPISODE: Brain Versus Brawn Walker's Fire Engine.

Currently owned by and on display at Bressingham Steam Museum

REG No: FPW 280
MAKE: Unknown
EPISODE: Round & Round Went the Great Big Wheel.
Army motorcycle.

▲ Current owner unknown.

REG No:ATO 574
MAKE: 1936 Brough Superior 1150cc
EPISODE: Round & Round Went the Great Big Wheel.
Currently on display at the London Motorcycle Museum, Greenford.

▲ Currently owned by Jeff Gikes, Uxbridge.

REG No: PW 1714
MAKE: 1923 Charles Burrell 8 Ton Steam Road Roller No3962
EPISODE: Everybody's Trucking.

▲ Supplied by and currently on display at Bressingham Steam Museum, Diss.

REG No: UR 6962

MAKE: 1930 Star Flyer

EPISODE: Time on my Hands & Brain Versus Brawn.

Used in general road scene.

Currently owned and used by M Galliers, Shrewsbury.

REG No:G 4547271

MAKE: 1941 Matchless G3L 350cc

EPISODE: The Honourable Man Platoon Motorcycle.

The owner supplied and rode this motorcycle for filming.

Currently owned by Philip Basey MBE, Rackheath, Norwich.

MAKE: 1933 Saddle Tank Engine (Colwyn)

EPISODE: The Royal Train 'Snettlefold Stopping Train'.

Currently under restoration at Chatham.

Currently owned by the Northampton & Lamport Railway Station, Chaple Brampton, Northampton.

REG No: None ▲
MAKE: Wellerhaus Mechanical Pipe
Organ.
EPISODE: Everybody's Trucking.

▲ Supplied and currently on display at Thursford Museum, Nr Fakenham.

REG No: None ▲
MAKE: (Pump Truck origin unknown)
EPISODE: The Royal Train.

▲ Supplied by and filmed at the North Norfolk Railway, Sherringham.

REG No: JVB 454 ▲
MAKE: BSA Motorcycle & Sidecar
EPISODES: Everybody's Trucking,
Gorilla Warfare & The Captain's
Car.

REG No: TEA 20 ▲
MAKE: 1950 Ferguson Tractor
EPISODE: Operation Kilt.

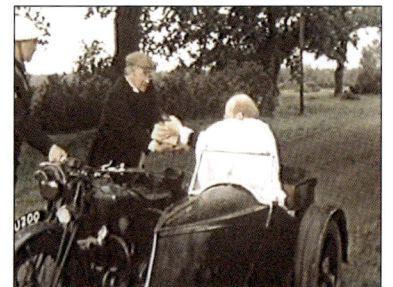

REG No: XAU 2006 ▲
MAKE: Unknown
EPISODE: Number Engaged.

REG No:CT 6902

MAKE: 1902 Aveling & Porter Steam Road Roller.

EPISODE: Museum Piece.

Supplied for filming and driven by Richard Parrett, Weeting, Suffolk.

△ Currently owned by Ian Clayton, Hallaton, Leicestershire.

△ Machinery supplied for filming by Mr Hoskins, Felsfield, Norfolk.

MAKE: Marshall △

TYPE: 1940 54" Threshing Drum.

EPISODE: All Is Safely Gathered In. There is an identical drum and elevator on display at Bressingham Steam Museum, Diss.

REG No: CF 3440 △

MAKE: 1909 Charles Burrell 7 ton Single Crank Traction Engine 'Bertha'.

EPISODE: All Is Safely Gathered In Harvesting takes place on Walnut Tree Farm, Bressingham.

△ Supplied by and on display at Bressingham Steam Museum, Diss.

▲ Currently owned and run by the Patrick Automotive Museum, Kings Norton, Birmingham from where it reguarly attends road runs and events.

REG No: BUC 852   ▲
MAKE: 1935 Fordson
Used as Jones' Butchers Van throughout the series. Originally owned and modified by the BBC, it was later put up for auction.
Purchased by The Patrick Museum, Kings Norton, Birmingham, it makes regular appearances at events and rallies and has appeared in Dad's Army documentaries.

▲ Bardwell, filming 'Wake Up, Walmington'

Above: Filming of 'The Battle of the Giants' at STANTA.

Left: On display at Bressingham Steam Museum Dad's Army day 2000.

REG No:PMP 782

MAKE: 1939 Bedford K Type

EPISODES: This vehicle was used in all episodes featuring Hodges' Grocers Van. The vehicle is a flat bed type so the top box was a prop made of wood especially for the programme. Sharp eyed viewers will notice the radio aerial, and the removable mirrors!

Supplied by Jack Mulley, who supplied many other vehicles for filming and transporting the cast and production team. Mrs Mulley is still the current owner.

The vehicle no longer has its box on the back, this being added for the programme. The vehicle didn't always appear as Hodges' van!

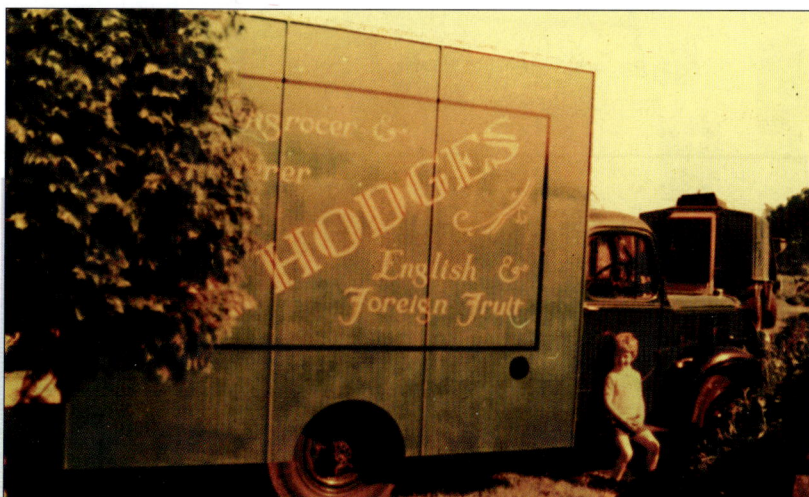

Left: East Wretham, filming 'Is There Honey Still For Tea?

Below: Everybody's Trucking. Filmed at STANTA.

▲ Currently stored at Castle Risng, Norfolk

REG No: RV 676
MAKE: Bedford Lorry
SCENE: Bert King's lorry used to collect the Vicar's bells. Filming took place at St. Mary Magdelen Church and Old Common Road, Shepperton ▲

REG No: BPL 73
MAKE: Shelvoke & Dewry Dustcart
SCENE: Mainwaring and the platoon hitch a lift in this vehicle after their disastrous weekend exercise.

▲ Owned by the Southern Counties Historic Vehicle Trust, Copthorne

▲ Currently owned by Mr Albert White, Lincolnshire.

REG No: KR 9378 ▲
MAKE: Ford AAF 13cwt Van
SCENE: This vehicle was used as Jones' Butchers Van. Why it was used instead of the original vehicle is open to debate, was it contractural?

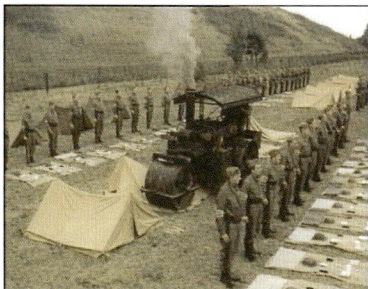

REG No: OU 5264
MAKE: Wallis & Stevens Steam Roller
SCENE: Used to pull Jones' incapacitated van to the campsite.

Currently owned by Mr Malcolm Randall, Andover.

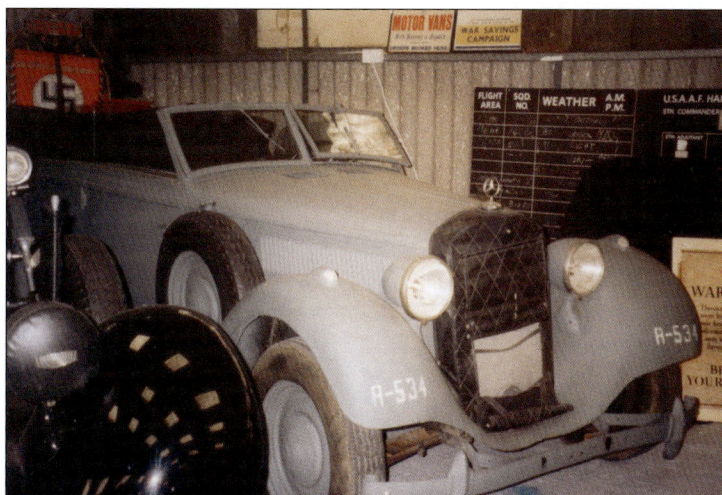

Currently on display at Tony Oliver's History on Wheels Museum, Eton Wick, Near Windsor.

REG No: WH611131A
MAKE: Mercedes
SCENE: The German General's staff car driven to the cliffs to watch England's coastline.

REG No: 77RA29
MAKE: Humber
SCENE: Major General Fullard's staff car, seen arriving at Mainwaring's Bank.

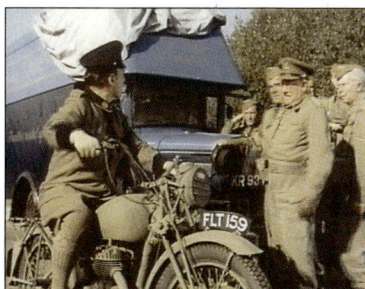

REG No: FLT 159
MAKE: Unknown
SCENE: The AA patrolman who cannot help the platoon with their leaking gas bag.

REG No: SMK 483
MAKE: BSA Bantam
SCENE: Warden Hodges' motorbike.

Above: East Wretham.

Above: STANTA MOD.

Left: Lynford Hall

Below left: Thetford, Guildhall.
Below: East Wretham.

Above: Blackrabbit Warren, STANTA
(Everybody's Trucking)

Right: Walnut Tree Farm, Bressingham
(All Is Safely Gathered In)

Left: Nether Row, Thetford.
(Time On My Hands)

A History of the Dad's Army Cartoon Strip.
March 1972 - Autumn 1998
by Andy Howells

British Television was still very much in its infancy in 1951. Many families could barely afford the new entertainment medium which was beginning to spread across the country, Television's popularity was still a few years away and would not receive full acclaim until the Coronation of Queen Elizabeth II in 1953.

However, the publishers of the UK's weekly Sunday newspaper, The News of the World recognised the potential of television early on, particularly transferring TV characters to the cartoon page. Following a formula originally laid down in a comic entitled Radio Fun (which successfully transferred Radio Characters to the cartoon page) TV Comic was first published on November 9th 1951. TV Comic featured such early TV favourites as Muffin the Mule and Mr.Pastry. Its content was very junior at this time and concentrated on stories for small children, but it's content began to grow up with its readership as the 1950s moved into the 1960s.

The popularity of Gerry Anderson's TV Series, Supercar and Fireball XL5 saw TV Comic angle their target readership to a slightly older audience. TV Comic reflected the popular TV trends of the era, the emergence of the BBC Sci-fi series Doctor Who saw the Doctor begin his own TV Comic time travels in November 1964.

Serious TV adventure stories such as The Avengers, Tarzan and Skippy the Bush Kangaroo were frequently complemented in TV Comic's pages with cartoon humour from popular TV Series such as Whacko, Tom and Jerry, Basil Brush and Bugs Bunny. In March 1972, Jimmy Perry & David Croft's Dad's Army joined the pages of TV Comic. Dad's Army already had a proven track record on British Television of nearly three and a half years' success, the cast having completed over forty television episodes and a feature film. All the characters and the stars were now well and truly household names and the series had captured the imagination of the younger generations as well as the old.

Arthur Lowe, who played Captain Mainwaring in the series told Radio Times in March 1972, "We expected the show to have limited appeal, to the age group that lived through the war and the Home Guard. We didn't expect what has happened - that children from the age of five upwards would enjoy it too." Dad's Army's transfer to the cartoon page seemed almost inevitable. TV Comic's immediate rival, the glossier TV Times produced Look-in was only able to license the use of ITV programmes within its pages; it would appear the door was open for Dad's Army - a BBC programme - to join the ranks of TV Comic.

Dad's Army debuted in issue 1058 dated 25th March 1972 and appeared in full Colour on page 6. These early strips were drawn by artist Bill Titcombe who had a long established career in cartooning for titles as numerous as Beezer, Hotspur,

Knockout and Top Spot.

Describing himself as a 'bit of a hack', Bill already illustrated Tom and Jerry for TV Comic, but he welcomed the chance to illustrate some new adventures for Walmington-on-Sea's Home Guard, which would be scripted by writer Nobby Clarke.

The Dad's Army strip formed the basis of a weekly serial, allowing time for the seven central characters to establish themselves within each plot and storylines to develop. Bill Titcombe's style progressed with the strip, and aided with an invitation to Thetford where Dad's Army was filmed; Bill had a chance to make more detailed studies of the series stars. He became very much at ease capturing the likenesses of Captain Mainwaring, Sergeant Wilson, Lance-Corporal Jones and Privates Frazer, Walker, Godfrey and Pike.

It is worth bearing in mind that back in the 1970s artists weren't provided with a lot in the way of resource to illustrate cartoon strips. So it is likely that much of the illustrations were drawn with the aid of a limited supply of publicity stills. Any extra material might have been culled from magazines such as Radio Times. The same could probably be said also for the script writing, as no input for the cartoons came from Jimmy Perry or David Croft.

The first Dad's Army serial involved a supply of live grenades accidentally dispatched to Walmington's Home Guard (erroneously spelt 'Warmington' periodically throughout the first year of the strip). During an air raid a German Spy lands on the Commanding Officer sent to warn Captain Mainwaring. This results in the officer being mistaken for a German Spy.

In some cases, incidents occasionally mirrored the TV goings on of Dad's Army. In one story a barrage balloon almost escapes carrying away Warden Hodges (as opposed to Captain Mainwaring in the TV episode "The Day the Balloon Went Up"). Another serial dealt with the platoon's removal of a Cromwell Gun from the local museum (shades of "Museum Piece"?). Mainwaring's hopes to use the gun as an anti-tank device literally back fire, but not before upsetting Warden Hodges and a local cricket team.

The Dad's Army strip also sported its fair share of German invaders, generally taking the form of spies, attempting to infiltrate the duties of the platoon.

At one point three members, Jones, Walker and Pike are kidnapped and taken to France. Later, a patrol boat containing Mainwaring, Wilson, Frazer and Godfrey accidentally drifts across the English Channel behind enemy lines. This is almost in a vein similar to the TV episode "Sons of the Sea", in which the platoon only get as far as Eastbourne, though for a while they do believe they're in France.

Other characters from the TV Series also appeared in the strip from time to time. These included ARP Warden Hodges, the Verger, the Vicar and Captain Square who - in one story - characteristically tries to show Captain Mainwaring up by tricking him into entering an area command shooting competition when he knows perfectly well Mainwaring is a lousy shot.

Mainwaring and Wilson's roles in the bank are frequently reinforced as the scene often shifts from the characters' lives in the Home Guard to their normal working day occupations. This illustrated an essential tie-in with the goings on of the TV Series and even transferred the spirit of Arthur Lowe and John Le Mesurier's wonderful scenes together to the cartoon page.

The main characters were well developed and portrayed in these early strips despite the occasional error. Continuity was probably the last thing on the writers' mind when aiming the strips for juvenile consumption. It is also very difficult to establish several characters to the confines of a single page weekly strip, but both Titcombe and Clarke did this well through the serial medium.

Such was the popularity of these early stories, six serials were rehashed and reprinted (though only in black and white) in a book published by Piccolo in 1973. Bill Titcombe was unimpressed with the finished result of this book and quite rightly so, as the strips have a rather unfinished patchy look in the book and on some pages the artwork isn't reproduced very well at all. Still, the Piccolo Dad's Army book remains possibly the easiest way of collecting some of these early stories and the book remains a popular collectable amongst Dad's Army fans today.

By January 1973, after ten months at TV Comic, the Dad's Army strip stood down and Bill Titcombe was dispatched for other cartoon duties. However, it was not the end of the line for the Dad's Army strip, as readers of TV Comic's sister publication, TV Action would soon see.

Serial / Story Checklist - 1972
TV COMIC
One page, published weekly in colour from issue dated March 25th 1972.
Stories by RAG Clarke & Drawn by Bill Titcombe.
Issues 1058-1062
OPERATION SPYCATCHER* (March 25th 1972 - April 22nd 1972)
An Army ammunition dump accidentally sends a supply of real grenades to the Walmington-on-Sea Home Guard. An officer is dispatched to warn them, but when his arrival coincides with the landing of a German spy by parachute, confusion ensues and Captain Mainwaring has him placed under arrest.
Issues 1063 - 1068
OPERATION BLUNDERBUS* (April 29th 1972 - June 3rd 1972)
Following a visit to the museum to look at an anti-tank gun,

Private Walker 'borrows' it so Captain Mainwaring may test it under combat conditions. The Platoon's actions are observed by a German spy, but the Cricket Team from Plumpstead also take an interest when the platoon remove a WW1 tank from the green via their cricket pitch...

Issues 1069 - 1074
DAD'S ARMY GOES TO SEA* (June 10th- July 15th 1972)
Guarding defences at the Old Beach Café, Jones, Walker and Pike are kidnapped by Germans who mistake them for regular soldiers. They are taken to France but are inadvertently followed by Mainwaring, Wilson, Frazer and Godfrey who accidentally drift across the channel in their patrol boat and also end up behind enemy lines.

Issues 1075 - 1081
DAD'S ARMY IN THE RED* (July 22nd- Sept 2nd 1972)
Mainwaring and Wilson are looking for new accounts for the bank and when the Captain of the balloon site turns up they think they may have a new customer. However, he's reluctant to put his mess funds in the bank, especially when he feels they're guarded well enough already, so the platoon concoct ways of penetrating the balloon site defences.

Issues 1082 - 1089
OPERATION SPIT AND POLISH* (Sept 9th- Oct 28th 1972)
Captain Mainwaring brings in Sgt. Major Higgins to smarten up the platoon. Higgins quickly reduces Sgt. Wilson to the ranks and deafens the platoon with his constant shouting. A remedy to protect their hearing backfires and results in Private Walker – ever the instigator – getting busted. But even Higgins isn't perfect and Captain Mainwaring's command could hang in the balance if action isn't taken.

Issues 1090 - 1096
SURE-FIRE MAINWARING* (Nov 4th- Dec 16th 1972)
Captain Square dupes Captain Mainwaring into been picked by the Brigadier for the Shooting Team in the Command Cup competition. The platoon try methods to help improve the Captain's aim but these result in Police arrest, assault by a bank customer and eventual bed rest, but a bang on the head results in the Captain's aim improving.

Issues 1097 - 1100
ON PATROL WITH DAD'S ARMY (Dec 23rd 1972 - Jan 13th 1973)
Christmas Eve has arrived, and the Brigadier has selected the Platoon for Guard duty at GHQ. As Pike and Frazer do first guard, they suspect a shed is haunted unaware a wild goose is on the loose...

TV COMIC   HOLIDAY SPECIAL 1972
Two pages in Black & White. Published in Summer, 1972 by Polystyle publications. Story by RAG Clarke & Drawn by Bill Titcombe.
It's Bank Holiday and the Platoon is marching along the beach when Captain Mainwaring believes he sees signalling from afar. Sending members of the platoon to investigate they all begin to disappear one by one...

TV COMIC   ANNUAL 1973
Two pages in Duotone. Published in Autumn, 1972 by Polystyle publications.

Story by RAG Clarke & Drawn by Bill Titcombe.
The platoon is sent to guard Brigadier Brassbound's secretaries for the weekend at Buck House. The ARP Warden decides to investigate but gets greeted by something more ferocious than the Home Guard.
All stories marked * have titles attributed to them from the Piccolo book published in 1973, which included line reprints of the stories. Any other titles are purely for reference in this article.

TV Comic's sister publication, TV Action had grown out of Countdown, which was generated for the teenage market in 1971 by editor, Dennis Hooper. The focus of Countdown had initially been Science Fiction in orientation but by 1972 was including more Action based adaptations of TV programmes such as Hawaii Five O and The Persuaders as well as the ever-popular Doctor Who (which had been promoted to Countdown from TV Comic in 1971).

Undergoing another title change to the more descriptive TV Action + Countdown and subsequently just TV Action by January 1973, Polystyle relaunched the comic with the addition of Alias Smith and Jones, Cannon, The Protectors, Droopy and Dad's Army from issue 101.

The Dad's Army cartoon strip changed quite dramatically from its previous appearances in TV Comic, its page count was increased to two but gone were the serial format, the Colour and more notably Bill Titcombe's artwork. Bill Titcombe having stayed on at TV Comic, to carry on work with strips such as Animal Magic and Tom & Jerry.

Cartoonist Peter Ford took over the artist's pen and gave the Walmington-on-Sea Home Guard a much more caricatured feel. Peter's work had previously been featured in the Gerry Anderson Lady Penelope comic during the 1960's.

TV Action editor, Dennis Hooper's storylines were varied and in places sometimes more slapstick. The short stories Dad's Army would now take part in would frequently border on what Captain Mainwaring would have possibly described as "Realms of Fantasy".

It was quite common to see members of the platoon taking part in situations that would never occur on television, such as boarding aeroplanes and using parachutes. One story even resulted in Captain Mainwaring losing his trousers while demonstrating how to lift a sandbag correctly. An event that certainly would not have occurred in the TV Series as Arthur Lowe (Captain Mainwaring) had strictly forbidden any trouser jokes within his contract!

A mainstay of the television series the strip reflected was the continuing battle between Captain Mainwaring's platoon with Warden Hodges and the Verger. TV Action issue 126 illustrated the Warden's attempt to mount a surprise attack on the platoon, only for his bike and sidecar to tumble straight into a tank trap!

TV Action continued until August 1973, when dwindling sales caused the comic to end at Issue132. The Dad's Army strip returned to TV Comic from issue 1133 dated September 1st 1973. Peter Ford continued with the artwork but the strip itself was reduced back to a single page in black and white.

Dad's Army's involvement with TV Action was still not quite over though. A four page story involving a German Double Agent and Private Walker turning a German parachute into ladies negligee (echoes of the 1969 television episode Man-Hunt) turned up in the TV Action Annual for 1974 (published in Autumn, 1973).

Back in TV Comic, four regular characters were continually brought to the forefront of the weekly storylines. Captain Mainwaring and Sergeant Wilson were still at the helm although both characters were increasingly beginning to differ from their television counterparts. Mainwaring was certainly becoming more pigheaded and selfish; it was quite common for him to shirk responsibilities by trying to partake a few hours sleep whilst leaving others to do essential Home Guard duties.

Wilson's character was frequently at odds with his television counterpart and lacked sincerity and support for his Captain and other platoon members. He was likened to Hodges by often giving the punch line to the end of a weekly installment. Both Privates Pike and Walker seemed to do well from the strips; Pike was very much the soppy boy character Ian Lavender developed for television (he was never actually referred to in these later strips as "stupid"). While Walker was still the wide-boy persona created so wonderfully on-screen by James Beck. Due to the youthfulness of the characters it seems they were probably easily identifiable with the younger readership.

Jones, Frazer and Godfrey didn't seem to be well represented in the strips and at times they only had token lines or occasional things to do. Jones for instance, frequently tripped over with the customary yell of "Don't panic!"

The strip handled a diverse range of storylines on a weekly basis. These involved Captain Mainwaring gaining ideals of grandeur and attempting to move Home Guard HQ away from the Church hall, frequent run-ins with German Spies, the regular army, the U.S. Army, doodlebugs and his own personal Hitler - Warden Hodges.

Unseen television characters also made occasional appearances, or at least made their presence felt. Mrs. Mainwaring appeared courtesy of a speech bubble in issue

1142 when she required Captain Mainwaring to do some decorating in their home. Mrs. Hodges was also mentioned in the same strip, although it would be another ten years before the same character would even get a passing reference from her husband in the radio series It Sticks Out Half A Mile. The Vicar and Jones also referred to having wives in other editions, though this was never clarified on television (In fact The Vicar said he wasn't married in the 1973 television episode "The Recruit").

With the sad loss of James Beck to the Dad's Army television series in August 1973, it could have been assumed that Private Walker's character would have ceased to appear in the weekly cartoon strip, however; this was not the case. Private Walker continued to regularly turn up for patrol for the next 18 months of the Dad's Army strip, which probably explains how well the character transferred to the cartoon page and was a vital ingredient to the plot lines.

Dad's Army remained unchanged within the pages of TV Comic throughout 1974, but in early 1975 the strip took an interesting turn when Bill Titcombe returned as artist after an absence of two years. Bill's return coincided with the arrival of Private Cheeseman who duly replaced Private Walker in the strip as he had done on television.

The style of the artwork seemed to return to its former glory days of 1972, although still in Black and White, the feel was very much what readers expected from the humour of Dad's Army. An example from issue 1240 in September 1975 had Frazer and Jones handing in their resignations unless Captain Mainwaring got rid of the other, a scene not uncommon in the television series.

The regular Dad's Army cartoon strip ended in TV Comic issue 1275 dated 22nd May 1976, prior to another relaunch of TV Comic and another reshuffling of cartoon strips. The Dad's Army strip did resurface in the TV Comic Annuals for both 1976 and 1977, this time, two page Colour strips drawn by Bill Titcombe. The 1976 annual features a story where the platoon - on manoeuvres - fall victim one winter's night to a local farmer, while the 1977 annual saw the platoon put on a production of Aladdin with Warden Hodges and the Verger.

After the 1977 TV Comic annual (published in autumn, 1976), the end of the Dad's Army TV Series in 1977 and the final World Distributors Dad's Army annual for 1978, fans may have assumed that they had seen the last Dad's Army cartoon strip. However, this was not to be the case.

The 1979 TV Comic annual (published in autumn 1978) contained three strips (Dad's Army's largest ever page count in a TV Comic annual), which were unaccredited but appear to have been drawn by Peter Ford, including one strip in Colour. More curious was the reappearance of Private Walker. A possible explanation for the strip's reappearance (and possibly Private Walker's) could be that these were either reprints or unused strips from TV Comic and TV Action.

The final strip in the 1979 TV Comic Annual concerned a story in which the platoon obtains a goat as regimental mascot (this in itself was not unlike a television episode broadcast eight years earlier entitled "The Big Parade"). The goat (obtained by Private Walker) catches sight of Warden Hodges and promptly chases him into a nearby river, looking back at a gloating platoon Hodges gets the last say "Bah! I'll get you lot for this!"

Obtaining the Dad's Army strips today is rather difficult, various editions of TV Comic and TV Action do survive in many collectors hands, but unfortunately frequently exchange hands at high prices due to the highly collectable nature of each edition's content. Popularity of TV Series such as The Avengers and Doctor Who make tracking down copies of these comics considerably difficult and rather expensive for the collector.

Presently, it is unlikely that all of the strips will ever be reprinted as the artists and the respective publishers burned much of the original artwork due to lack of storage space.

However, good examples of the Dad's Army cartoon strip can be found in 5 TV Comic Annuals and 1 TV Action Annual. These can generally be picked up at comic fairs, second hand bookstalls and quite frequently the Internet auction site, 'ebay'. Prices can vary between £2 to £5, depending on condition. The annuals are great for nostalgia buffs who want to relive a very special era in comic strip history.

Comic Strip Checklist 1973 - 1979

TV ACTION
Issues 101-132   20th January 1973 - 24th August 1973
Two pages, published weekly in Black & white from issue dated January 20th 1973.
Stories by Dennis Hooper & Drawn by Peter Ford.
Issue 104   February 10th 1973
On the seafront, Captain Mainwaring splits his trousers while demonstrating how to carry sandbags correctly to the Platoon and is forced to give orders while keeping his hands in his pockets. Then a female Army officer turns up...
Issue 105   February 17th 1973
Captain Mainwaring is taking a flight with the Wing Commander, however when their plane flies over the cliff top Café the platoon mistake it for an enemy plane, Pike takes drastic action with a rock cake!

Issue 124   June 30th 1973
Captain Mainwaring receives a stone gnome from his Aunt Nelly, which he decides will be useful for target practice. Pike is assigned to take it to the beach, but confusion ensues when the gnome gets mixed up with the ARP's supper!
Issue 126   July 14th 1973
The platoon are digging a tank trap, but are frequently disturbed by unwanted visitors, first by the regular Army and then by Warden Hodges and The Verger.

TV ACTION ANNUAL 1974
Four pages in Duotone. Written by Dennis Hooper & Drawn by Peter Ford
A new clerk arrives at the bank - but is Miss Smith all she seems? Meanwhile, Walker puts a German parachute to good use by converting it into ladies undergarments...

TV COMIC   SUMMER SPECIAL 1973
Although Dad's Army was appearing in TV ACTION at the time a Dad's Army strip appeared in the TV COMIC Summer Special for 1973.

TV COMIC   Issues 1133- 1202
1st September 1973 - 28th December 1974
One page, published weekly in Black & white from issue dated September 1st 1973.
Stories by Dennis Hooper & Drawn by Peter Ford.

Information on known installments:
Issue 1133   1st September 1973
The platoon goes on a parachute training course, Pike and Mainwaring land on an ARP tent.

Issue 1134   8th September 1973
The platoon is late for a combined services conference, as Jones' van is immobilised, they commandeer a horse and cart, and run Hodges off the road into a river.
Issue 1135   15th September 1973
On return from a cycle exercise the Platoon discover that Hodges' ARP have taken over the hall. Mainwaring insists a 24-Hour Guard is put into operation...

Issue 1136 22nd September 1973
Mainwaring volunteers the platoon to take part in training with the guards. When they arrive they find they're only there to peel spuds.
Issue 1137 29th September 1973
The Captain decides the platoon will put on a performance of Macbeth.
Issue 1139 13th October 1973
The platoon goes on an army assault course but a dog wreaks havoc.
Issue 1141 27th October 1973
The platoon are defending a jetty, however; the barge they are standing on drifts into the English Channel...
Issue 1142 3rd November 1973
Mrs. Mainwaring is complaining that the Mainwaring's house exterior needs painting. Captain Mainwaring authorises an Army unit of painters to do the job while he is away. Mrs. Mainwaring briefly appears in this edition. Mrs. Hodges is also mentioned.
Issue 1143 10th November 1973
Captain Mainwaring warns the platoon about German spies. Corporal Jones suspicions are aroused when a customer enters his butchers' shop with a strange accent enquiring about 'spies'...
Issue 1144 17th November 1973
Mainwaring thinks the Germans are tapping his phone line
Issue 1145 24th November 1973
Mainwaring is training the men in trench warfare
Issue 1146 1st December 1973
Driving in the van at night, the platoon get lost thanks to Mainwaring's map reading
Issue 1147 8th December 1973
The platoon build their own anti-aircraft gun and shoot down a Nazi bomber
Issue 1148 15th December 1973
The ladies sewing circle makes a flag for the Home Guard. This edition wrongly has Jones referring to his 'old lady', i.e. wife. He's a bachelor.
Issue 1149 22nd December 1973
The Home Guard has a new pillbox, on the cliff tops. But not for long!
Issue 1150 29th December 1973
The Vicar asks the ARP and Home Guard to raise funds to repair the church roof. The platoon forms a choir to sing Christmas carols.
Issue 1151 5th January 1974
Mainwaring gets himself a Very pistol so if the enemy tries to assassinate him he can fire a flare for help. On the way home in the blackout he slips on ice and it goes off.
Issue 1152 12th January 1974
Mainwaring discovers that the bells in the church tower have no ropes. He decides there is no time to lose in getting them fixed, in case the bells are needed in an invasion. The platoon use Hodges' ladder without his permission, and when he goes

to retrieve it the warden gets tangled in the ropes, setting off an invasion alert!
Issue 1153 19th January 1974
Mainwaring gets the platoon invited to gunnery school. But rather than firing 25 Pounders as he'd thought, they are instead drilled by a manic Sergeant Major, who makes them run about with the artillery piece
Issue 1154 26th January 1974
When a power cut in the hall causes Mainwaring to break his arm, he sets about making an alternative power source so it won't happen again – and ends up in hospital!
Issue 1155 2nd February 1974
During a blizzard, Mainwaring decides to equip the team for snow-bound warfare
Issue 1167 27th April 1974
Captain Mainwaring decides to move the Platoon Headquarters to the Waterloo Country Club. However as the platoon marches to their new HQ an air-raid alert sounds...

TV COMIC SUMMER SPECIAL 1974
A Dad's Army Cartoon Strip is known to have appeared in the 1974 edition of the TV COMIC Summer Special.
Issue 1178 13th July 1974
The platoon is on exercise and risk being captured by American troops. However, Jones' van saves the day when its noisy engine makes the Americans believe they themselves have been captured!
Issue 1182 10th August 1974
A doodlebug lands in the woods during an air raid; the Home Guard and the ARP begin to search for it. During the search, Mainwaring's lack of trust in Godfrey's judgement means he detonates it by accident.
Issue 1183 17th August 1974
'B' Squadron leaves the Home Guard a tank that has no ammunition or engine for exercises. When finding some ammunition a Jerry Fighter descends on them.
Issue 1191 12th October 1974
Mainwaring spots a mine floating perilously close to the pier and aided by Wilson & Pike attempts to take action to blow it up.
Issue 1192 19th October 1974
Captain Mainwaring dupes the platoon into doing some farmwork in return for personal provisions. But the Captain's selfish actions backfire...
Issue 1193 26th October 1974
The platoon's latest recruit Private Hoskins is stirring up trouble in every possible situation. While he panders to Captain Mainwaring's whims, Wilson and Jones concoct a plan to get rid of him.
Issue 1194 2nd November 1974
Captain Mainwaring fails his medical on grounds of being overweight. As Wilson and Walker accompany the Captain to the local steam baths they inadvertently leave his uniform in a steam cubicle causing it to shrink.

Issue 1195   9th November 1974
The platoon wreak havoc when they receive an invitation to visit a nearby Naval Base...

Issue 1196   16th November 1974
On a night manoeuvre, Captain Mainwaring accidentally signals his Very pistol to a regular army exercise also on manoeuvres in the area...

Issue 1197   23rd November 1974
Staff Sergeant Mussels from HQ attempts to train the Platoon in unarmed combat...

Issue 1198   30th November 1974
The Platoon and the Wardens attempt to repair a damaged bridge, but the Platoon come off worse when they lose Jones' van to the river!

TV COMIC
Issues 1203 - 1275
4th January 1975 – 22nd May 1976
One page published weekly in Black & white. Stories by Dennis Hooper & Drawn by Bill Titcombe.

TV COMIC   SUMMER SPECIAL 1975
A Dad's Army Cartoon Strip is known to have appeared in the 1975 edition of the TV COMIC Summer Special.

TV COMIC   SUMMER SPECIAL 1976
A Dad's Army Cartoon Strip is known to have appeared in the 1976 edition of the TV COMIC Summer Special.

TV COMIC   ANNUAL 1975
Two pages in Duotone. Written by Dennis Hooper & Drawn by Peter Ford.
Hodges gets promotion but Mainwaring finds the Warden's replacement even more intolerable than his predecessor. Jones & Walker hatch a plot to get their old Warden back...

TV COMIC   ANNUAL 1975
Two pages in Duotone. Written by Dennis Hooper & Drawn by Peter Ford.
The Colonel challenges Captain Mainwaring to a game of golf. After a short lesson from Wilson, Mainwaring thinks he's ready...

TV COMIC   ANNUAL 1976
Two pages in Colour. Written by Dennis Hooper & Drawn by Bill Titcombe.
The Platoon are on night Manoeuvres but fall victim to a local farmer...
(The character of Private Cheeseman appears in this story)

TV COMIC   ANNUAL 1977
Two pages in Colour. Written by Dennis Hooper & Drawn by Bill Titcombe.
Captain Mainwaring decides to stage a production of Aladdin for the children at Christmas Time. With Warden Hodges and the Verger as stagehands the Captain's production literally brings the house down.

TV COMIC   ANNUAL 1979
One page in Duotone. Written by Dennis Hooper & Drawn by Peter Ford.
The platoon goes on a parachute training course, Pike and Mainwaring land on an ARP tent. (This strip appears to be a reprint from TV Comic issue 1133 - 1st September 1973)

TV COMIC   ANNUAL 1979
Two pages in Duotone. Written by Dennis Hooper & Drawn by Peter Ford.
HQ sends Mainwaring a Lewis gun to defend the bank, however; the Bofar Battery is in his line of fire. When their CO won't co-operate Mainwaring decides to take drastic measures. (The character of Walker reappears in this story)

TV COMIC   ANNUAL 1979
Two pages in Colour. Written by Dennis Hooper & Drawn by Peter Ford.
Walker provides the platoon with a regimental mascot - a goat - that takes an immediate dislike to Warden Hodges!

Thanks to Bill Titcombe, Dave Homewood and Jack Wheeler for additional information, which has helped me complete this history of Dad's Army Comic Strip.

So far only eight jigsaw puzzles have come to light, each produced by Whitman UK, four with 350 pieces at 17" x 12" (43.2 x 30.5 cm) and four with 400 pieces at 18 x 13 inches (47 x 33cm).

350 piece puzzles

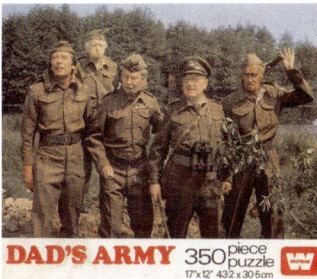

From 'The Big Parade', features Walker, Godfrey, Jones, Mainwaring and Frazer by Stanford Lake, West Tofts, just before they find Pike in the bog.

From the 1971 film at Monument Car Park, Chobham Common and features the platoon lined up ready to carry out the rifle drill. Wilson, Jones and Mainwaring are in discussion.

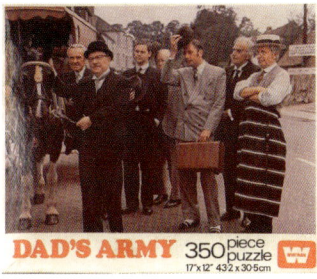

From the 1971 film - a posed picture as Arthur Lowe is wearing his own spectacles. It features the magnificent seven, in civvies, standing next to a horse and cart in the High Street of Chalfont St. Giles.

From 'A Soldier's Farewell' features John Laurie, John Le Mesurier and Bill Pertwee on horse back and dressed up as Wellington and his men.

400 piece puzzles

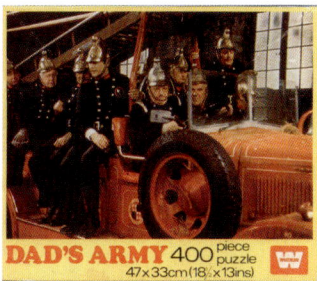

From 'Brain Versus Brawn' sees the seven including Colin Bean and Hugh Hastings on the fire engine inside Walker's shed. This is the only studio shot used in the jigsaw puzzle series.

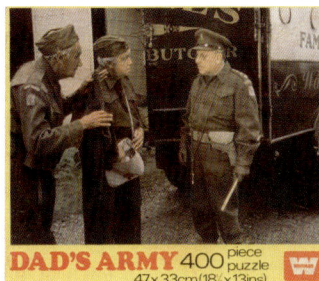

From 'Battle of the Giants' we have Frazer, Godfrey and Mainwaring at the back of Jones' van. Godfrey is looking to see what medicine he has for Jones.

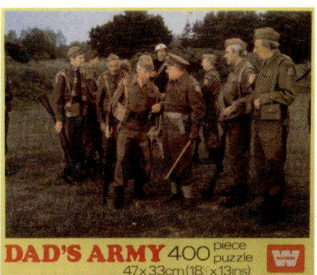

From 'Battle of the Giants' featuring the platoon with Jones the worse for Godfrey's 'elderly' wine and the Warden is about to give them the next set of instructions.

From the 'Captain's Car' the scene outside the Thetford Guildhall waiting for the French General to arrive.

Ovaltine Game

Advertised in 1972 as part of an Ovaltine promotion, this game was available by collecting special Dad's Army money tokens found inside Ovaltine products. A total token value for each game was not to exceed 60p, thus ensuring that at least 80p was paid in cash for the game. Tokens came in 10p & 20p values, depending on the product and tin size.

Tins of Ovaltine, Chocolate Time Extra, Drinking Chocolate and Instant Non Fat Milk all contained tokens and a promotional flash across the product label.

Adverts for the game included a 10p token 'to start you off' printed on the tear-off slip.

The Box

As this item was sent out by post, it is not surprising that the game is presented in a stiff envelope, all the playing pieces and board being flat items folded inside.

The cover is illustrated by caricatures of the platoon members, with the exception of Pike. He does, however, make an appearance on the playing board. Playing instructions are carried on the reverse.

This game is produced and illustrated by Peter Thurlow Ltd, although the images are quite different from those in the later cartoon strips they produced

Playing the Game

The story is that Pike has been sent out on patrol and has not returned, so other members of the platoon have to go out and look for him, making their way, via an assault course to the Church Hall.

Proceeding from the start in a clockwise direction, each player must land on at least one 'Capture' square to collect a paratrooper and bring him back to the hall. Only one prisoner is permitted.

The outer ring of the game contains various penalties, subject to the throw of the dice. The inner ring is the assault course leading to the Church Hall.

The winner is the first to arrive back at the church hall (with a paratrooper!) on the exact throw of the dice.

What's in the Box?
The game is presented in a stiff envelope, all the playing pieces and board being flat items. Aside from the 22" x 15" board, and dice there are six playing pieces, depicting Mainwaring, Wilson, Jones, Frazer, Godfrey & Walker. There is no playing piece for Pike, as he was 'sent out on patrol first and has not been seen since'. In addition to the platoon members are six 'Capture Cards' depicting enemy soldiers.

The Denys Fisher Board Game

Marketed under the 'Strawberry Fayre' name, which included other children's games, this game was released in 1974.

The Box

The box measures 490mm x 295mm x 44mm and when fully packed is surprisingly heavy. The full colour illustration on the box (also the board and playing pieces) are drawn by Peter Thurlow Ltd, the same company responsible for the Dad's Army Annuals, so the likenesses are pretty accurate. A caption on the box states "Crazy capers out on patrol as our redoubtable heroes prepare to hold off the Hun!"

Playing the Game

The object of the game is to 'get both your men to their map references. The first to do so wins'.

The character pieces have different backgrounds and are paired off accordingly. To choose the map reference, one of each of the 'Map Reference Cards' is chosen. This is then marked with the appropriate coloured 'Reference Marker'. Each character must visit at least one WD Top Secret' base on the way.

Your progress can be hampered in a number of ways, the most interesting is the fact that you can be 'Hodged' - using this character piece to swap positions with. If you happen to move to an air-raid shelter this results in a number of 'bombs' (Swastika markers) being dropped. The bombs can only be cleared by replacing them with the Union Jack markers.

Experience in playing the game is varied. Sometimes it can be over very quickly, but this is mainly due to your opponents not blocking your progress. It can also be very frustrating, being 'Hodged' so close to your reference marker.

Other games can last a considerable time and it has the added advantage of being able to make children win without it seeming too obvious.

What's in the Box?
The instructions for the game are written in the lid of the box - see 'playing the game'. Inside the box should be the following items:
Full colour Playing board - this measures 567mm x 468mm. As can be seen from the accompanying picture, the illustration depicts a 3D representation of a compound with various buildings marked on a (12x12) grid .
48 WD Top Secret Cards - 5 x blank, 7 x Union Jacks, 7 x Air Raids, 4 x Hodges, 3 x for each of the following - Mainwaring, Wilson, Jonesy (sic), Fraser (sic), Godfrey, Pike & The Vicar.
24 x Map Reference Cards - 12 red & 12 black.
14 x Swastika Markers, 14 x Union Jack Markers, 4 x Reference Markers.
1 x Dice.
9 Character Pieces & plastic stands - Mainwaring, Wilson, Jones, Fraser (sic), Godfrey, Pike, Vicar, Verger & Hodges. Cards and playing pieces initially came as individual sheets which the owner had to 'carefully press out' before playing. If you are offered a game with all sheets intact, it would be a rare item indeed, as the game would not have been played!

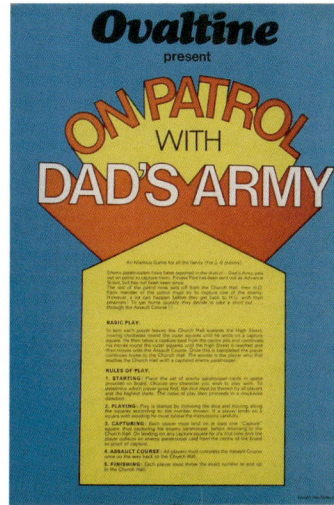

Below: Playing pieces depicting platoon members and examples of the 'capture' cards.
Left: Box (folder) and playing board.

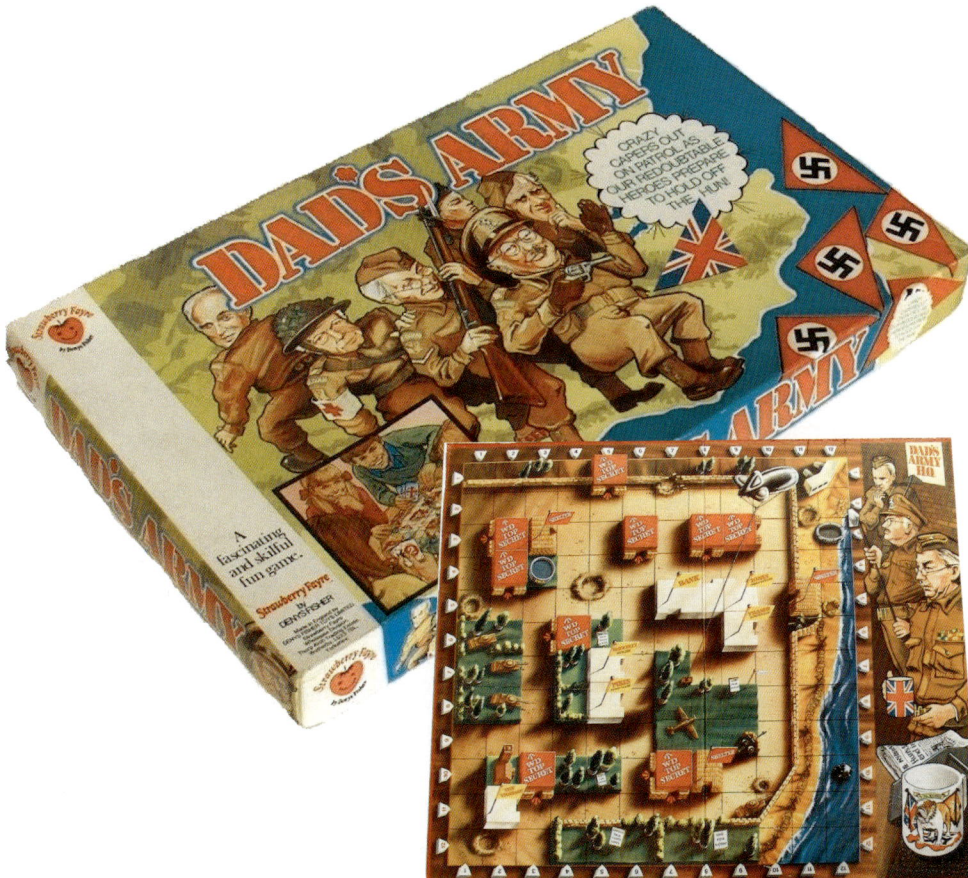

Above: Playing piece depicting platoon member (Wilson) and an example of each of the counters and cards.
Left: Box and playing board.

This section has been supplied by Dyllan Tappenden following his extensive research into the subject.
The compilers are indebted to him for allowing his findings to be published in the Companion.

BACKGROUND

The basis of writing this section of the companion was the demand for further knowledge about the various model vehicles which have been produced, and which are principally associated with the Dad's Army TV Series. However like most projects the subject matter expanded slightly to incorporate other vehicles which (although not connected to Dads Army) are linked to TV Comedy series of the same period of media history as you will see.
The contents are divided into the chronological order in which the models were manufactured or retailed. They are available either individually or as part of a set.
The following headings describe the title of model, followed by the LLedo cast number(in brackets) then the year of production/retail. Vehicle description (and correct description where different), colours, characteristics and details of models offered (and manufacturers model number) special comments and features. Box design, colours and wording (when appropriate). Authors comments
At this point I should add that in general the vehicles were mass-produced in batches running into several thousands. Models are known to have been distributed globally to Australasia and North America where there were extensive networks of collectors, and that is without the UK or European market! These models are now fetching premium prices, so it it worthwhile keeping an eye out for them.

Radio Times Dad's Army Exclusive Edition
(LP43/015A) produced 1990/1

This is the first production run for this vehicle as Jones Butchers van from the TV series. However as discussed by Dad's Army Appreciation Society in their quarterly newsletter the vehicle is correctly represented by a Ford Morris BB Box Van (Lledo reference LP43). The vehicle appears in a navy blue paint scheme with cream upper body sides, rear doors and roof. Lettering on side is in gold scroll with the correct wording " J Jones Butchers". The radiator and light fittings are silver plastic.
The original model was produced with a cast metal roof as a separate mould, and thus is distinct from later versions which had this item replicated in white (rather than cream) plastic. The model was produced as a result of co-operation with the BBC Radio Times who instigated an order for several thousand models, which were offered via that publication. The model proved very popular, and as a result those not sold via the Radio Times found their way onto the "open market" and prompted a further run of vehicles to be produced independently by Lledo via their own retail outlets. A donation was made from the sale of each piece to The Motor and Allied Trades Benevolent Fund.
They are packaged in French blue boxes with red lettering.

The Radio Times legend is printed on a red banner across front of the normal Lledo style box.

Special Radio Times - Dad's Army Twin Set
Jones Van & Hodges Van
(LP43/015A & LP59/001A) believed produced 1991/92

Although I have only verbal indications that this set was produced (and no personal experience), it is believed that after the success of the first Jones Van production run, Lledo then produced a twin set which included Jones and Hodges vans together in a single box (again I do not have any details of the colour/style of the packaging - so anything further is pure speculation). However whether its appearance in the chronology of vehicles is before the 1991 set or after is unclear. If anyone has details or photographs of this set please let me know via the Dad's Army Appreciation Society. I have yet to see this set and thus cannot comment, however whether its appearance in the chronology of vehicles before the 1991 set or after is open to discussion. If so the likelihood is the dark green body and cab, with correct yellow lettering & lining for the business is seen. The radiator is in metal (unusual for most Lledo trucks), with attached headlight fittings in silver. The box body roof is dark plastic with ridges to denote the roof supports.

First Dad's Army Set (1991)

The same designed box as above, but without the Dad's Army legend across the front of box and no special edition lettering & Home Front Die cast title on rear;
This set builds on the initial success Lledo had with the single issues of Jones Van as an individual item, and also as the Limited Edition Radio Times versions described previously. The Jones Van is joined by a series of other vehicles which capture the wartime spirit, in drab colour (in comparison to the prettier colours of Jones'), perhaps the Salvation Army Canteen vehicle is the other exception. The NFS Dennis Escape Ladder Fire Engine is correctly painted in grey with appropriate allocation panel, whilst the dark green Dennis outside broadcast vehicle looks good, but cannot be authenticated as accurate by its owners! The American Stake Truck is another mythical beast I fear, but completes a nice set. As the set has a secondary branding as 'Home Front

Die casts' I guess the Dad's Army title was more of selling point?

Jack Jones' Butchers Van - Ford Morris BB Box Van (LP43/015A)

The vehicle retains all the features of the original batches, with cream roof, made of die cast metal, thus making the van a solid piece of engineering, and crisp lettering and lining of the bodywork.

BBC Outside Broadcast Van - Dennis Limousine (LP35/003A)

A simple model in BBC green (dark/olive mix), with minimal lettering printed in gold on the side panel and door. In some instances the vehicle can be found with interior glazing unit thus adding to the final finish. The piece is somewhat spoilt by the fact the bottom and top moulds are joined together across the middle of the vehicle making an unsightly join. On the roof a brown plastic ladder is attached (for that birds eye camera angle of course!)

National Fire Service - Dennis Fire Engine (LP12/027A)

Correctly painted in NFS drab grey, with data panel (indicating its allocation to London Fire region), the vehicle is supplied with a wheeled escape ladder in dark brown plastic. The running boards are black plastic.

Queens Messenger Fast Food - American Mack Tanker Truck (LP42/006A)

Supplied in light grey paint scheme, incorporating lettering in red transfers, the tank section is a separate casting enabling the vehicle chassis to be interchangeable for the purposes of a differing loads that Lledo used the vehicle for.

Salvation Army - Dennis Mobile Canteen (LP16/110A)

Produced in dark blue paintwork, with white 'mobile canteen' lettering, there is in addition a wartime poster in white, and some lettering towards the rear of the body, and on the door of the cab. The 'Salvation Army' badge is picked-out in red, and all this detail is crisply embossed on the model.

Vintage Series Radio Times Comedy Classic (1993)

Consisting of six vehicles from various BBC TV comedy programmes. The vehicles (and the series they originate from) are in light blue boxes in the Radio Times series (some boxes have BBC logo others Comedy Classic letter on front); This set was produced to extend the marketability of the Lledo range after the success of several other themed series, which they produced around this time (including Darling Buds of May). By extending this set to include vehicles attributed to other Comedy Series they increased the collectability four-fold.

Some of the items in the set are now more rare in comparison to others. The set includes a repeat appearance of the Jones & Hodges vehicles. However they are joined in this instance by unique models representing the Grace Brother delivery van, Maplins Holiday Camp bus (later to appear in differing colours as a Walmington on Sea vehicle) and the Army Truck from It Ain't Half Hot Mum. However the rarest piece; mainly because various parts get lost or damaged (namely the horse or Harry H Corbett figure) thus devaluing the item is the Steptoe and Son rag and bone cart. This always seems to be the one everybody is missing in their set – perhaps fewer were produced but whatever the reason, this is my preferred set. Whenever I look at the vehicles together I can recall watching all the various series first time around.

Hi-De-Hi - Maplins Holiday Camp Bus (LP17/190A)

Cream and green livery, with fine lettering on the side indicating the holiday camp, this is a nice piece completely die cast in construction with only minor plastic ancillaries (radiator). The bus is not glazed, and has a light beige interior seating arrangement.

It Ain't Half Hot Mum - American Mack Canvas Roofed Army Truck (LP28/032A

Khaki paintwork to the truck cab and body, and a plastic green tarpaulin covered area, the vehicle has white graffiti transfer to the side, and is another nice item. Some of the vehicles have internally glazed cabs.

Yellow Are You Being Served? - Grace Brothers Delivery Van (LP16/130A)

Red paintwork, with art-deco style lettering on a cream panel on the body side relating to the identity, the roof is a cream plastic fitting.

Steptoe & Son - Horse and Cart
(PM113/001A)

This 'vehicle' consists of a cart made of metal, with dark blue bodywork, the cart floor is dark brown with lettering in silver along the side of the cart, the seat for 'Harry H' forms part of the mane moulding. The forks for the harness are plastic in matching blue, and can be brittle, the horse is brown, with white maine and tail although, white, and black have been sighted! Horse and figure are also plastic this time in cream. Finally the wheels are red rimmed.

Dad's Army - Jack Jones' Butchers Van
(LP43/015A)

The standard version, with some models having metal roofs other plastic.

Dad's Army - William Hodges' Greengrocers Van
(LP59/001A)

Standard version, although some versions have been glazed, the finish normally included a silver footplate too.

Dad's Army Second Set (1995)

The boxes are light blue with union jack arrowhead and black arrowhead logos on side and rear,.

This set was designed to capture the feel of the TV series by specifically associating vehicles with the Walmington on Sea brand name, within a recognisable Dad's Army logo box. However it fails to complete the challenge by missing the opportunity to replicate vehicles, which actually appear in the series or film. The two old stalwart (Jones' & Hodges') vehicles appear accurate enough (as discussed elsewhere), but the taxi and newspaper vehicles are completely wide of the mark. The bus (a late addition to this set when Lledo

realised the interest and retail value to collectors) could just about pass for that seen in the episode 'Everybody's Trucking', however the paint scheme is thus incorrect. It certainly is rare in comparison with the others in the set however, never having been produced to the same volumes. The LDV truck reminds me more of the vehicle from the film used by Bert and his mate to collect the vicar's bells – but only at a passing glance.

I often think that a nicer item might have been a reproduction of the Dennis Fire Engine in red (as seen in the episode 'Brain versus Brawn') at least this would more accurately reflect a vehicle actually seen in the series!?

Jack Jones' Butchers Van - Ford Morris BB Box Van
(LP43/015A)

Standard version except that the lining and transfer lettering are beginning to look a little tired!

Green William Hodges' Greengrocers Van - Bedford 30 cwt Van
(LP59/001A)

This appears to be the first sighting of a lighter green paint job for the box body.

Black Walmington Taxi - Ford Model T saloon car
(LP33/012A)

Black overall, some white mudguard versions have been alleged (but not seen), whilst the lettering is picked out in white, silver bumper and light fittings are fixed to the radiator which is also made of silver plastic. Front windscreen fitting and light handsome cab lamps are also similarly produced.

Blue Walmington Recorder - Ford Model A Newspaper Delivery Van
(LP13/261A)

The dark blue van has radiator, light fittings in the normal silver plastic. The van has a room advertising board with appropriate beige lettering, whilst the bodywork also has ownership lettering and reproduction poster from the war period.

Brown Local Defence Volunteer - Ford Stake Truck with Load (LP20/049A)

The vehicle is produced in drab dark brown livery, with white lettering on the side of the body, another poster is reproduced on the side, whilst the load of milk style churns is in grey plastic (perhaps they contain some secret weapon?!).

Blue Walmington on Sea Bus Co - single deck bus (LP17/209A)

This is the late addition to the set, and appears not to have been produced in the same quantity as the previous vehicles, the livery is a dark blue with light blue around the window surrounds, gold lettering indicating the Walmington Bus Co is crisp, and the advertising board along each edge of the roof has various images suitable from the time. The front lights and radiator are silver fittings. There is no glazing unit on the vehicle, but the interior seating mould is in light blue plastic (matching the external livery).

Dad's Army Limited Edition (1997)

Produced in a Perspex box and sitting on a "mock" plinth,

with a picture of the TV Series cast on the rear, 17,000 were produced despite the Limited title! The majority of vehicles were produced with a rather whiter roof made of plastic, than the original versions, however some can have a cream version, and some made from die cast metal (using the original tooling) There are a considerable number of variants of this model – see later section.

Jack Jones' Butchers Van - Ford Morris BB Box Van
The final run of our old faithful, draws the Lledo production run to an end, during 1998 Lledo came under extreme financial pressure, especially from cheap foreign imports of toys, and the changing toy retail environment. The firm finally succumbed to administrative receivers, and the assets of the business were sold-off. Corgi bought some of the 'Days Gone' moulds and the Lledo name, whilst the remaining stock was auctioned off to specialist dealers for reselling to collectors – I managed to collect a whole box of this particular version only a few months before the curtain fell. Some spares (especially the plastic moulds for radiator and light fittings were purchased by Oxford Die Case (who continue to manufacture small vehicles of similar dimension to Lledo from their UK factory (in fact they have produced a Home Guard set – but that is another story, and is unrelated otherwise to Dad's Army).

Finally some of the casting moulds not purchased were

dumped (it is unclear who currently has those for Jones' & Hodges Van or even if they survived). Corgi stepped in and purchased some of the Lledo manufacturing items, and quickly indicated their desire to produce a Dad's Army related vehicle or two, as it fitted the ambition to produced Film and TV related vehicles. As you will see in the next section this came to fruition, and two really nice vehicles have been produced (to a much larger scale and finer finish), as part of a whole range including James Bond, Only Fools and Horses, Fawlty Towers, Last of the Summer Wine, Minder, etc

Corgi Film & TV Series
Dad's Army Vehicle (2000), Jones' Butchers Van
Produced in a light blue cardboard box with hand painted figure depicting of Cpl Jones holding a bayonet (made from

polished thin metal). The figure is produced in white metal, and the attention to detail of the hand painting is most professional, and very effective in portraying Jones. The vehicle is to 1:50 scale, whilst the figure is to the larger 1.43 which rather spoils the effect of placing the figure alongside his vehicle. However the van is correctly liveried despite being an inaccurate vehicle type - a Thornycroft rather than the Fordson. By and large the beautifully produced van and figure using new tooling commissioned by Corgi, does justice to this new model venture, which is manufactured in China. For the year 2004 the vehicle no longer appears in the Corgi range and has now been discontinued.

Model Ref: CG09002 - Jack Jones' Butchers Van - Thornycroft Box Van with figure of Corporal Jones.

Corgi Film & TV Series
Dad's Army Vehicle (2000), William Hodges Greengrocers Van

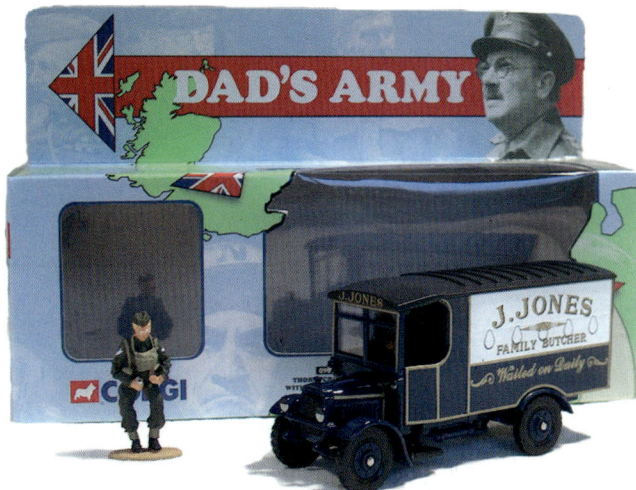

Produced in a similar light blue cardboard box with a hand painted figure of Warden Hodges (complete in ARP uniform and white tin hat) and depicted as pointing his finger (threateningly!). The vehicle is again slightly inaccurate as it is depicted as an O Series Bedford (post war) Box van. A fact that is in keeping with the vehicle used in the TV series, but not appropriate in fact, for the war time period (but who really cares?). The vehicle is in 1:50 scale although it appears smaller than Jones' Van (which will create problems for those wishing to display both alongside each other) and the figure is again in 1:43 scale to match Jones (but neither of the vehicles!). As with the previous model, the livery and detail are excellent, and the hand painted figure really captures Hodges character. Again the finish is nice, and Corgi are to be congratulated in undertaking this venture into Dad's Army territory.

Model No: CG18501 - William Hodges Greengrocers Van - Bedford O Series Box Van with figure of ARP (Hodges) Warden.

DIFFERENCES IN VEHICLE FINISHES

This section concentrates on some specific models that have been subject to 'adulteration' over the years, either accidentally or deliberately (due to a manufacturing change) from the original version, these are above and beyond those comments already made earlier.

Walmington Taxi Variants:

A somewhat understated vehicle this, Lledo produced many version over the years for their general range, whether they were for 'Sponsors', Limited Edition specials or like our own version as part of a themed set. In this instance the vehicle appears in only two guises; one as the standard black taxi (displayed here), and another I am led to believe with the mud-guards and footplates picked-out in white paint (et al Wartime paint scheme). It has not been possible to ascertain whether this was a deliberate attempt to add some authenticity to the product or just over zealousness by a member of the Lledo paint workshop! Whatever the reasons the white/black versions are extremely rare and a definite collector piece!

Jones Van:

The versions of Jones' van are the most numerous variants, to my own knowledge there are more than half a dozen types, with various parts or castings changing from metal to plastic as the years rolled on. The first version produced had both a die cast metal chassis, cab, body and roof. When the last version was produced by Lledo as the Anniversary Edition in the Perspex box, the roof had become white/cream plastic and the transfer lettering, somewhat smudged in comparison with the early versions with their 'crisp' lining.

Some models during the 'middle period' of production had a slightly differing lining on the doors, and Lledo collectors have even indicated to me that a batch of vans was produced with a differing style of lining due to a printing error on the transfer, which went unnoticed for a considerable time (and rather than lose an expensive batch of vehicles Lledo continued to sell them to retailers) – if you have one of these vehicles, they are indeed unique!?

Hodges Van Variants:

There are several variants of the Hodges Van, not least is the lighter green paint finish which may include both the body, cab or a combination of either. This appears to be a trend in both 1993 and 1995 sets and can only be attributed to a lack of continuity within the paint mixing. Similarly some vehicles are glazed internally, whilst others (for cost savings by Lledo) are not. Finally as displayed here, to display the paint version, some had the footplate finished in silver, whilst again other remain in black! There is no record of which versions were produce in which year, but certainly those of the lesser quality finish appear to relate to later versions!

Dennis NFS Fire Engine Variants:

The Dennis Fire Engine from 1991 was produced with at least one variant. In some cases the wheeled escape ladder was produced in dark brown plastic, a much more accurate colour scheme than the other offering off–white/cream. The vehicle has proved popular as part of the Dad's Army series but also with Fire Engine enthusiasts, and thus is fairly rare.

AND FINALLY

The final comment regarding all these items relates to a final variation on the packaging. Lledo produced the standard size box with cream plastic moulded interior in which to fit the models, for most of its range (the Anniversary Perspex box being an exception). Using this standard box you may come across vehicles described in this guide in 'Days Gone' or plain 'Lledo' boxes, this is likely to be explained by (i) a replacement box due to the original being lost or damaged or (ii) more vehicles produced by the manufacturer than correctly printed boxes were available (as shown above). There is no certainty in these final remarks, but certainly the latter has been given as one explanation.

The author would like to acknowledge the considerable help over the months, if not, years it has taken to complete my own sets of vehicles, and obtain that small "gem" of information that fits all the pieces of the jigsaw together for this section. Mark Usher, John Ward, former employees of Lledo plc, and the numerous contacts in the die cast fraternity, not forgetting the assistance from Sarah at Corgi (Customer Services), all have provided useful background data and enabled me to bring this data together. Lastly, all of my fellow DAAS members, who have given positive feedback and comment on my previous articles and letters

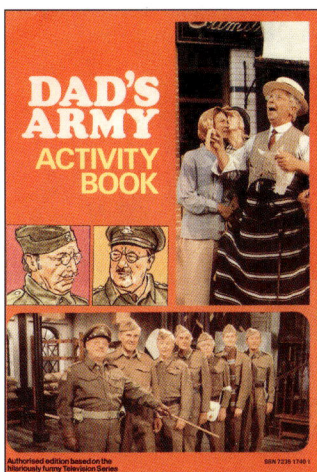

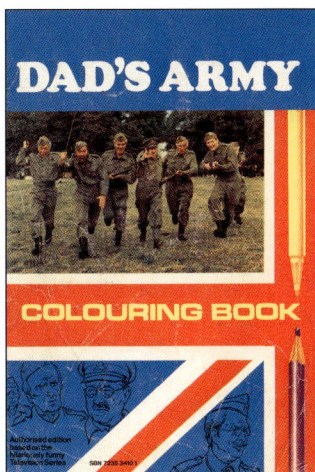

Dad's Army Activity (1973) and Colouring Books (1977)

Produced by World Distributors, Manchester.

The illustrations were drawn by Peter Thurlow, who created the characters for the cartoon strips.

The activity book (originally priced at 10p!) contains puzzles, join the dots and exercises with a Home Guard/Platoon theme. The Colouring book contains black and white line drawings of the characters.

Very rare to find, especially if unmarked.

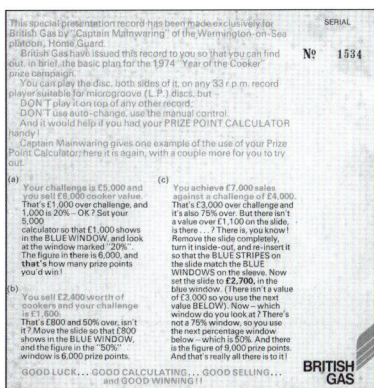

British Gas Promotional Record

The wording on the back cover reads: 'This special presentation record has been made exclusively for British Gas by "Captain Mainwaring" of the Warmington-on-Sea (sic) platoon, Home Guard.

British Gas have issued this record to you so that you can find out, in brief, the basic plan for the 1974 "Year of the Cooker" prize campaign'

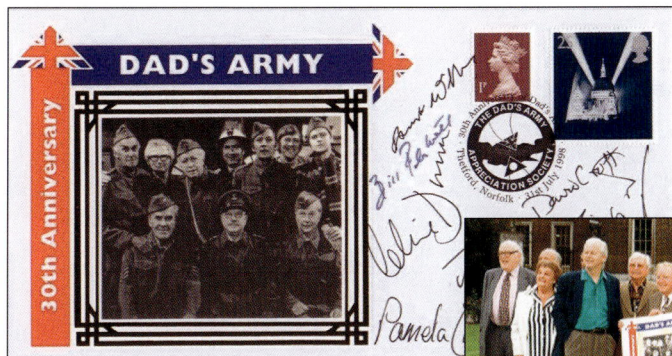

Dad's Army 30th Anniversary Souvenir Cover

Produced by Benhams and designed in association with the Dad's Army Appreciation Society, the cover featured a photograph of the cast printed onto a silken fabric and mounted within a gold-blocked border, and was signed by writers and stars of the show. The postmark is placed at Thetford and dated 31 July 1998, the anniversary of the first television transmission of Dad's Army.

Limited to a run of 1,000 editions.

Right: First Day Cover launch held at The Imperial War Museum, London. Guests included David Croft, Jimmy Perry, Clive Dunn & Ian Lavender.

Dad's Army Garden Characters

Produced (unpainted) on the Isle of Wight, cast in concrete and standing about 3 feet high, they make an unusual alternative to garden gnomes!

Daddies Ketchup Mug

Produced in 1977 by a pottery in Newton Abbott.

3 labels had to be collected from sauce botles and each was personalised by having your own photograph fired onto it.

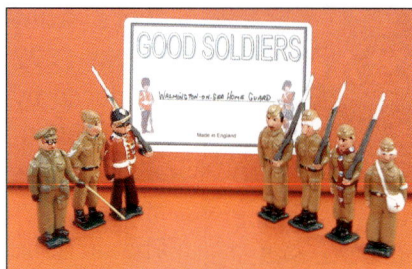

GOOD SOLDIERS
'Walmington-on-Sea Home Guard

Die cast set of the main seven members of the platoon, painted and measuring 60mm high.
Manufactured by 'Good Soldiers', 246 Broadwater Cresecnt, Stevenage, Herts SG2 8HL

Unpainted White Metal Cast Soldiers
These 50mm high Dad's Army die cast figures were originally made by Mr John R Howarth for 'Toy Soldier Magazine'.
Unfortunately they were unable to obtain a licence and therefore they were never produced commercially.
One set from the original moulds is on display at the Dad's Army Collection, Bressingham, Norfolk.

HOME GUARD HEROES
Die cast box sets of unpainted figures, approximately 30mm high.
Although not marketed as 'Dad's Army', set WWII 1/1 'Home Guard Heroes'(above left) has clearly been modelled on the cast members, whilst set WWII 1/6 'Characters, 5th Columnists & Civil' (above right) contains good representations of the Vicar, Verger, ARP Warden and Mrs Fox, complete with fox fur!
Another set WWII 1/3 'Home Guard in Forage Caps' is also available, but they do not depict any characters from the series.
Produced by Foundry Miniatures, 23-24 St. Marks Street, Nottingham NG3 1DE.
www.wargamesfoundry.com

Following an unsuccessful attempt in 1990 to form an appreciation society, Bill Pertwee approached avid Dad's Army fan Tadge Muldoon to form a society following the many requests he had received for information since publication of his book 'Dad's Army, The Making of a Television Legend' in 1989.

The New Dad's Army Appreciation Society (the 'new' was dropped in 1995) was formed in 1993 after Tadge had written to the many names Bill had supplied and the first newsletter, entitled 'Permission to Speak, Sir!' was issued in September 1993.

Tadge had made a conscious decision to produce a good quality newsletter, rather than the usual photocopied news sheet.

The first Appreciation Society event was held at the Victory Services Club, London and featured special guest Colin Bean.

Following 5 issues of the newsletter and having run the Society for just 2 years, Tadge died following a tragic accident. Bill Pertwee stepped in again and asked another well informed follower of the series and retired civil servant, Jack Wheeler to run the society. Since then, the society has gone from strength to strength and has now in excess of 1,500 members, including many who live outside the UK.

A parallel society was formed in New Zealand by Dave Homewood, based in Cambridge. His first newsletter 'Platoon Attention' was produced in April 1995 and although membership is not a large as the UK branch, the quality of the research and content of the newsletters, written in the main by Dave, ensures that they are read not only in New Zealand but many UK members who have subscribed to receive copies.

One of the features of the UK society is its close contact with those involved with the series, and this has helped in arranging the many local events and conventions at which some of the stars and writers of both the TV and radio series have attended.

1998 was the 30th Anniversary of the series and this was celebrated by holding a Convention in the Banqueting Suite at the Oval Cricket Ground, London. Many of the surviving cast attended, including Clive Dunn who flew in from his home in Portugal.

With newsletters appearing at regular quarterly intervals, the society issued a Dad's Army Handbook following demand from members wanting information which was then unavailable at the time in any publication.

Many events have been staged, including the hugely

York 1996. Frank Williams, Bill Pertwee and Eric Longworth

Oval 1998. Dad's Army Convention

Bressingham Dad's Army Day 1999. Pamela Cundell, Bill Pertwee and Frank Williams.

Locations Tour 1998. Bury Sugar Beet Works

successful Thetford weekend when the Dad's Army Collection was opened at Bressingham Steam Museum in May 2000. What follows is a brief list of all events arranged by the Appreciation Society:

4 March 1995
Meet Private Sponge, The Victory Services Club, London.

19 October 1996
York Convention, The Bonding Warehouse, York.

27 April 1997
Tour of Locations (Suffolk & Norfolk).

18 April 1998
30th Anniversary Convention, The Oval, London.

12 September 1998
York Convention, The Bonding Warehouse, York.

26 - 27 September 1998
Tour of Locations (Suffolk, Norfolk & Stanta MOD).

10 April 1999
Basingstoke Local Event, May Bounty Cricket Ground.

25 July 1999
Dad's Army Day, Bressingham Steam Museum.

13 May 2000
Dad's Army Parade, Thetford.

14 May 2000
Opening of Dad's Army Collection at Bressingham.

16 September 2000
Maidstone Local Event, Beltring Hop Farm, Kent.

30 September 2000
Newcastle Local Event, Station Hotel, Newcastle.

14 October 2000
Bristol Local Event, The Hatchet PH, Bristol.

13 May 2001
Dad's Army Day, Bressingham Museum.

15 September 2001
Cardiff Local Event, The Pendragon PH, Cardiff.

22 Spetember 2001
Wigan Local Event (Meet Private Sponge), Wigan Pier.

20 - 21 April 2002
Locations Tour (Suffolk,Norfolk & Stanta MOD).

Locations Tour 2002. Army rations at STANTA MOD.

Street Party 2003. Jimmy Perry addresses the membership.

Locations Tour 2002. Coffee at David Croft's.

4 May 2002
Feature Film showing, The New Olympus Theatre, Gloucester.

11 May 2002
Society Street Party, Bressingham Museum.

12 May 2002
Dad's Army Day, Bressingham Museum.

27 July 2002
Portsmouth Local Event, The New Theatre Royal, Portsmouth.

16 November 2002
Coventry Local Event, Walgrave Hospital Social Club.

26 - 27 April 2003
Locations Tour, (North Norfolk & Stanta MOD).

10 May 2003
Society Street Party, Bressingham Museum.

11 May 2003
Dad's Army Day, Bressingham Museum.

12 July 2003
Worthing Local Event, The Richmond Room, Worthing.

13 September 2003
Dad's Army Exhibition, Thetford Heritage Weekend.

4 October 2003
DAAS 10th Anniversary Convention, Pendley Theatre, Tring.

To join the Dad's Army Appreciation Society, visit the website at:
www.dadsarmy.co.uk
to view subscription rates and download a membership form, or write to:
DAAS,
8 Sinodun Road,
Wallingford,
Oxon,
OX10 8AA
enclosing a sae for further information, or email
info@dadsarmy.co.uk

Below are some items produced by the Appreciation Society for its members

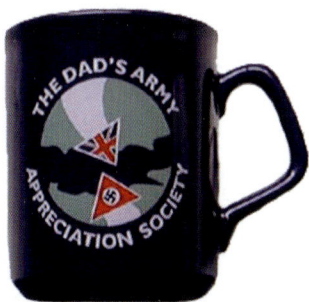

A popular item - the DAAS mug!

This plate was produced in limited numbers to celebrate the 30th Anniversary of the programme

A bottle of Dad's Army Ale was given to all attending the Society's 10th Anniversary event

The ticket to the opening of the Dad's Army Collection doubled as a card/pass holder

On a glorious 11 May 2000, the Dad's Army Collection at the Bressingham Steam Museum was opened in front of a crowd of about 5,000 people by the writers and creators of the series, Jimmy Perry and David Croft, exactly 60 years after the formation of the Home Guard during the second World War.

The origins of the museum go back to 1997 when Bill Pertwee suggested to the Appreciation Society that it would be nice if there were some way to display some of the Dad's Army items that have been produced over the the years, from books and records to stage programmes, original scripts and models. It could also enlighten people, especially the young about what actually took place during those dark days.

The Society had established contact with the Bressingham Steam Museum in Norfolk principally because they had originally supplied some of the vehicles used in the series. It was during discussions with Jonathan Wheeler, the Collections Manager, that the idea for a small display of Dad's Army items was first put forward. Nothing grand, just a couple of display cabinets alongside some of their permanent displays, some of which were used in the series. It was as a result of these discussions that the first Dad's Army Day, was held at the museum in July 1999.

Below: Crowds queue up for autographs at a 'Dad's Army Day. The exhibition is in the large hall.

The society organisers were called back to the museum for another meeting, this time in the presence of Spencer Chapman, a gentleman who had worked on the original Dad's Army sets in the early seventies, and who now worked freelance in set design. He presented a number of drawings (some of which have been reproduced here) showing the transformation of a large hall into a life size replica of Walmington-on-Sea, complete with Jones' Butchers Shop, Bank, Church Hall, Railway Station (to display some of the museums collection), Post Office and Frazer's Funeral Parlour.

This was to be a major project with a lot of investment from the museum. Before any work could commence, permission had to be obtained from Messrs Perry and Croft, who have subsequently been 100% behind the project and were the first to offer manuscripts and items to the Society for display. The BBC, although supportive of the project, would not allow exact replicas to be built.

The opening date was arranged well in advance and the set builders got under way once the hall had been cleared of some large pieces of machinery that occupied it. They worked flat out during the winter months and finished about a week before the opening weekend. The Appreciation Society had put out a request to members willing to donate items for display, to which many responded, and several display cabinets have been filled to date.

The Railway Station in the plans didn't make it, which was a shame, as it would have allowed period carriages and engines to be displayed alongside the museum's substantial railway collection. However, audio visual units were included at placed at intervals around the hall, showing wartime information films on request, and a large screen was available for use in the church hall for educational purposes.
Press coverage was enormous, and on the friday

Below: David Croft cuts the tape to open the Dad's Army Collection.

before the opening, a live broadcast was transmitted from the collection, attended by Clive Dunn, Jimmy Perry, David Croft, Bill Pertwee, Pamela Cundell and Frank Williams. It was during this transmission that Bill Pertwee was presented with a greengrocers cart emblazoned with the name of 'W Hodges'!

The opening day went "like a smooth well oiled machine" to quote Captain Mainwaring, helped in no small way by Howard Stephens at the museum. The previous day had seen the cast members paraded around nearby Thetford in front of vast crowds, on a very hot day. Undaunted by this, they all re-gathered for the special Society members only preview of the museum before it was officially opened to the general public who then could talk to the cast and obtain autographs etc.

The Dad's Army Collection is open all year round and a Dad's Army Day has become an annual event. There are plans to extend the displays when time allows, and incorporate additional items from the Steam museum's collection.

For more information contact:
General enquiries and bookings 01379 686 900
info@bressingham.co.uk
www.bressingham.co.uk

Above: The church hall, containing displays of the original cast's uniforms.
Below: 'Mrs Prentice's' Post Office, and Frazer's Funerals next door.
Below Left: General view showing the Fire Station Entrance, Jones' Butcher Shop, Bank and Hodges' hand cart.

Original sketches

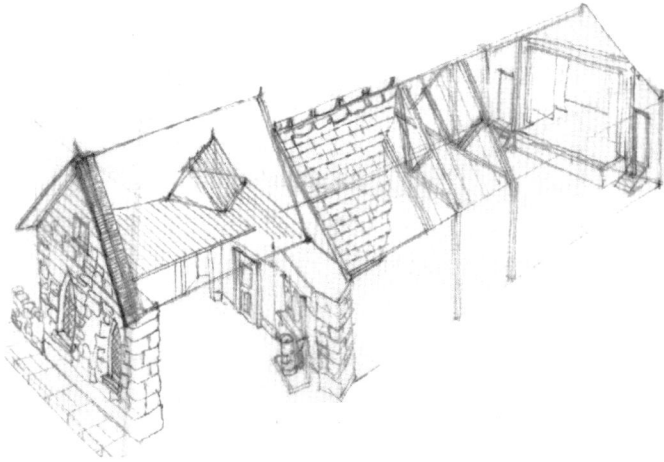

Above: Construction details of the church hall, complete with stage.

Below: Main entrance, the church building was replaced by an exhibition area for steam rollers etc.

Above: View to the rear of church hall, with Anderson shelter. The shop was replaced by the fire station entrance.

Above: The fire station entrance next to Jones' Butchers Shop

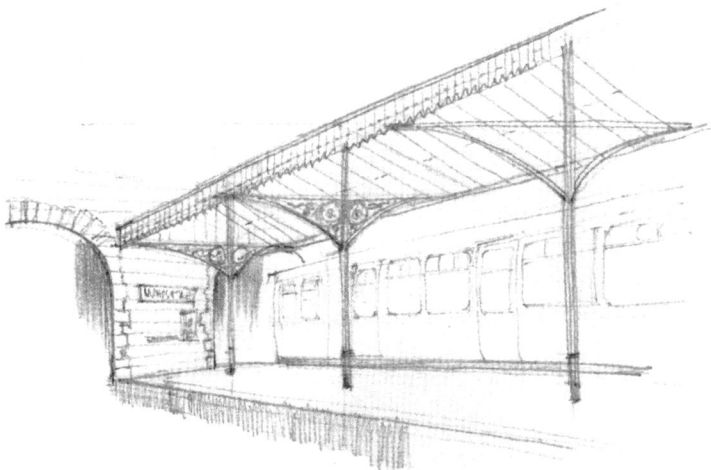

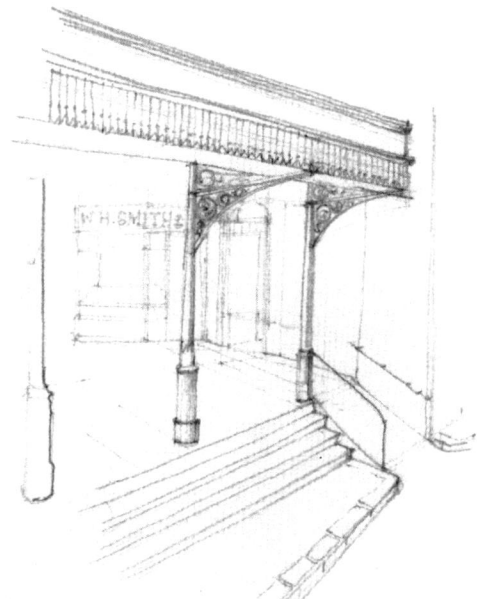

Above and right: The proposed station platforms and buildings, showing one of Bressingham's display carriages in the platform and old 'W H Smith' newsagents shop front.

Ring Dem Bells, Bardwell.

The Deadly Attachment, Thetford.

We Know Our Onions, Honington.

Menace From The Deep, Great Yarmouth Pier.

A Soldier's Farewell, Kilverstone.

Come In, Your Time Is Up, Stanta Lake.

Battle Of The Giants, STANTA, MOD.

Time On My Hands, Nether Row, Thetford.

Round & Round Went The Great Big Wheel, Wacton.

Everybody's Trucking.

The Royal Train, Weybourne Station.

Is Ther Honey Still For Tea?, East Wretham.

Here we pay our last respects to the many actors no longer with us who have made the Dad's Army experience so memorable.

Roger Avon
1914 - 1998

James Beck
1929 - 1973

Harold Bennett
1899 - 1981

Tim Barrett
1933 - 1990

Ronnie Brody
1918 - 1991

Peter Butterworth
1919 - 1979

Desmond Cullum-Jones (back row)
1924 - 2002

Hugh Cecil (back row)
1913 - 2004

Erik Chitty
1907 - 1977

Joan Cooper
1923 - 1987

Leon Cortez
1898 - 1970

Janet Davies
1930 - 1986

Robert Dorning
1913 - 1989

Arthur English
1919 - 1995

Don Estelle
1933 - 2003

Edward Evans
1915 - 2001

William Gosling (back row)
1912 - 1981

Jack Haig
1913 - 1989

George Hancock (back row)
1906 - 1992

Nigel Hawthorne CBE
1929 - 2001

Fraser Kerr
? - 2004

John Laurie
1897 - 1980

John Le Mesurier
1912 - 1983

Arthur Lowe
1915 - 1982

Geoffrey Lumsden
1915 - 1984

Jimmy Mac (back row)
1903 - 1984

Fulton Mackay
1922 - 1987

Larry Martyn
1934 - 1994

Olive Mercer
1906 - 1983

Arnold Ridley
1896 - 1984

Fred McNaughton
1903 - 1981

Michael Moore (back row)
1909 - 1979

Verne Morgan
1900 - 1984

Robert Raglan
1906 - 1985

Anthony Sagar
1920 - 1973

Anthony Sharpe
1915 - 1984

Edward Sinclair
1914 - 1977

Campbell Singer
1909 - 1976

John Snagge
1904 - 1996

Vic Taylor (back row)
1924 - 1972

Talfryn Thomas
1922 - 1982

Edward Underdown
1908 - 1989

Drake Vernon (back row)
1897 - 1987

Patrick Waddington
1900 - 1987

Queenie Watts
1920 - 1980

Peter Whitacker (back row)
1921 - 2002

Martin Wyldeck
1914 - 1988

Dad's Army - a companion

Cover Design - Paul Carpenter

Images and Information Prepared by Tony Pritchard

Design and Layout by Paul Carpenter